IMAGES
of America

SMYTH COUNTY REVISITED

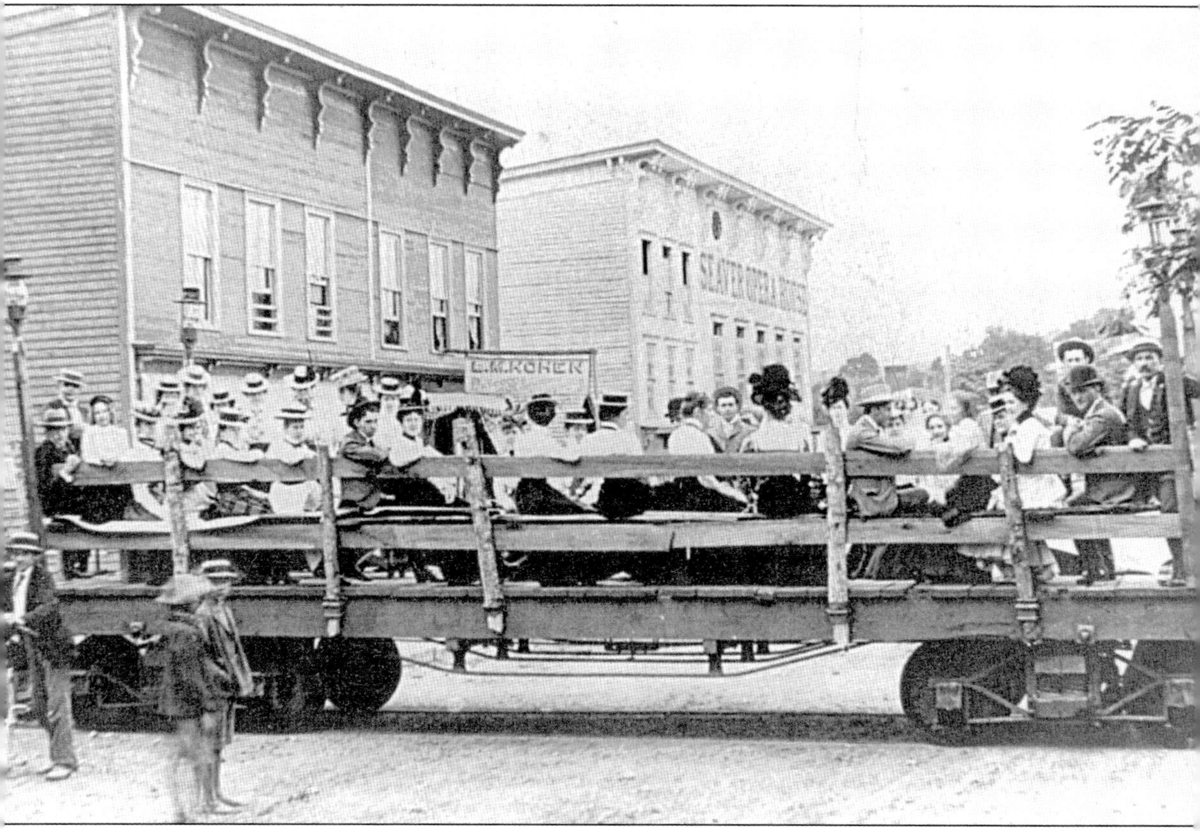

ON THE COVER: MARION AND RYE VALLEY'S SUNDAY TOUR. This open train car, pictured here and on the cover, was a means of transportation for numerous people to view the area. Some of those who were on this ride included Nannie, Janie, and Katie Preston; John and Mrs. F. Copenhaver; Mr. and Mrs. W. L. Lincoln; Mr. and Mrs. C. C. Lincoln; Mr. and Mrs. A. T. Lincoln; Dr. Tom Staley; Mrs. G. W. Richardson; J. B. Richardson; and Nancy Apperson. (Courtesy Mack Sturgill Collection.)

IMAGES
of America

SMYTH COUNTY REVISITED

Kimberly Barr Byrd and Debbie J. Williams

ARCADIA
PUBLISHING

ISBN 978-0-7385-4409-0

Published by Arcadia Publishing
Charleston, South Carolina

Printed in the United States of America

Library of Congress Catalog Card Number: 2006936684

For all general information contact Arcadia Publishing at:
Telephone 843-853-2070
Fax 843-853-0044
E-mail sales@arcadiapublishing.com
For customer service and orders:
Toll-Free 1-888-313-2665

Visit us on the Internet at www.arcadiapublishing.com

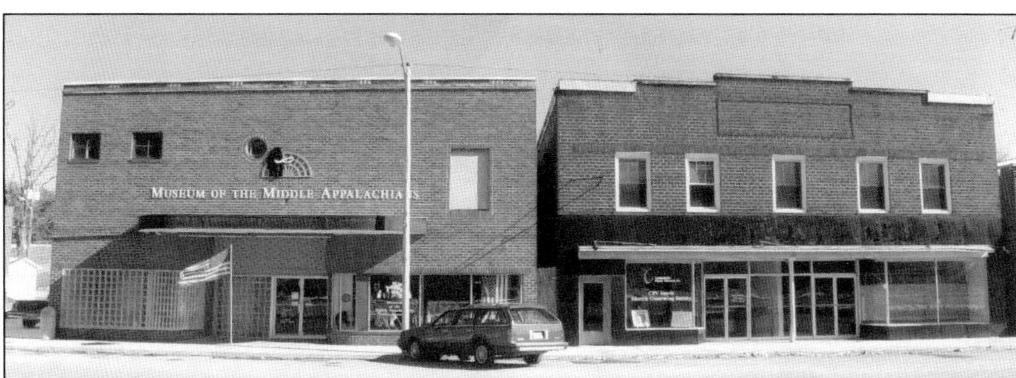

MUSEUM OF THE MIDDLE APPALACHIANS. Located in the old Salt Theatre building, the Museum of the Middle Appalachians is a true jewel. An interactive model of the Saltville Valley is on display in Singleton Hall along with permanent exhibits featuring geology, the Ice Age, the Civil War, Woodland Indians, and Company Town. The Museum Store has over 4,000 vintage photographs available for viewing and purchase. (Courtesy Museum of the Middle Appalachians.)

Contents

ACKNOWLEDGMENTS

Even though efforts have been made to verify the facts and dates included in this book, in many instances different dates have been found for the same event. None of the contributors, including the Museum of the Middle Appalachians, are responsible for the dates given or the contents of this book. This volume is not intended to be a formal or thorough history of Smyth County but merely a visual tour of the many changes in Smyth County's development through the years. This book also includes a few places of interest that border Smyth County and may have been within the county borders at one time.

High-quality prints of images supplied by the Museum of the Middle Appalachians in Saltville are available for purchase by contacting them. We encourage you to help preserve our rich heritage for future generations by allowing your local historical society to scan your old photographs, letters, or other materials.

Please take a moment to look at the names of those who contributed photographs for this book. We would like to express our sincere appreciation to everyone who provided materials and information. Without their generosity, this project would not have been possible.

We would like to express our sincere appreciation to the following people: Larry Barker, Tom Burkett, Sam Campbell, Mildred Clark, F. Joseph Copenhaver Jr., Tim Crawford, Connie Dalton, Dewey Davenport, Beverly Evans, Zollie Fowler, Gene Groseclose, Harry Haynes, Ken Heath, David Henderson, Atwood J. Huff, Mel Leaman, Bob McKinney, Kathy Miller, Judy Millsaps, Juanita Mitchell, Lisa Mitchell, Megan Mitchell, Judy Moore, G. C. Musser, B. Gayle Neely, Michelle Powers, Jeff Richardson, Lawrence Richardson, Carol Rosenbaum, Joe Sayers, Debbie Schwartz, Charles W. Seaver, Carol Shepherd, Dr. O. O. Smith, Nancy Smith, Robert Stump, Jimmy Warren, Jeff Weaver, James Wood, and Charles Wassum III.

This book is dedicated to the people of Smyth County who have made this second edition possible by purchasing the first edition and making it such a huge success. Secondly, we dedicate this book to our husbands, Mark Byrd and Joey Williams, and our families for their love, support, and encouragement.

So catch a rainy day, grab a warm drink, find a cozy corner, and prepare to sit a spell as we reminisce of times gone by.

INTRODUCTION

In 1748, James Patton led a group of men to this area to survey 120,000 acres of land granted to him by the king of England. Charles Campbell, Dr. Thomas Walker, and John Buchanan were part of this expedition. Charles Campbell claimed the Buffalo Lick Survey, and John Buchanan later settled in the Rich Valley area.

Smyth County, named after Gen. Alexander Smyth, who represented this area in Congress, was formed in 1832 from parts of both Washington and Wythe Counties. The breathtaking mountains, wide river valleys, and rich natural resources have contributed greatly to Smyth County's development. The Holston River, which naturally directed the paths of those who settled here, divides the county into three valleys.

Nestled in the mountains of Southwest Virginia, Smyth County is rich in history. Many towns can trace their history back only a couple hundred years, but because of excavations, Saltville's history can be traced back more than 14,000 years. One of the most complete musk-ox skeletons ever found in North America outside of Alaska has traced Saltville's history back to the Ice Age. The earliest reference regarding archaeological artifacts in the Smyth County area is from Thomas Jefferson's journal notes of a mastodon tooth from Saltville given to him by Arthur Campbell of Marion.

In 1750, Samuel Stalnaker built his home near present-day Chilhowie. Later Town House was built as a fort and eventually expanded to become a stagecoach inn. Due to Native American raids, many early settlers were driven back east. Town House offered early frontiersmen protection against the Native Americans and later served as a meeting place for the soldiers of the Revolutionary War, War of 1812, and Civil War. Permanent settlers began to establish in this area following the French and Indian War.

Industry played an important part in the county's early development. Mills, which were necessary for grinding wheat and grains and for providing power, sprung up at various locations in the county. In 1770, Arthur Campbell built the first recorded mill in this area, which was located on Staley's Creek. This was also the first mill recorded west of New River. Soon every community of any size with water frontage had a gristmill. In 1835, three years after its formation, Smyth County was reported to have 16 gristmills, 14 houses of worship, a cotton factory, 3 iron works, a courthouse, a jail, several mercantile stores, and 8 taverns. Soon many other industries began to form.

The economy was boosted in 1884 when the Virginia legislature established the Southwestern Lunatic Asylum in Smyth County at a cost of $2 million. Attorney D. C. Miller was an active participant in persuading the committee's decision of Marion over other communities. Miller did all the paperwork needed, traveled to Richmond, and encouraged the legislature members to extend their work day before their Christmas break long enough to decide on which county would receive the largest public building in Virginia at that time.

The state hospital was located on the Atkins farm in Marion and opened in 1887 for patients, with Dr. Harvey Black as superintendent and Dr. Robert Preston as first assistant physician. The institution maintained its own electricity and power plant on-site, had access to four springs, and maintained several gardens and a farm to be totally self-sufficient. The monthly payroll for its employees was considerable with most of it being expended within the county. The institution also purchased most of its supplies in the community. It did and has continued to employ a large number of residents of this and surrounding counties with decent wages and benefits.

Religion was very important to Smyth County's early settlers. The first church in this area was built in 1766 in the Royal Oak section, which is present-day Marion. It was constructed by Arthur and John Campbell at their sister's request and named Royal Oak Presbyterian Church. The Methodist camp meetings that began in 1818 at Sulphur Springs were the beginning of the Chilhowie Methodist Church.

Smyth County has been home to several governors, delegates, senators, and Supreme Court justices. Many brave and famous leaders have resided here. From two of the county's first families came Virginia's governors: David Campbell and Henry C. Stuart. Campbell wrote of Smyth County's settlers, "The first settlers on Holston River were a remarkable race of people, for their intelligence, enterprise, and hardy adventure."

Smyth County was of great importance to the Confederacy during the Civil War because of the large salt deposits in Saltville, the nearby lead mines in southern Wythe County, and its close proximity to the railroad. By 1862, Saltville provided most of the salt for the Confederacy. It was essential for food preservation, tanning hides, and human consumption. After marrying Elizabeth Henry Campbell, Gen. William Russell moved his new family to Buffalo Lick, later called Saltville, and began producing salt. In 1799, William King expanded production to begin the first commercial salt making industry.

In the early 1800s, the Chatham Hill community was the location of a shipbuilding industry. These ships provided the quickest means of transporting goods prior to the railroad's arrival in Smyth County in 1856. Flat barges, measuring from 60 to 90 feet in length and up to 16 feet wide, were manufactured here and used to transport goods to the newly opened markets along the Ohio and Mississippi Rivers. These barges were floated down the North Holston to Kingsport and Knoxville, Tennessee, and, at times, as far away as New Orleans, Louisiana. In 1838, the Holston Navigation Company was incorporated.

The Home Guard, a group of men who were either too young or too old to join the armed forces, defended the Smyth County area until December 1864. Gen. George Stoneman and his 4,000 troops penetrated the county, destroying the railroad bridges and the Thomas Iron Works. The saltworks were disabled for a brief period of time.

In 1982, Smyth County celebrated its sesquicentennial. Although at times faced with its share of adversity, Smyth County continues to move forward. With new employment opportunities filtering into the area and the expansion of tourism, Smyth County is winning the battle and the future looks very positive going into the 21st century.

Thousands of years ago, God placed his hand upon an area of land in Virginia and decided that it would be one of the most beautiful places on the planet, alive with natural beauty. He created rolling hills, lush valleys, and tumbling creeks. One has only to visit a large city, return home, and gaze at the natural beauty that surrounds us to realize how God has truly blessed Smyth County's residents.

One

Ghost Stories and Local Legends

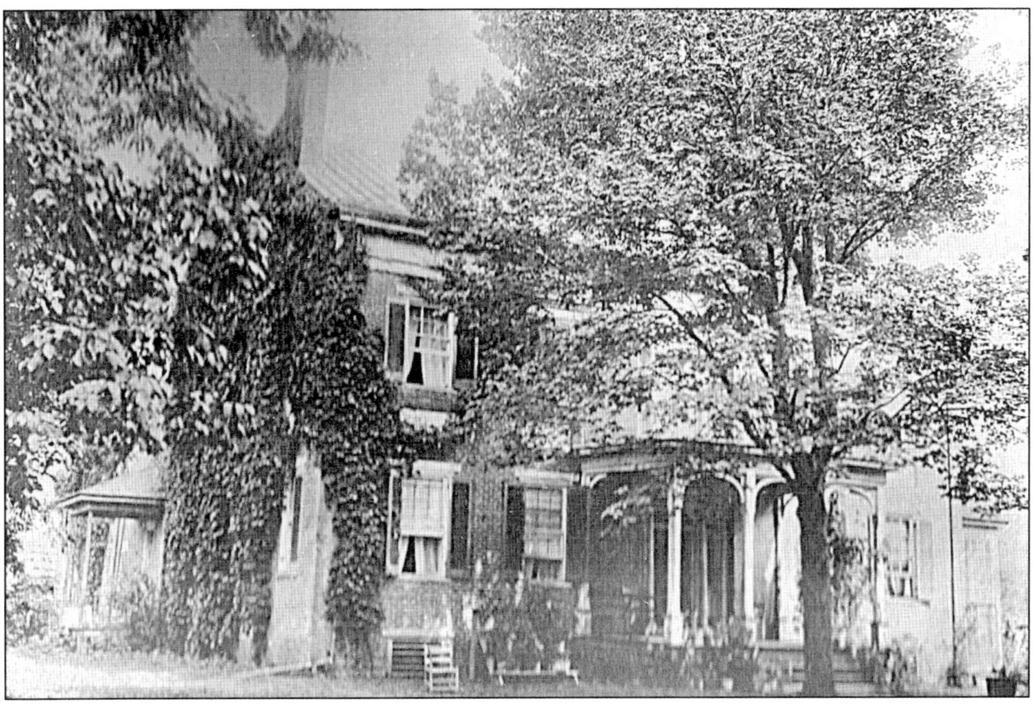

John Montgomery Preston House. Named Herondon by a recent resident, author Lucy Herndon Crockett, this Greek Revival–style mansion was built in 1842 as a tavern and stagecoach inn. In 1864, the dwelling became temporary housing for Union general George Stoneman and his troops. In a newspaper interview, Crockett and her mother, Nell, spoke of resident ghosts who could be heard in both sawing and cloth ripping contests. (Courtesy Elizabeth Harkleroad.)

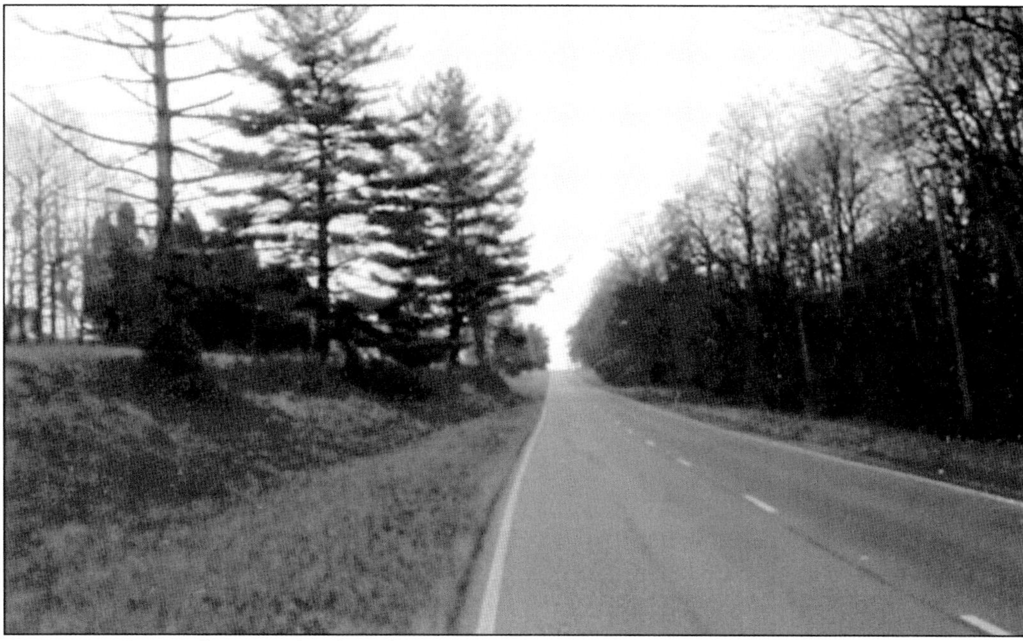

PRESTON HILL. This stretch of Highway 11 on Preston Hill is the location of many mysterious sightings. Sometimes on a clear night, a luminescent and transparent young boy and girl can be seen standing in the middle of the road and then fade away into the darkness. Several people have reported seeing thousands of eyes glowing in the dark on stormy nights. (Courtesy Debra Williams.)

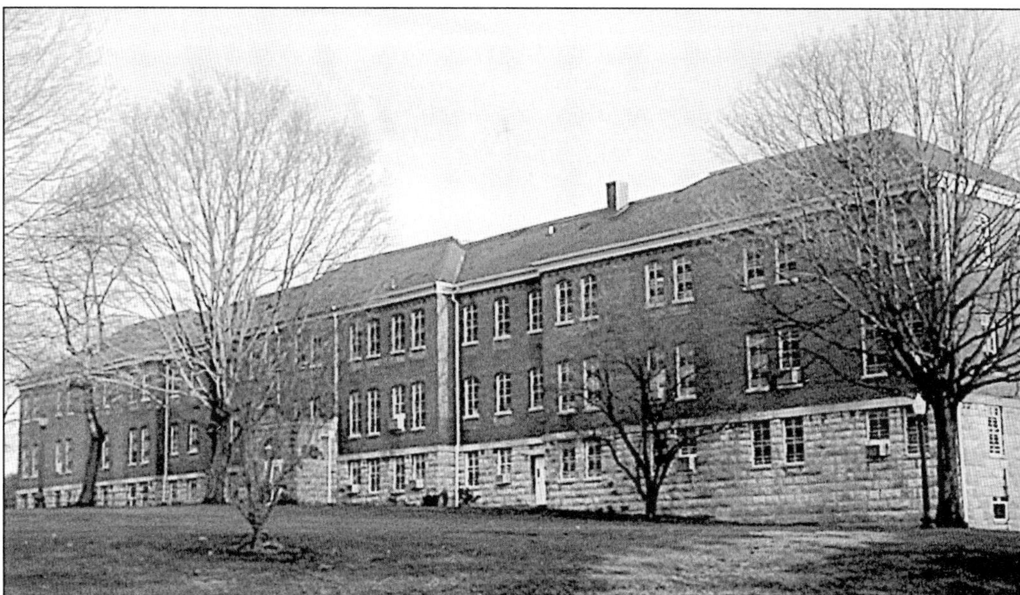

CRIMINAL INSANE BUILDING. Around 1910, this two-story structure with a basement was constructed to house the criminally insane. The inmates were moved to the Finley Gale Building in 1972. Present and former employees say they have witnessed strange occurrences, such as locked doors slamming, commodes flushing, and lights turning on and off when no one else was there. (Courtesy Southwest Virginia Mental Health Institute.)

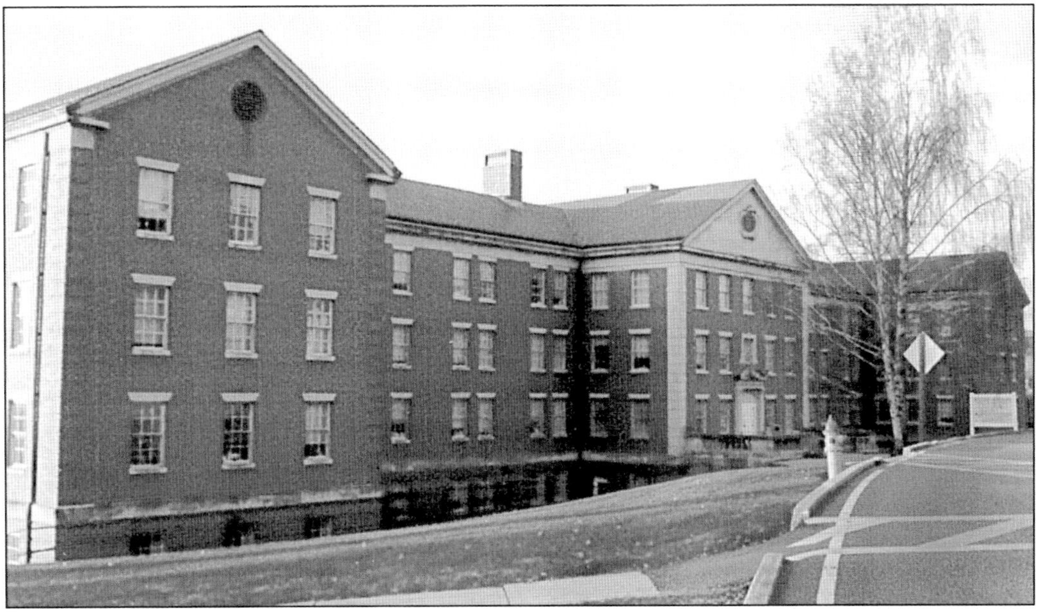

GHOST ROAMS THE MORRISON BUILDING. County employees swear this building is haunted by a woman wearing a yellow housecoat. This ghost has been seen by several people who claim that she turns computers on, adjusts the thermostat, and slams doors shut. This building was built *c.* 1953 as part of the state hospital and housed patients until the 1990s, when it was converted into county offices. (Courtesy Debra Williams.)

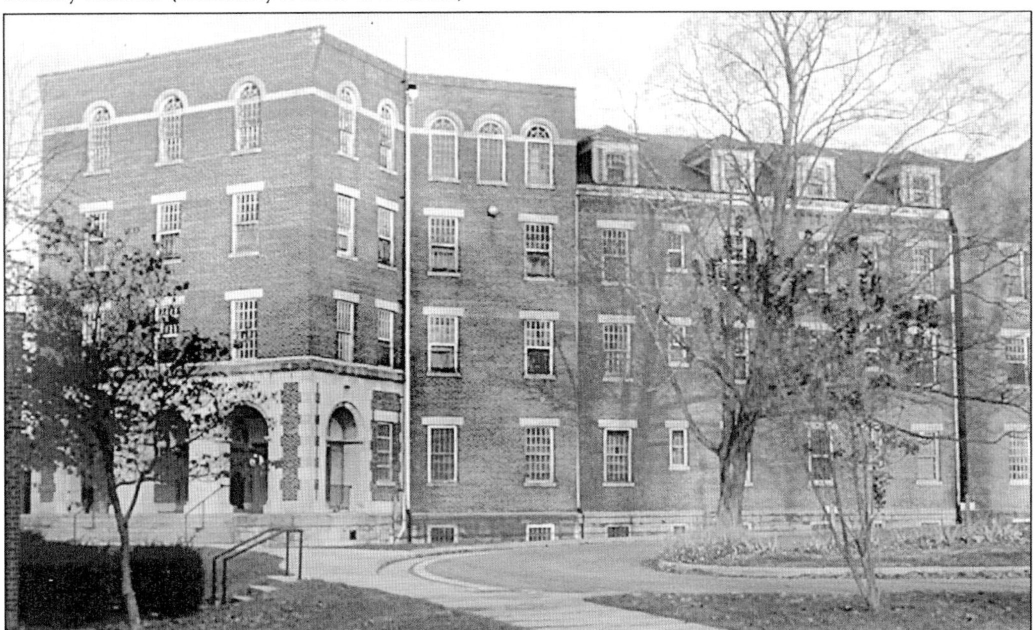

HARMON BUILDING. Around 1933, this building was erected as a hospital on state hospital grounds for patients with physical illnesses. Many surgeries, including lobotomies, were performed here. A morgue was on the bottom floor. Local legend has it that even though it is now abandoned and locked, the third-floor lights turn on and off and sometimes two dark silhouettes can be seen in the window. (Courtesy Southwest Virginia Mental Health Institute.)

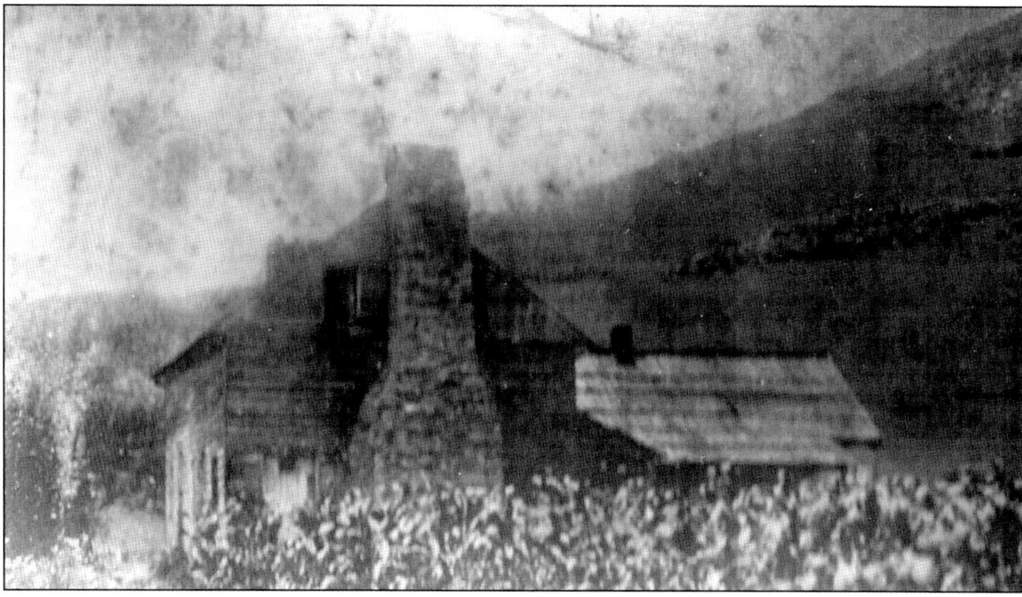

GHOSTS IN MADAME RUSSELL HOUSE. The two upstairs rooms in the Madame Russell house were separated with a partition and a door. This door was locked every night, but by morning, it would be open. Even though chairs and rock doorstops were placed against it, by morning the door could be found ajar. Many residents reported hearing chains rattling across the floor upstairs. (Courtesy Elizabeth Harkleroad.)

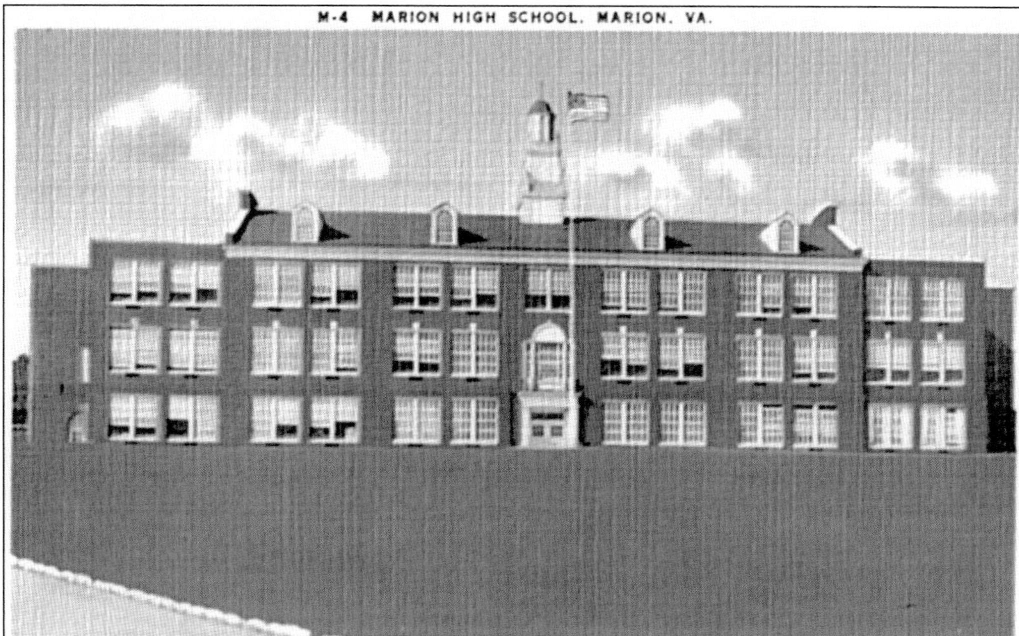

MARION MIDDLE SCHOOL. This three-story institute was erected in 1939 originally as a high school. The facility included a cafeteria, gymnasium, library, home economics room, and a huge auditorium for its time. In 1961, this became the middle school. Employees and students report hearing mysterious noises and lights turning on by themselves. Could these sounds really be from a ghost or the heating system? (Courtesy Debra Williams.)

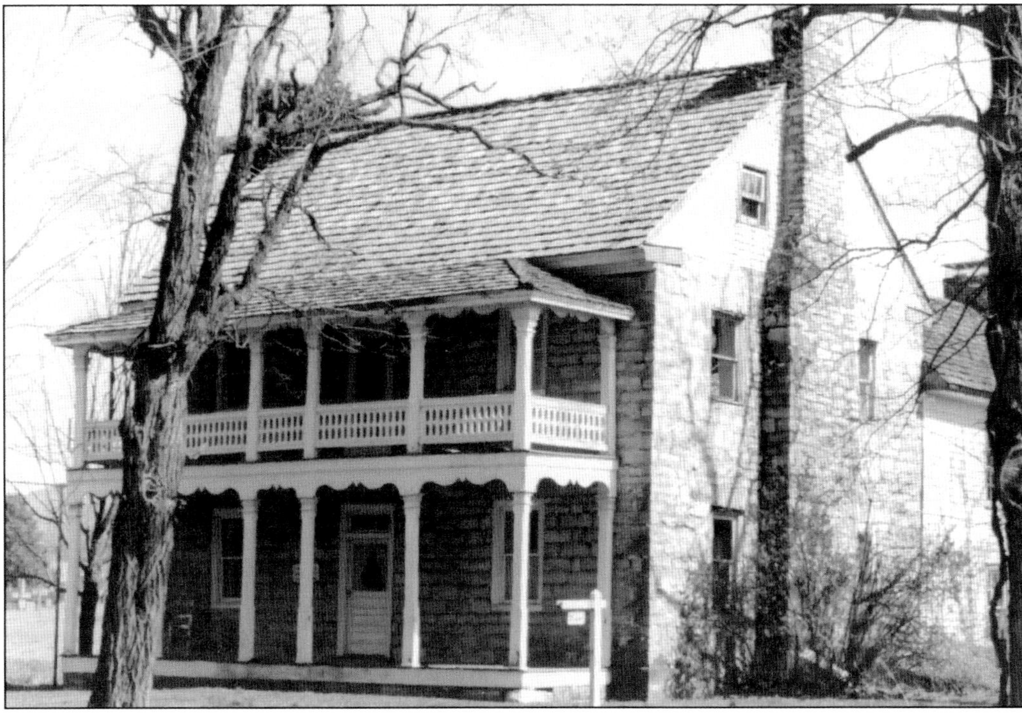

CULLOP STONE TAVERN. Located west of Atkins, Fredrick Cullop operated this limestone structure as a coach stop in the early 1800s. In 1825, Cullop committed suicide here. It is said his ghost still roams the hallways. While building Interstate 81 near this structure, a descendant of Cullop, operating a dozer, dug up Cullop's grave. The casket was placed into the drainage ditch and construction continued. (Courtesy Smyth County Chamber of Commerce.)

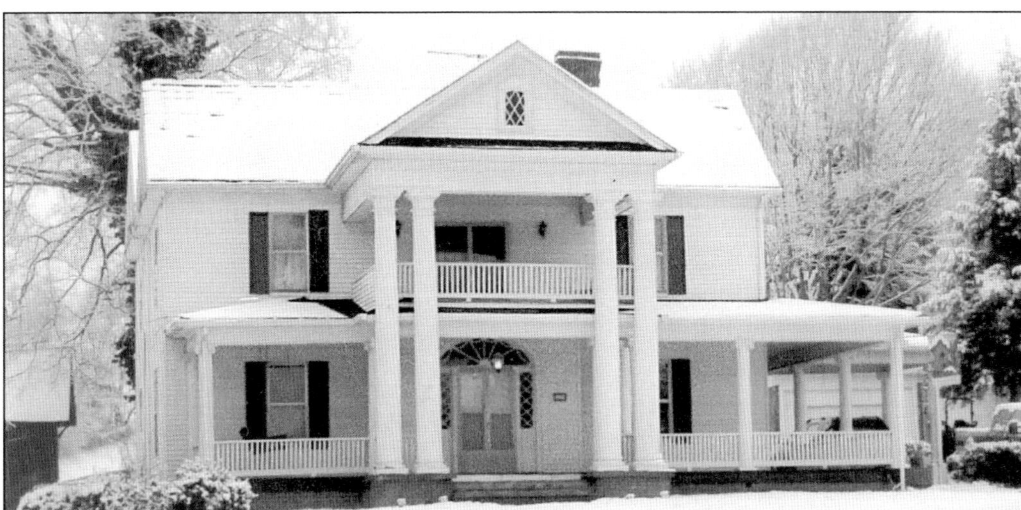

AMICABLE APPARITION AT APPERSON HOUSE. Built in 1869 by Civil War surgeon Dr. John S. Apperson, this stately home has changed hands six times through the years. Several years ago, a prospective buyer saw a ghostly woman dressed in an old-fashioned blue dress in the upstairs hall. The current owners enjoy the friendly lady, who shuts the dining room doors and turns on the lights frequently. (Courtesy Shannon Simpson.)

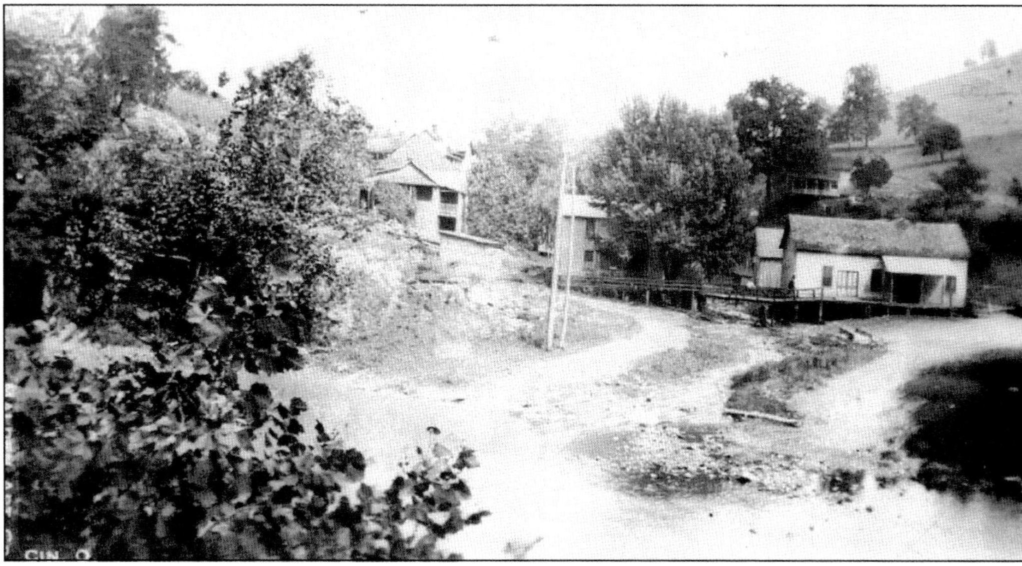

Ghostly Echoes From Battle of Saltville. In the Cedar Creek section of Saltville, during the month of October, legend has it that one can hear the commands of officers, cries of wounded soldiers, and sounds of cannons exploding. These are said to be the ghosts of the battle fought here nearly 150 years ago when Burbridge's army invaded the valley. (Courtesy Museum of the Middle Appalachians.)

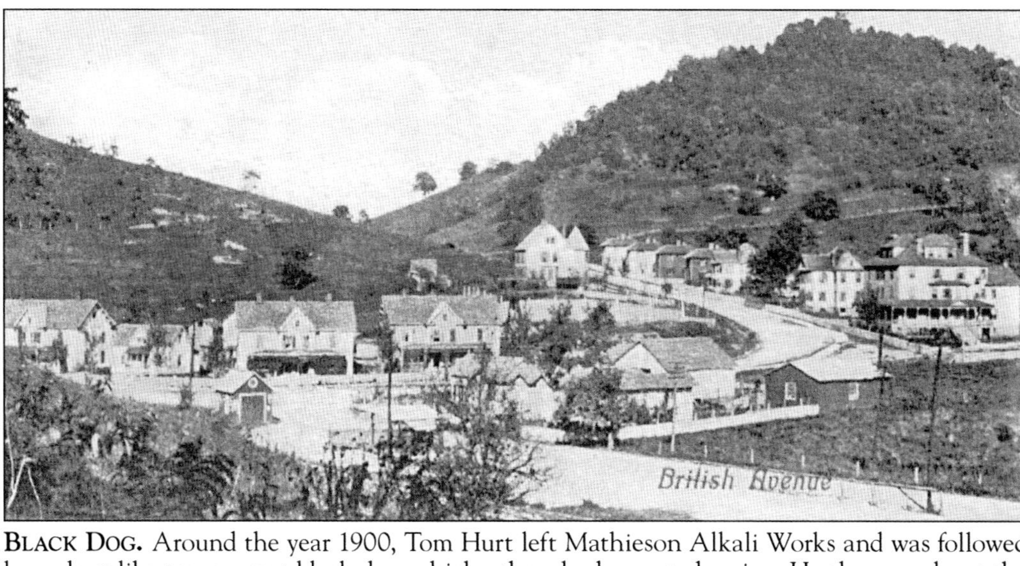

Black Dog. Around the year 1900, Tom Hurt left Mathieson Alkali Works and was followed by a ghost-like transparent black dog, which others had reported seeing. He threw rocks at the black dog and then shot it five times. Tom heard the sounds of a woman being tortured near a bridge at British Row. Upon inspection, there was no evidence of the woman or the black dog. (Courtesy Dr. Paul Brown.)

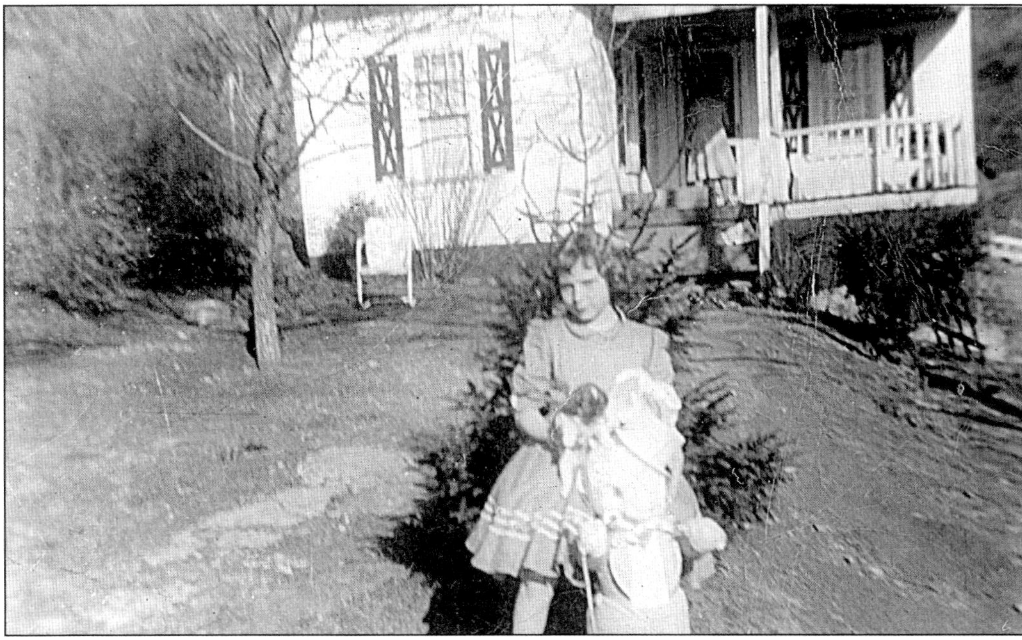

GHOSTS OF THE IRON WORKS. The Litton home was located where Stoneman's Raiders destroyed the Thomas Iron Works along Staley Creek in 1864. While constructing the home, the family, pictured, found many Civil War uniforms, bayonets, and other trinkets. They reported hearing someone sawing wood and grating the furnace in the basement, but there was no one or any wood found. (Courtesy Marlene Cornett.)

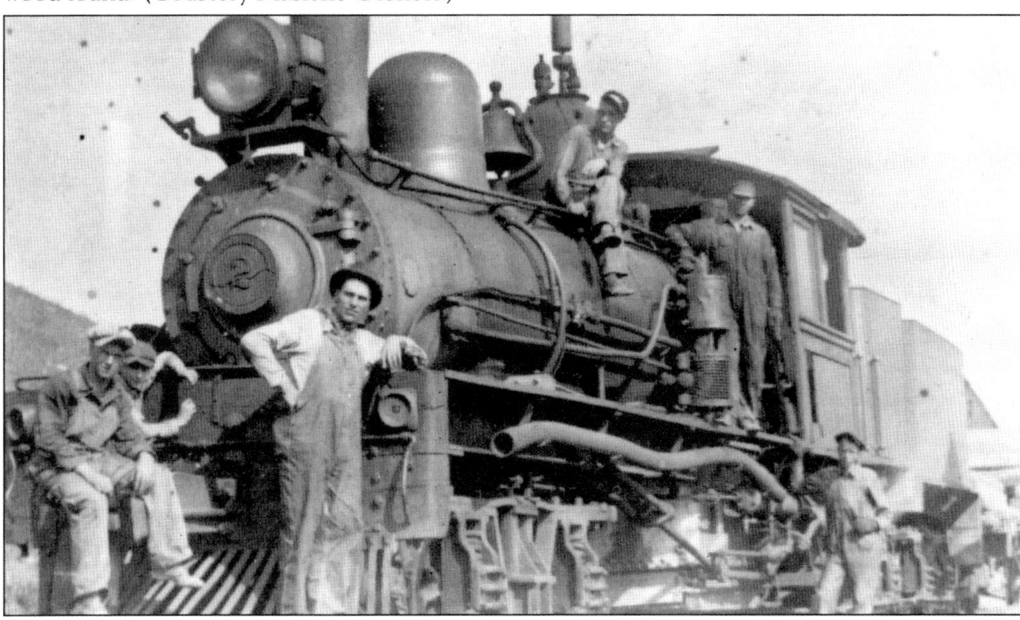

RYE VALLEY BURIED TREASURE. This crew—James Schwartz, Ed Adams, Pete Woods, Clair Delp, Buck Woods, and Jack Commer—told of picking up a passenger before stopping at Rye Valley to take on water. While they were stopped, the passenger got off and buried his money belt, then rode on into Marion. He was found dead the next day. The money belt is believed to still be buried. (Courtesy Rick Schwartz.)

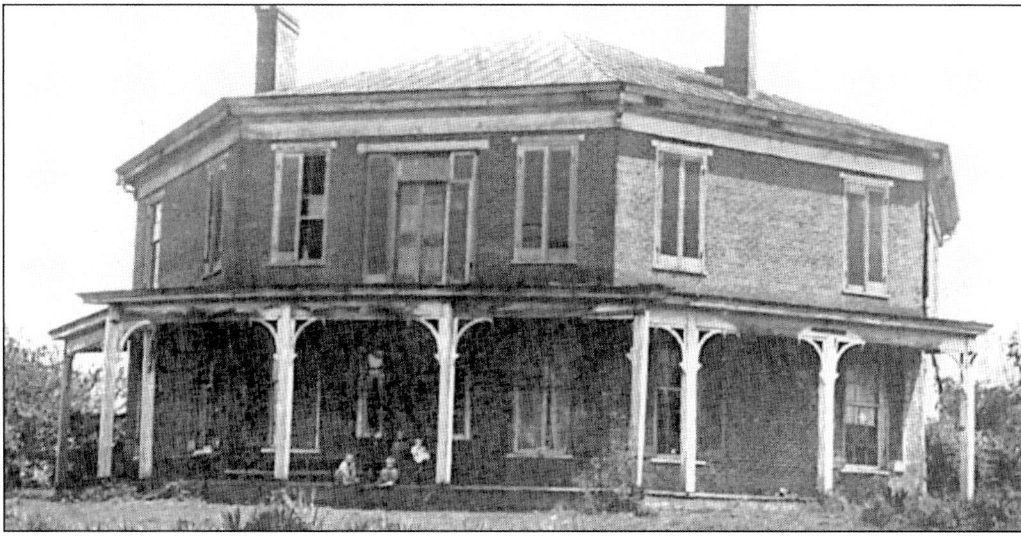

DARK ROOM AT MOUNTAIN VIEW. In the heart of this eight-sided house is a strange, windowless room. It is called "the dark room" by locals and harbors dark stains on the floor alleged to be the blood of slaves who were whipped there. Mack Sturgill shed some light on this local legend in his book, *Abijah Thomas and His Octagonal House*, stating that the stains were probably caused by food spills from the canning jars stored there. (Courtesy Mack Sturgill Collection.)

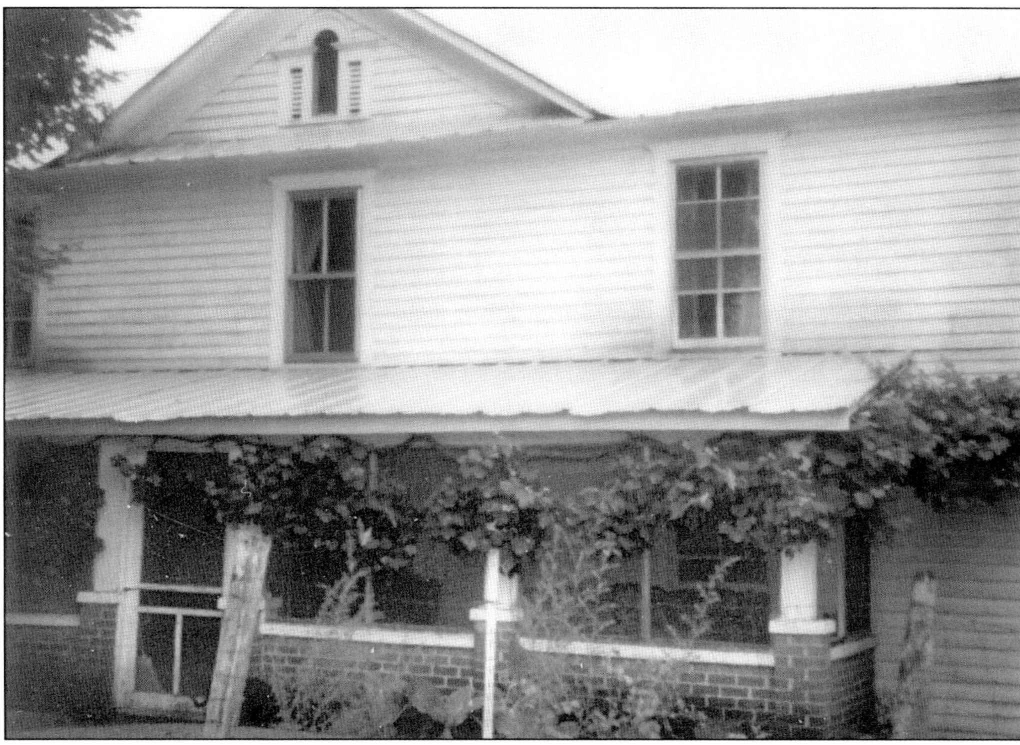

MYSTERIOUS SOUNDS AND MOVEMENT. The McClure home, *c.* mid-1800s, once stood on Mill Creek. Its occupants have told of a glass tumbler full of water turning over while sitting on the floor and no one close to it. They have also reported hearing sounds of items being dragged across the floor in an empty room upstairs. (Courtesy Freida Shupe.)

Two

LEISURE AND ENTERTAINMENT

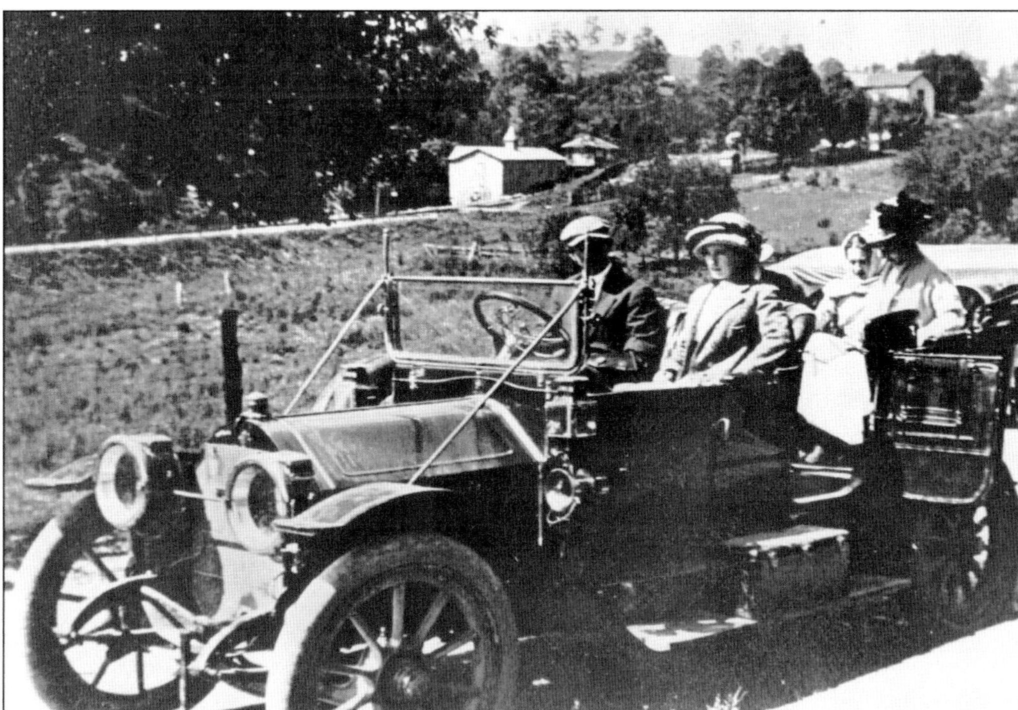

SUNDAY TOUR. The locals in this photograph are enjoying a Sunday tour in this stylish convertible. For decades, motorists have enjoyed road trips throughout Smyth County, including White Top Mountain, Mount Rogers, and Big Walker Lookout. The ladies pictured here are wearing fine hats to keep their hair in order. Notice the suicide door on this vintage automobile. (Courtesy Kenny Sturgill.)

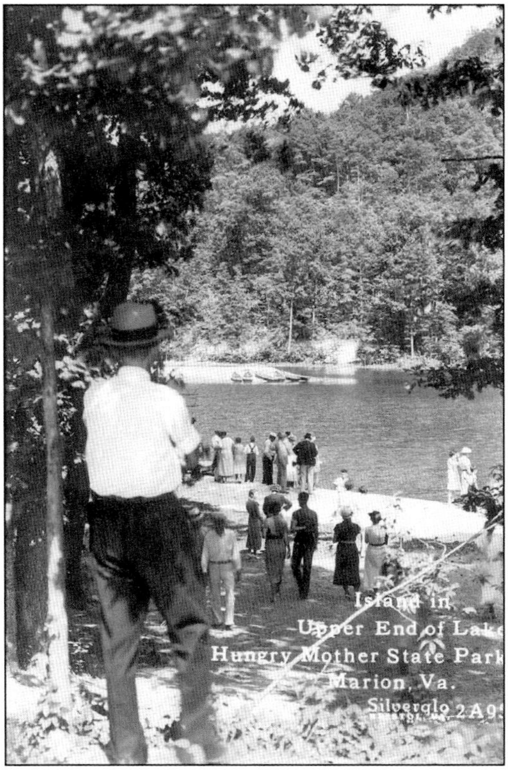

HUNGRY MOTHER ISLAND. At the upper end of Hungry Mother State Park is an island that has been the location of many weddings, plays, and family reunions. The island, which has log benches for seating, can be reached by a wooded bridge that expands across the lake. Animals roam freely, accustomed to visitors in the park. Wild flowers and foliage add to the natural backdrop. (Courtesy Dr. Paul Brown.)

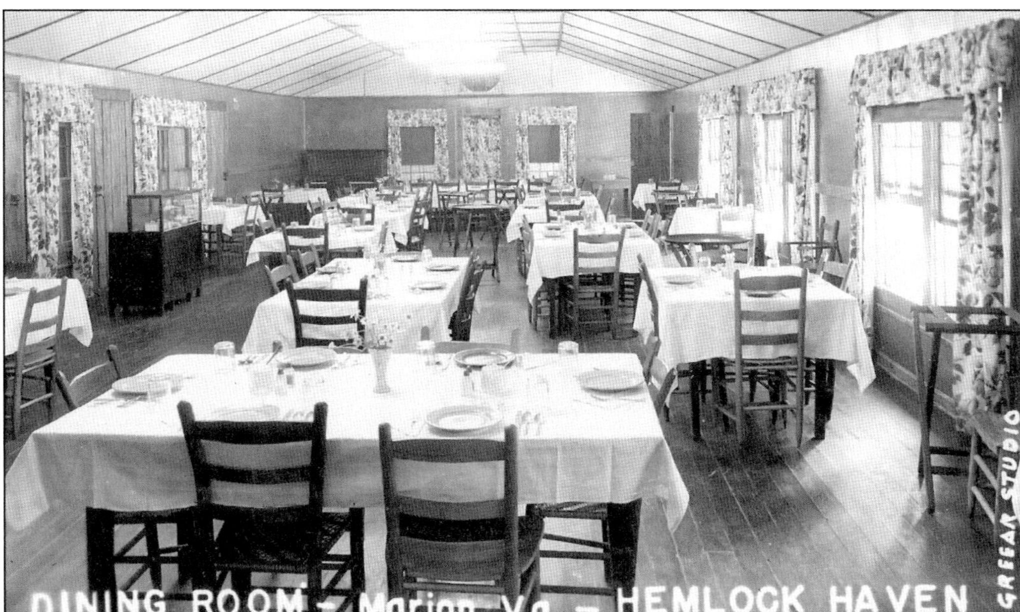

HEMLOCK HAVEN DINING ROOM. This dining room has now expanded into a conference center, but not so long ago, patrons at Hemlock Haven were treated to tasty meals cooked on-site. Located inside Hungry Mother State Park, Hemlock Haven offers cabins for lodging, baseball, volleyball, horseshoes, and nature hikes. Swimming, dining, fishing, boating, shopping, and more are offered at Hungry Mother State Park. (Courtesy Dr. Paul Brown.)

ENJOYING HUNGRY MOTHER STATE PARK. Horseback riding at Hungry Mother State Park was a popular pastime for vacationers. There were many trails those interested in nature could ride. For vacationers who wanted to stay over, a cabin could be rented for $15 per week for two people, $20 per week for three to four people, and $5 per additional person. Within the five years between 1936 and 1940, attendance grew from 68,505 to 93,889. Prior to World War II, the most popular activities were swimming, boating, horseback riding, and picnicking. (Courtesy Dr. Paul Brown.)

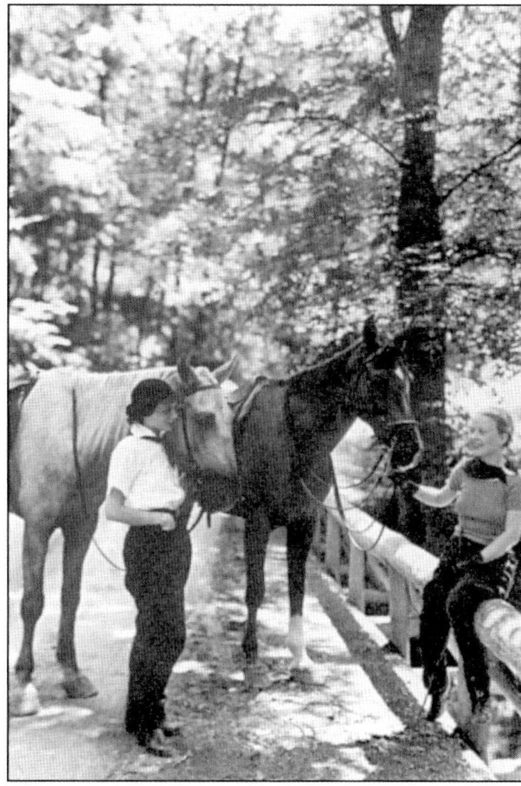

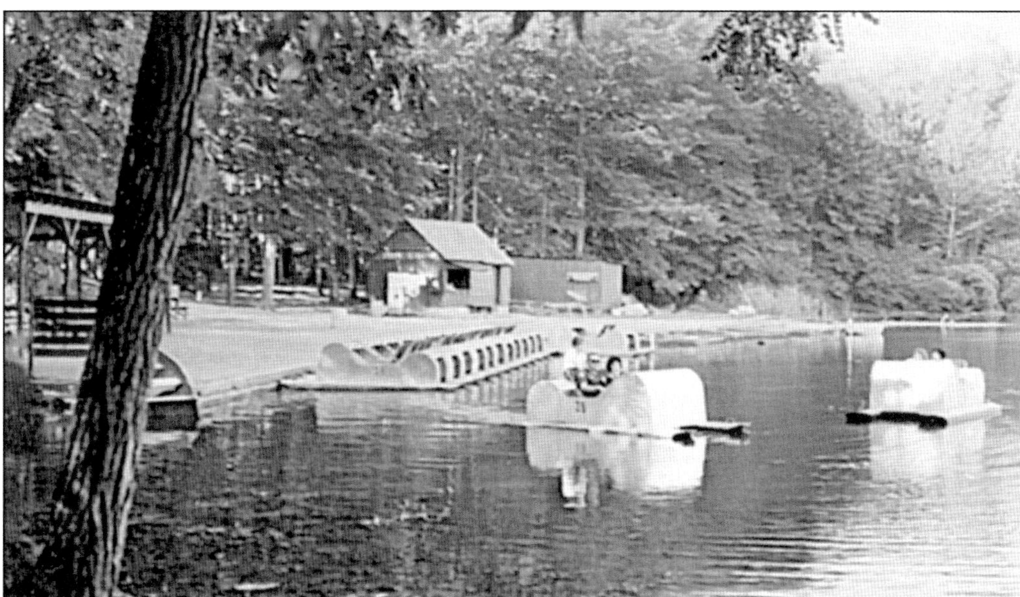

HUNGRY MOTHER STATE PARK. From the time Hungry Mother State Park opened on June 15, 1936, it was clear that the park had something for everyone. It was the most popular of all parks in Virginia. On June 21, 1936, over 1,500 people visited the park. Over 400 of these visitors went swimming at a cost of 15¢ for adults and 10¢ for children. Paddleboats and canoes could be rented at the boathouse. (Courtesy Dr. Paul Brown.)

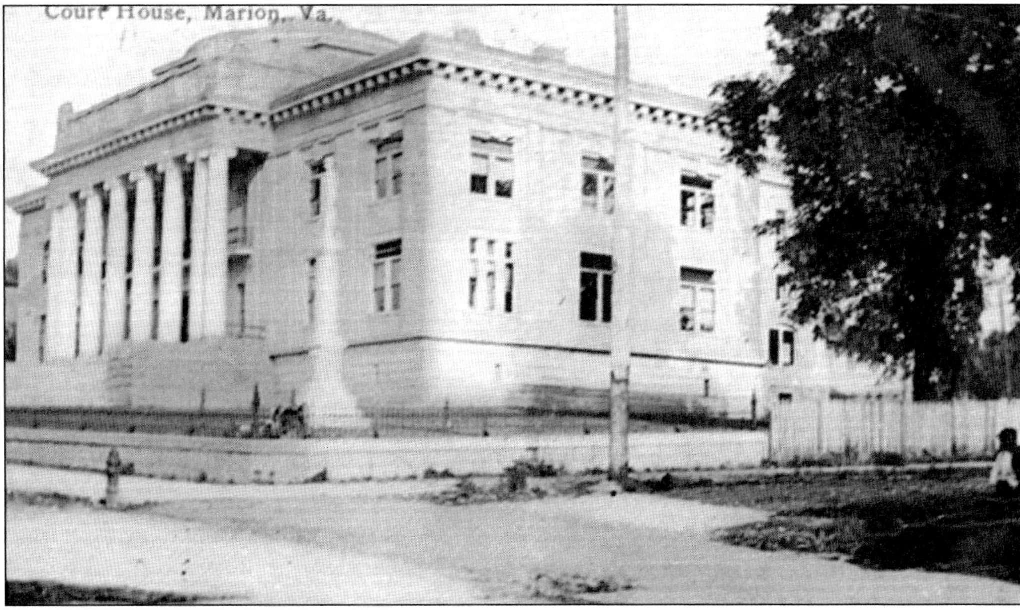

MARION'S FIRST MOTION PICTURE THEATRE. Built in 1905 as Smyth County's second courthouse, the upstairs of this building contained an auditorium for community productions. Patrons from all over attended the theater, which boasted of modern amenities such as electricity, stage, dressing rooms, and balcony. In 1909, the area's first motion picture show was viewed here by patrons. (Courtesy Dr. Paul Brown.)

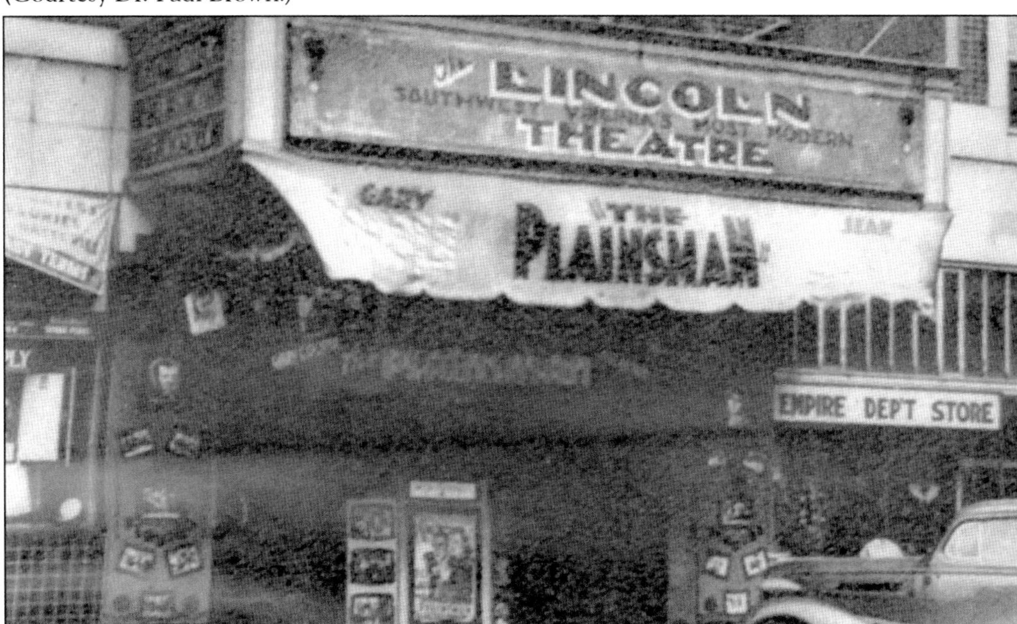

***PLAINSMAN* AT THE LINCOLN THEATRE.** This vintage photograph of "Southwest Virginia's Most Modern Theatre" advertises *The Plainsman* starring Gary Cooper and Jean Arthur portraying Wild Bill Hickok and Calamity Jane. The movie made its debut in 1936. The Lincoln Theatre was built in 1929 by C. C. Lincoln and his sons, John D. and C. C. Jr., at a cost of $150,000. In May 2004, the theater opened following a $1.8-million renovation. (Courtesy Mack Sturgill Collection.)

LINCOLN THEATRE ARTIST REVEALED. Amidst ancient Mayan Indian motifs stand six 15-by-20-foot murals, which were painted by artist Lola Poston exclusively for the Lincoln Theatre. From the time the theater opened in 1929, the name of the artist was a secret until Mack Sturgill discovered the truth in 1995. Charles C. Lincoln Sr. paid Poston $50 for each mural. (Courtesy Mack Sturgill Collection.)

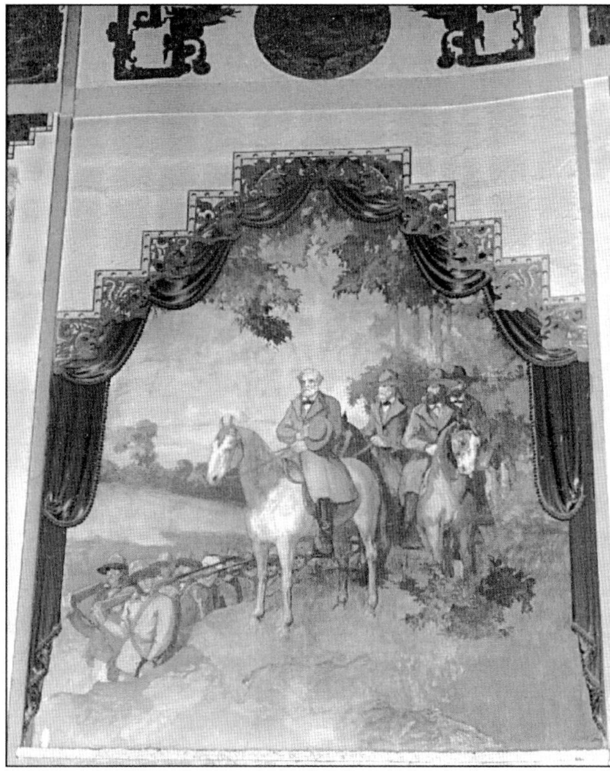

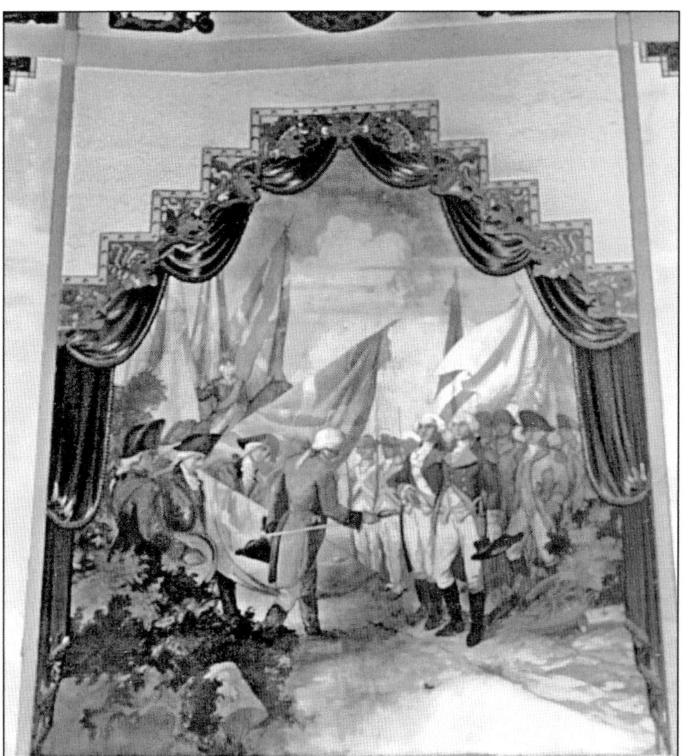

LINCOLN THEATRE MURALS. The beautiful hand-painted murals mounted at the Lincoln Theatre depict important aspects of history. These murals are titled the *Landing of Columbus in America*, *Surrender of Cornwallis at Yorktown*, *Daniel Boone with Indians on the Virginia Frontier*, *Smyth County's Cattle Industry*, *Robert E. Lee Reviewing his Troops*, and *Industrial Progress in the County*. (Courtesy Mack Sturgill Collection.)

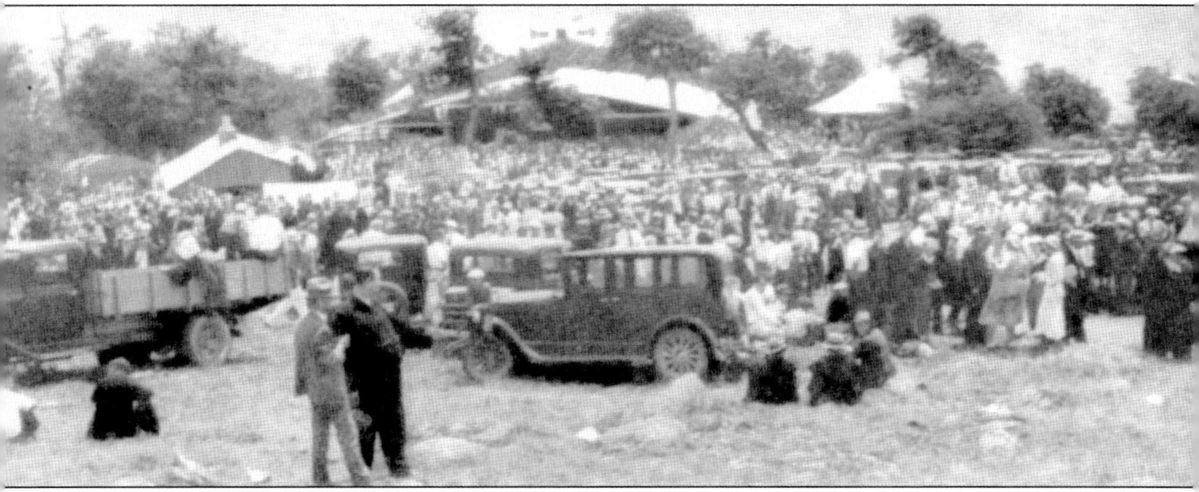

WHITE TOP FOLK FESTIVAL. This is an early photograph of the White Top Folk Festival in neighboring Grayson County, which began on August 15, 1931. In 1933, First Lady Eleanor Roosevelt attended the festival and invited several of the musicians to perform at the White House. Designed to celebrate and promote traditional music, the festival was organized by Annabel Morris Buchanan, John Powell, and John Blakemore. The festival consisted of both instrumental and singing contests and recreational dancing for the spectators the first year. Afterward, it expanded to include craft exhibitions and a conference relating to Appalachian mountain culture. Because of repeated flooding, the final festival was in the year 1939. (Courtesy Mack Sturgill Collection.)

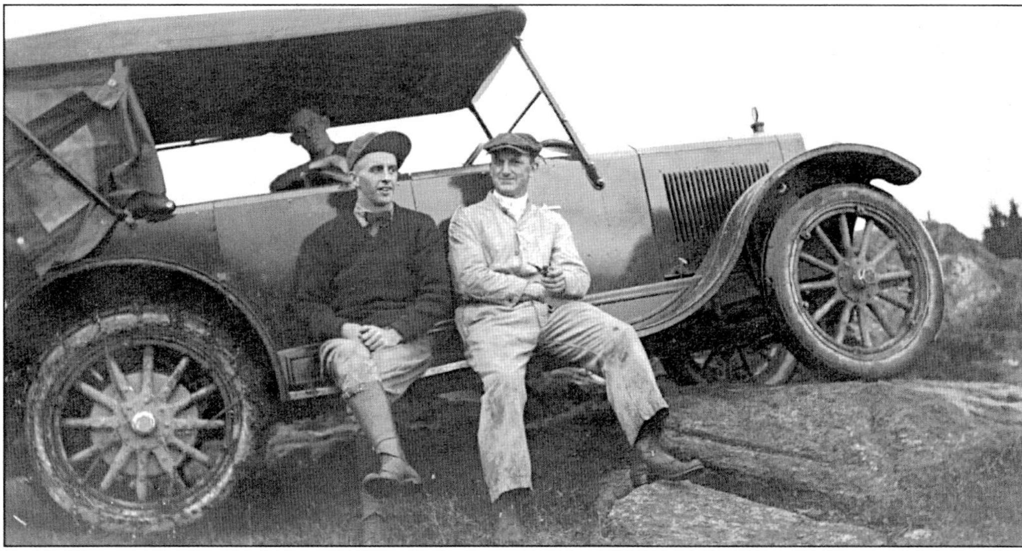

First Auto on White Top. Generations of Smyth Countians have enjoyed a day trip and picnic to White Top Mountain, the second highest mountain in Virginia. One can view the states of Virginia, Tennessee, Kentucky, West Virginia, and North Carolina from its peak. Pictured here is the first automobile to climb White Top Mountain. Notice the chains on the rear tire. Seated on the running board are Art Slear (left) and Charlie "Skinny" Burch. (Courtesy Charles Wassum III.)

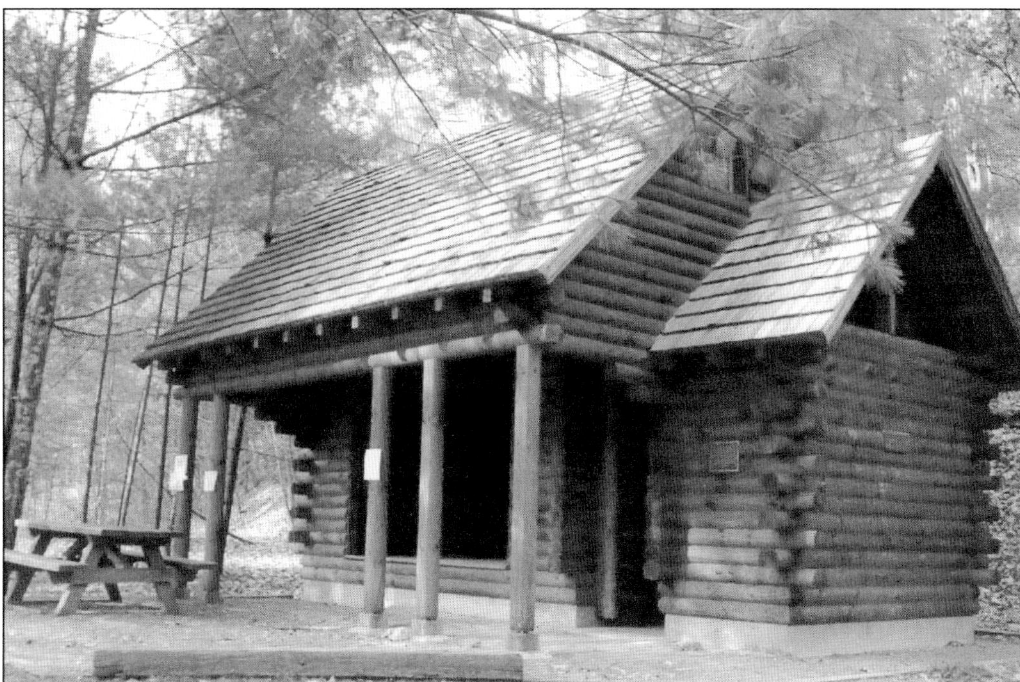

Trail Bathhouse. The Appalachian Trail, which extends from Maine to Georgia, runs through Smyth County, entering just north of Groseclose, crossing Sugar Grove onto White Top. Hikers from all over the world travel this trail that offers over 2,000 miles of nature for exploration by anyone, regardless of experience level. Pictured is a bathhouse located along the trail on Brushy Mountain. (Courtesy Debra Williams.)

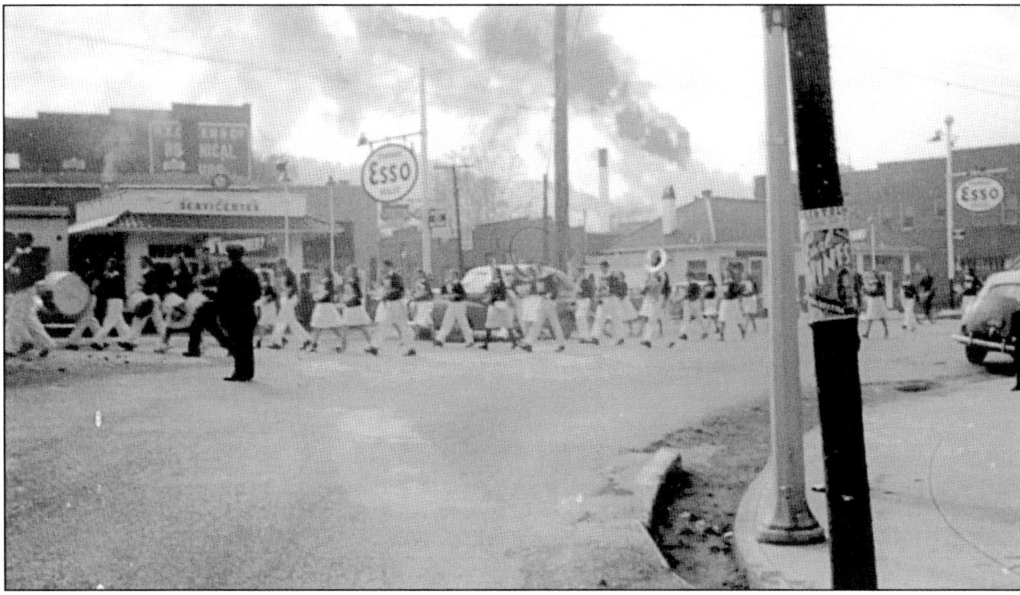

HOMECOMING PARADE, 1941. In the midst of World War II, locals found enjoyment in the annual homecoming parade on Main Street in Marion. Notice the R. T. Greer and Company billboard on the side of their building advertising botanical herbs. The flyer on the pole at the right of the photograph advertises popular jazz pianist Earl Hines and his Grand Terrace Orchestra Band. (Courtesy Charles W. Seaver.)

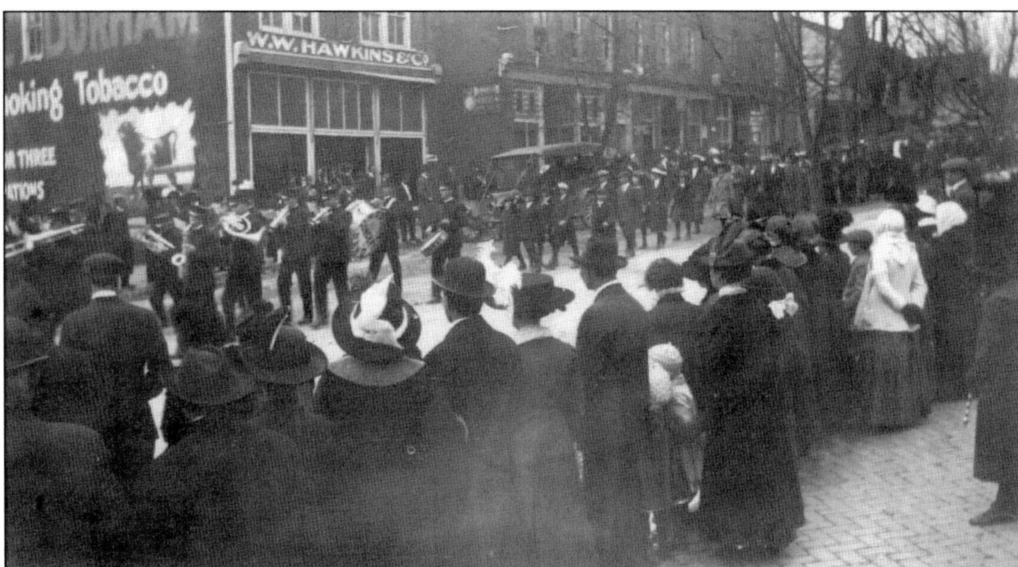

MARION CONCERT BAND. Notice the local ladies dressed in coats and their finest feathered hats as they braved the cold to view the parade. This photograph was snapped as the Marion Concert Band passed in front of W. W. Hawkins and Company. The attire of many of the men in this photograph probably came from W. W. Hawkins and Company because they sold stylish clothing for gentlemen. (Courtesy Dr. Paul Brown.)

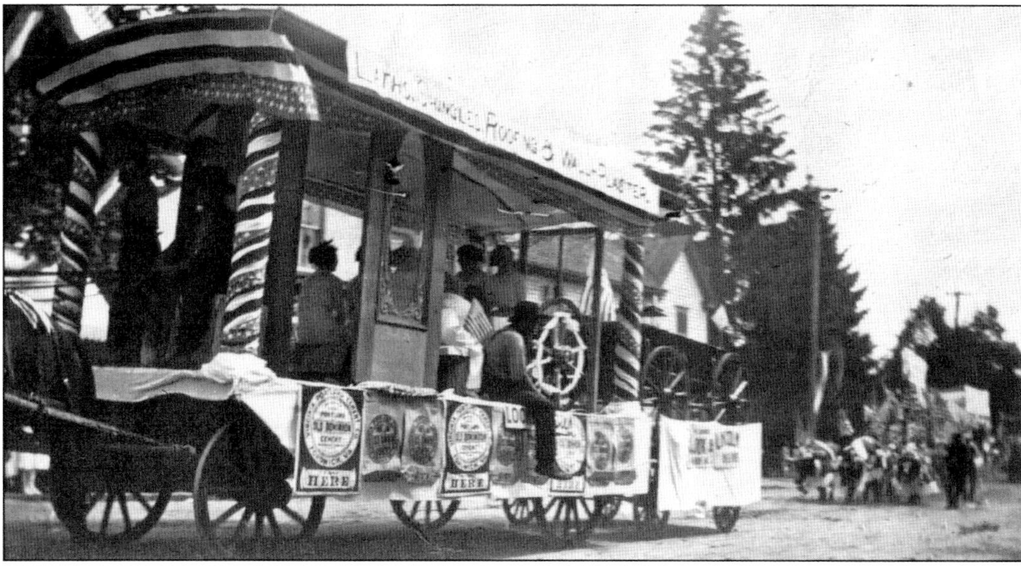

LOOK AND LINCOLN PARADE FLOAT. Around 1946, the banners located on this Look and Lincoln parade float advertised laths, shingles, roofing, wallpaper, and Dominion Cement. Notice the new wagon in tow that advertises Look and Lincoln's line of wagons. This is probably a Fourth of July parade because of the stars and stripes decorations and the flag being flown. (Courtesy Dr. Paul Brown.)

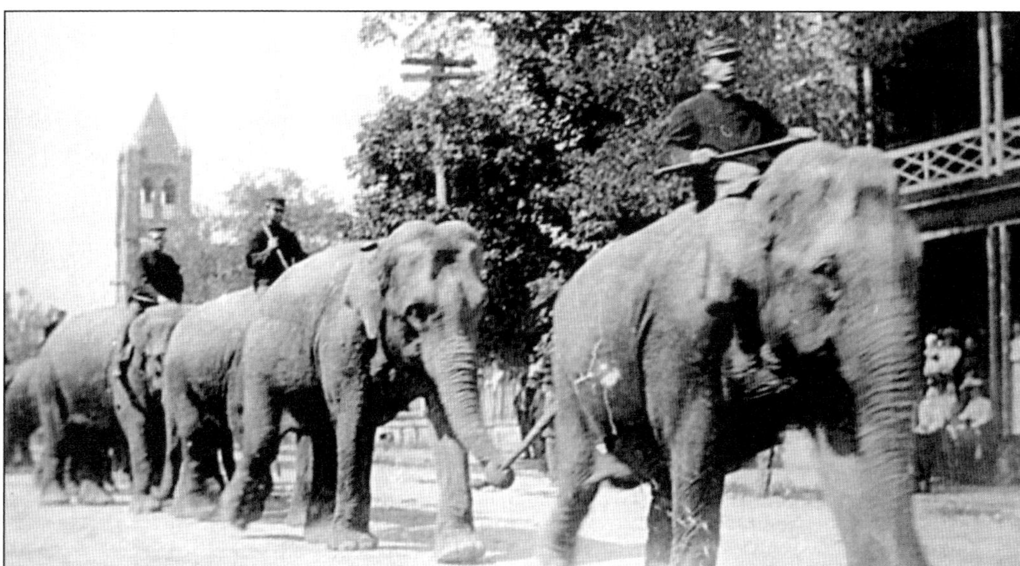

CIRCUS IN MARION. Not many elephants have walked the streets of Marion, but this *c.* 1910 photograph is proof that they have visited at least once. Notice the local spectators gathered on the porch of the Jackson Building (right), which was built *c.* 1857. Many locals hid their treasures here during the Civil War. The steeple of the Royal Oak Presbyterian Church can be seen in the background. (Courtesy Mack Sturgill Collection.)

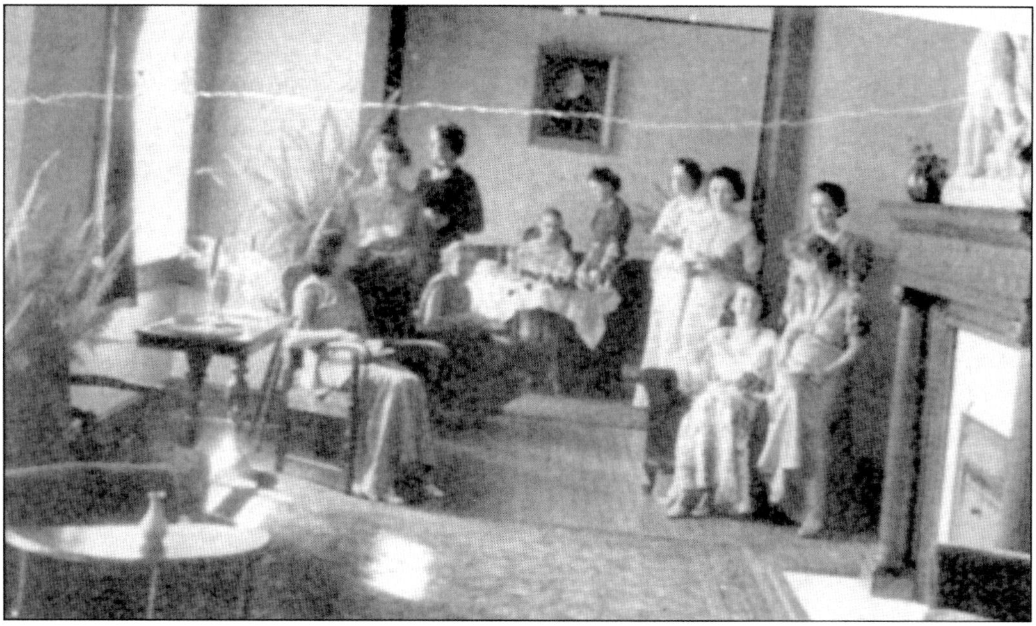

MARION COLLEGE AFTERNOON TEA. At Marion College, afternoon tea was a tradition. It was a time for the girls to socialize and bond, which helped foster more cohesive relationships. Sometimes tea was held next door at Rosemont, which had the reputation of harboring a family atmosphere and always having open doors for the students. (Courtesy Mack Sturgill Collection.)

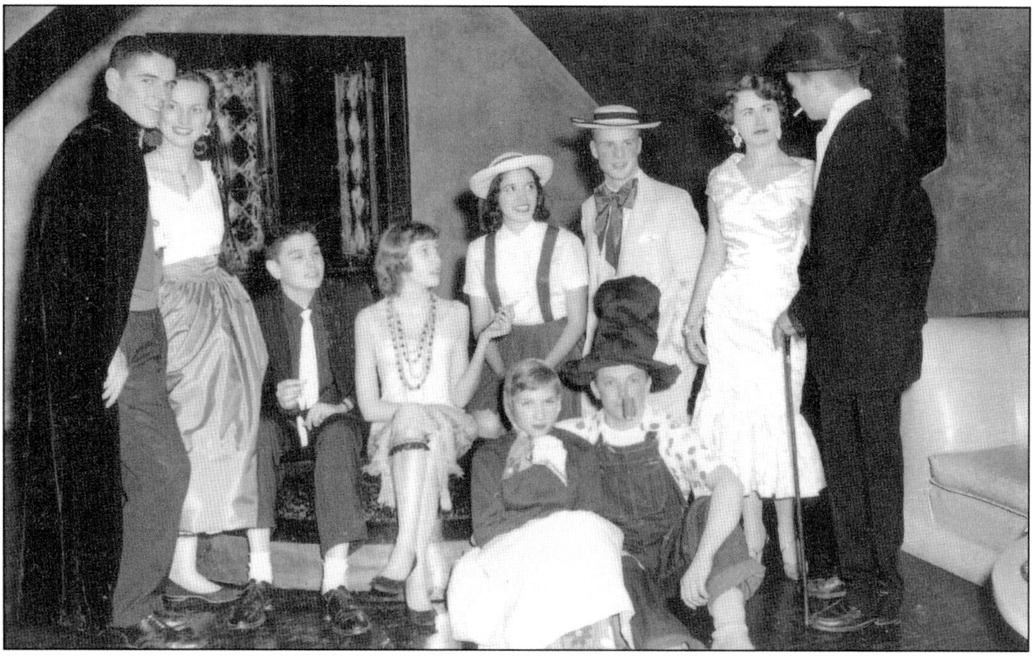

COSTUME PARTY AT GREYSTONE MANOR. In December 1957, Judy Greer and Erwin Wassum hosted a costume party in the ballroom at the elegant Greystone Manor, which sat where the Best Western is now. Pictured from left to right are (first row) Carol Manning and Kenny Greer; (second row) Robert Fray, Judy Greer, Bobby Estep, Kennon Hopkins, Erwin Wassum, Bill Thompson, and two unidentified. (Courtesy Erwin Wassum Rowland.)

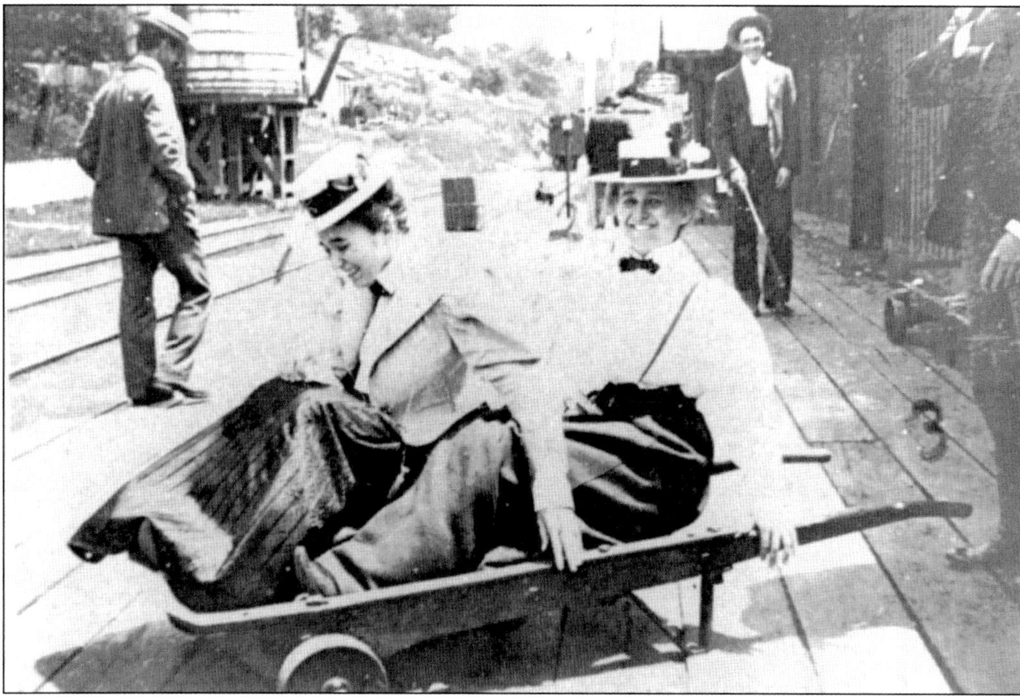

A Barrel of Laughs. These two ladies are having the time of their lives at the Marion Train Depot, as are the spectators who are laughing at their antics. There aren't many metal wheels on wheelbarrows anymore. Notice the water tank to the left, where steam-operated trains stopped to retrieve their water. (Courtesy Mack Sturgill Collection.)

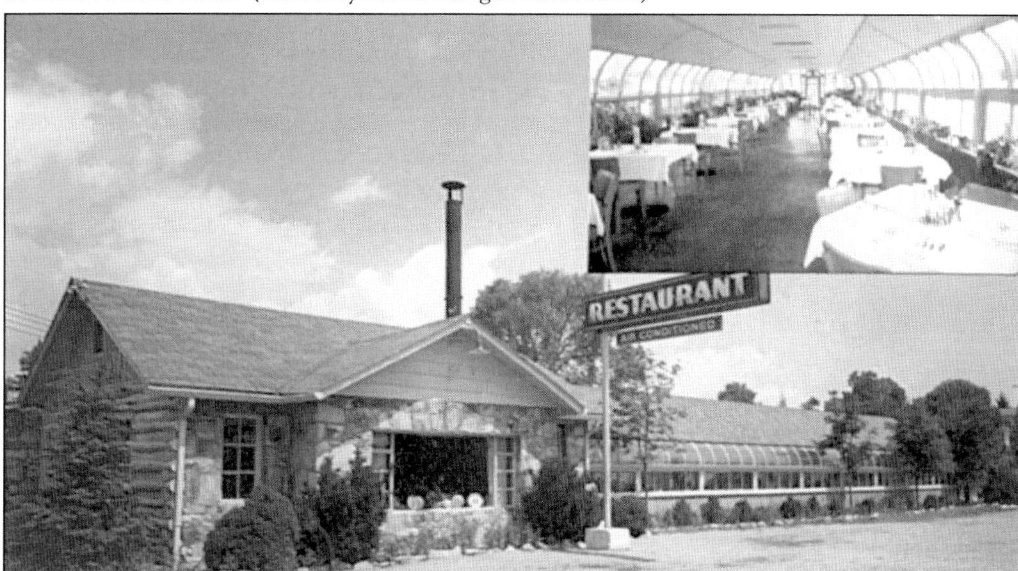

Virginia House Restaurant. Charles Wassum Jr. added a greenhouse to a log cabin service station to form a floral shop. Wassum partnered with George Greer Sr. and turned the shop into this restaurant. When the building burned in 1956, the restaurant operated in the Wassum home until Greystone Manor was acquired and transformed into the restaurant. Bill Lemon bought Greystone and later sold it to Holiday Inn. (Courtesy Atwood J. Huff.)

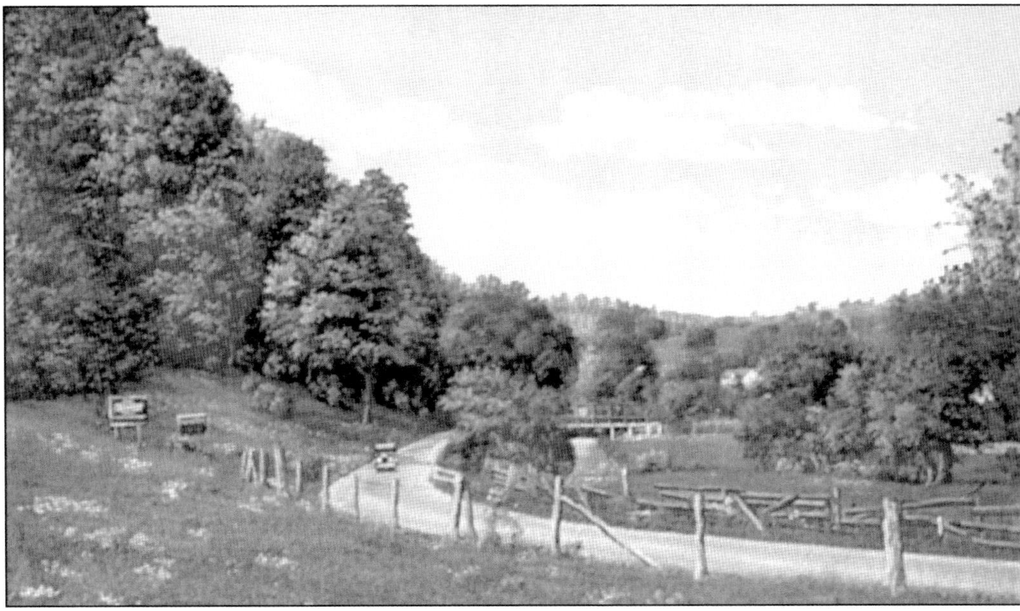

Lee Highway. Lee Highway was named as a national memorial to Gen. Robert E. Lee, who used his leadership power to rebuild the nation after the Civil War. What was once a game trail and Native American warpath became a narrow road used by trains of pack animals, wagons, and stagecoaches. Motorists enjoy a Sunday drive along this main highway. (Courtesy Dr. Paul Brown.)

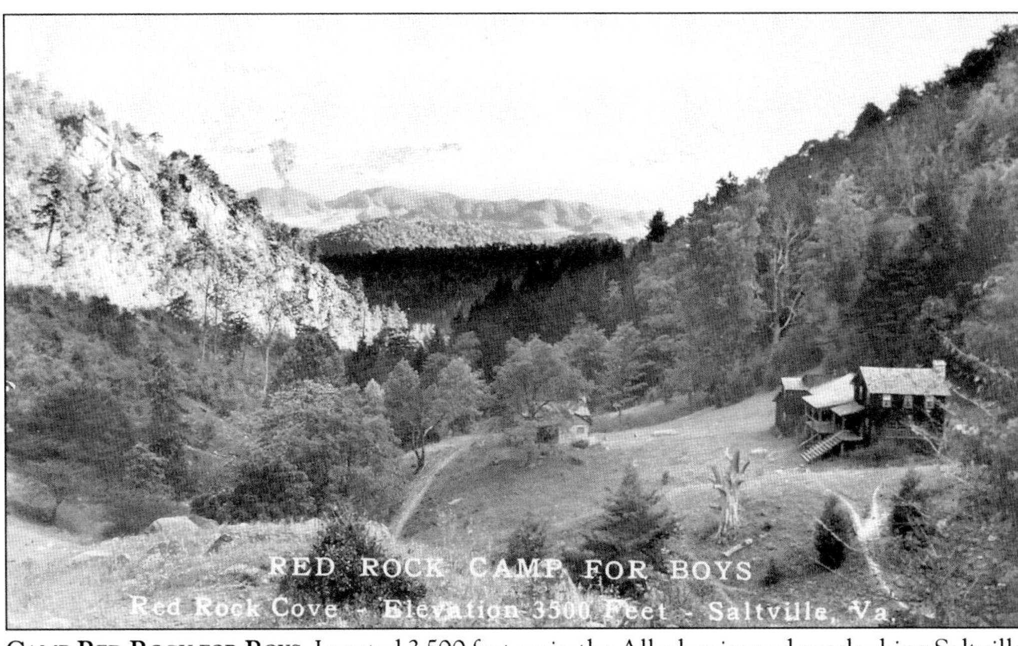

Camp Red Rock for Boys. Located 3,500 feet up in the Alleghenies and overlooking Saltville, Camp Red Rock was built on an old Native American camping ground. Their 1,000 acres of land made possible activities such as badminton, hiking, horseshoes, track, archery, wood-crafts, Ping-Pong, and the study of birds. Up to 25 boys attended at one time. (Courtesy Dr. Paul Brown.)

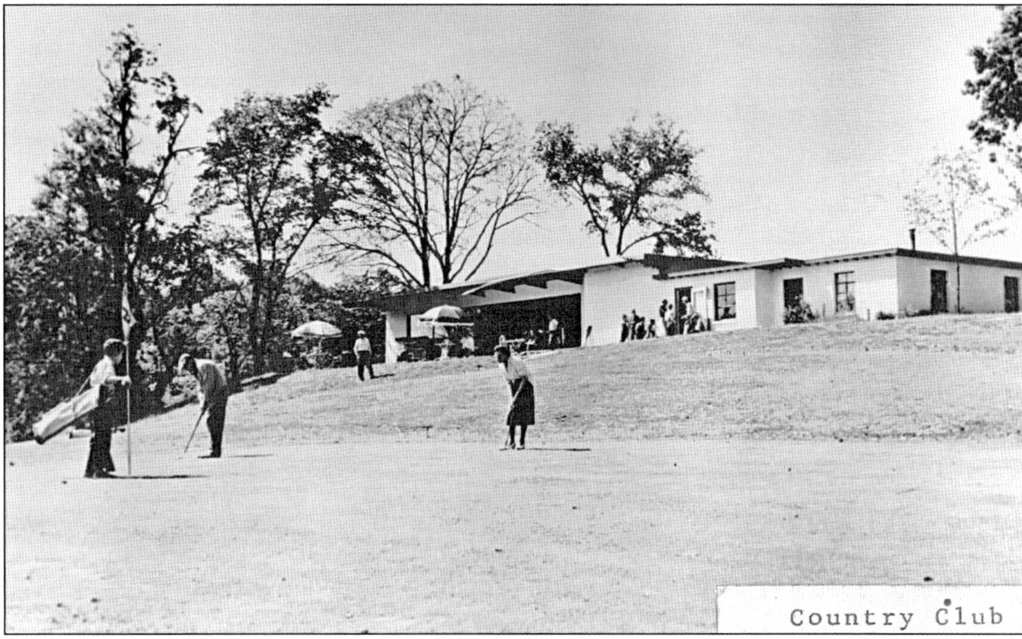

TEEING OFF. Holston Hills Country Club opened in 1946 and expanded from 9 to 18 holes in the late 1960s. The original clubhouse was a 16-foot-square cinder-block building. The present-day clubhouse was completed in 1998 at a cost of over $1 million. A prior golf course, built by Charles Wassum Sr. was located near Park Terrace Apartments, with the first hole located on land occupied by the Smyth County Community Hospital. (Courtesy Chamber of Commerce.)

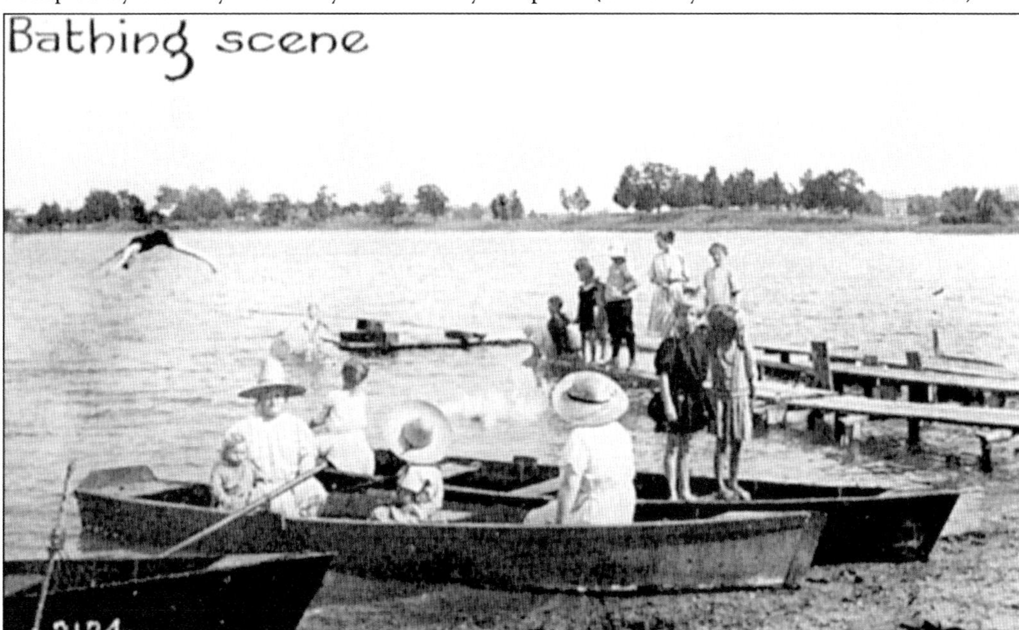

DANCING ON WATER. Here at Lake Mount Airy, near Groseclose, locals gathered for sunbathing, fishing, swimming, boating, and dancing during the 1930s and 1940s. A wooden platform placed over the water allowed local bands to perform while those in attendance danced on the water. This was a favorite spot where families gathered to picnic and play. (Courtesy Jeff Weaver.)

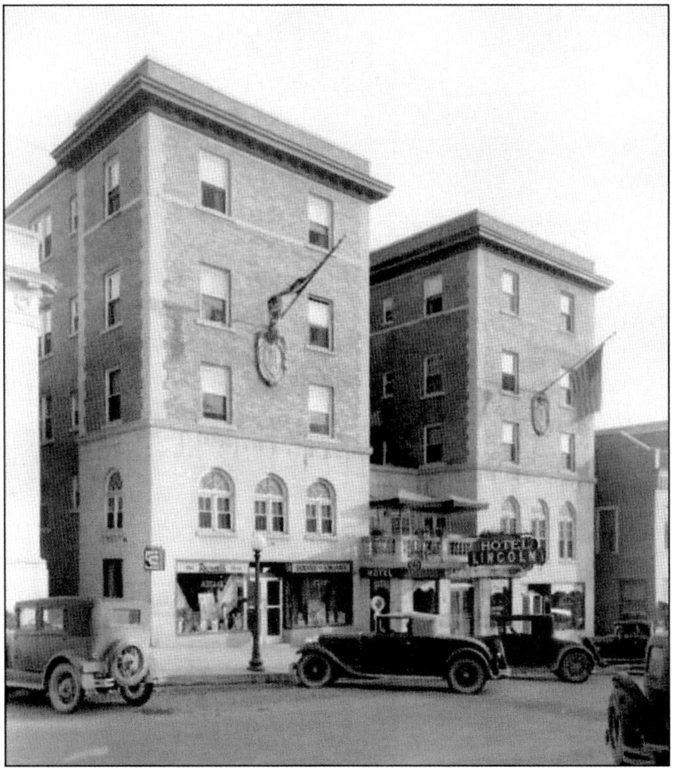

HOTEL LINCOLN. The original front desk is back in service at the General Francis Marion Hotel, which opened in April 2006 after a $4.5-million renovation. In 1928, this $175,000 hotel was renamed the Hotel Lincoln because of confusion with the similarly named Hotel Marion located across the street. Tourists have frequented the hotel through the years after watching a movie at the Lincoln Theatre. (Courtesy Mack Sturgill Collection.)

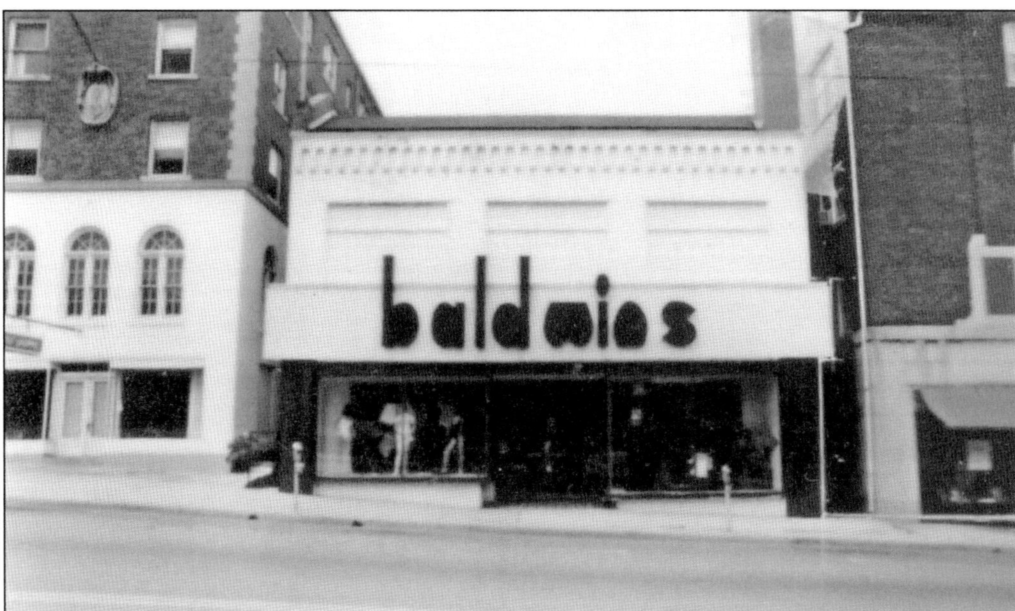

FRANCES OPERA HOUSE. Located between the Lincoln Hotel and the Lincoln Theater, this building has always been a department store. However, during the early 1900s, it was also an opera house. Here many locals were entertained by traveling theatrical companies, local bands, and political debates. During the construction of the new courthouse, trials and other county meetings took place here. (Courtesy Bill Huber.)

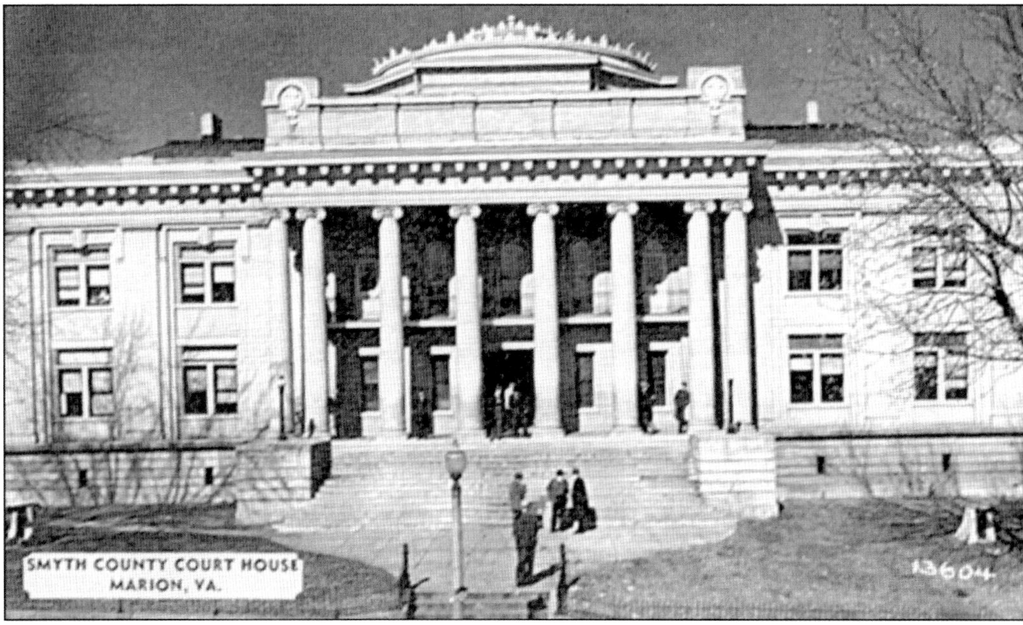

MARION'S FIRST PUBLIC LIBRARY. The ladies' room on the second floor of the courthouse was opened to the public on Saturdays from 3:00 to 5:00 p.m. so one could choose a book from the library that was also housed there. Marion's first public library was formed in 1922 by the local Women's Club. Florence Fell was the first librarian. In 1935, the library moved to the newly built Municipal Building. (Courtesy Dr. Paul Brown.)

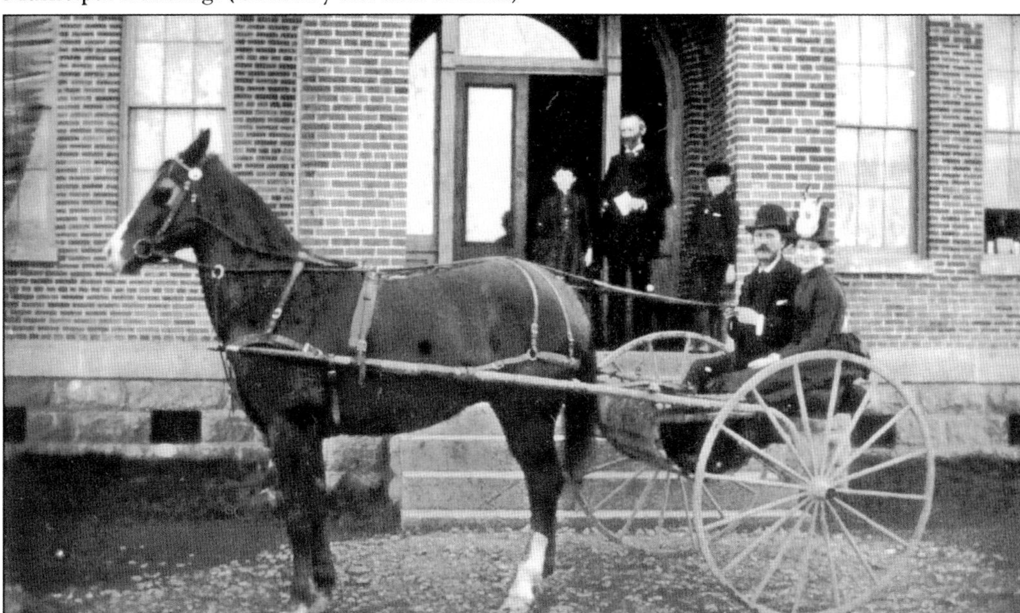

BUGGY RIDE AT STATE HOSPITAL. Most Southwestern Lunatic Asylum employees and their family members lived on the grounds. Their coming and going off the hospital property was restricted. Single women were permitted to leave the grounds only on Sundays and with special permission. In this *c.* 1890 photograph, this couple in the buggy are posing as others look on. (Courtesy Southwest Virginia Mental Health Institute.)

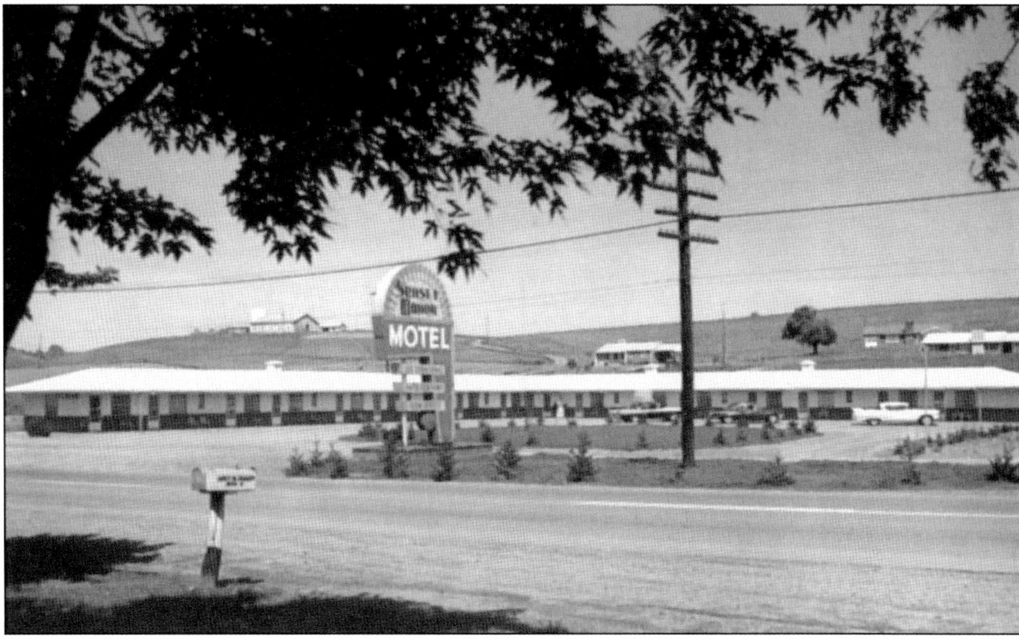

SUNSET MANOR MOTEL. Located on Highway 11, west of Chilhowie, the Sunset Motel was a popular stopover for those traveling through Smyth County. As modern conveniences became available, the motel offered color televisions and telephones in every room. This later became Maple Grove Retirement Home. Notice what few homes were located in what now is a subdivision. (Courtesy Dr. Paul Brown.)

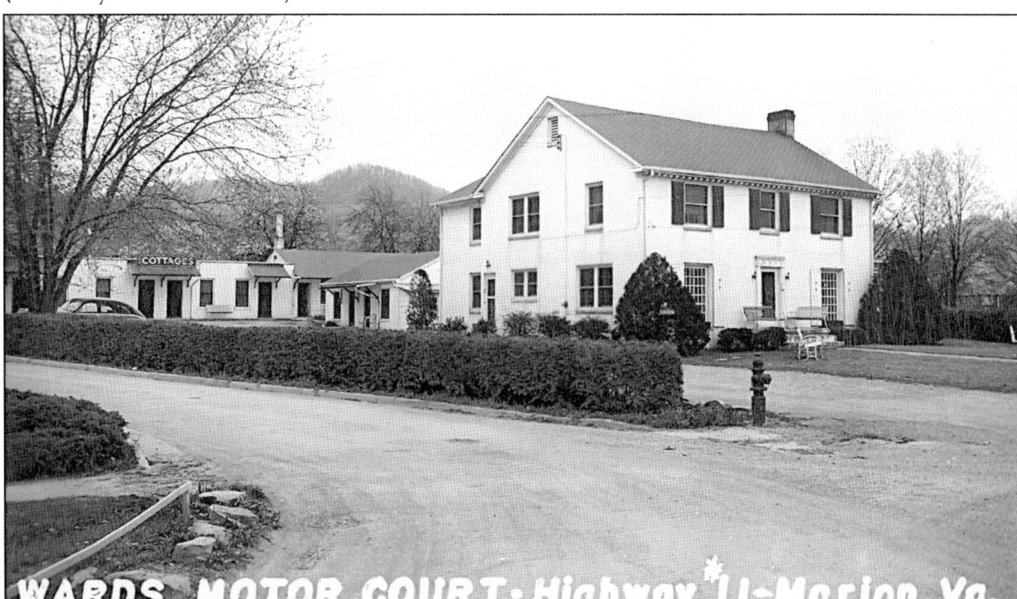

WARD'S TOURIST HOME AND COURT. Erected as Marion's first motel c. 1940, the Ward's Tourist Home and Court was owned by J. L. Ward. It contained 33 beds including those inside the home where guests also boarded. The name was changed by new owner Charles Lorenzen in the 1970s to Lorenzen's Motel. Notice how the dirt road goes off of Lee Highway into a curve. (Courtesy Clegg Williams.)

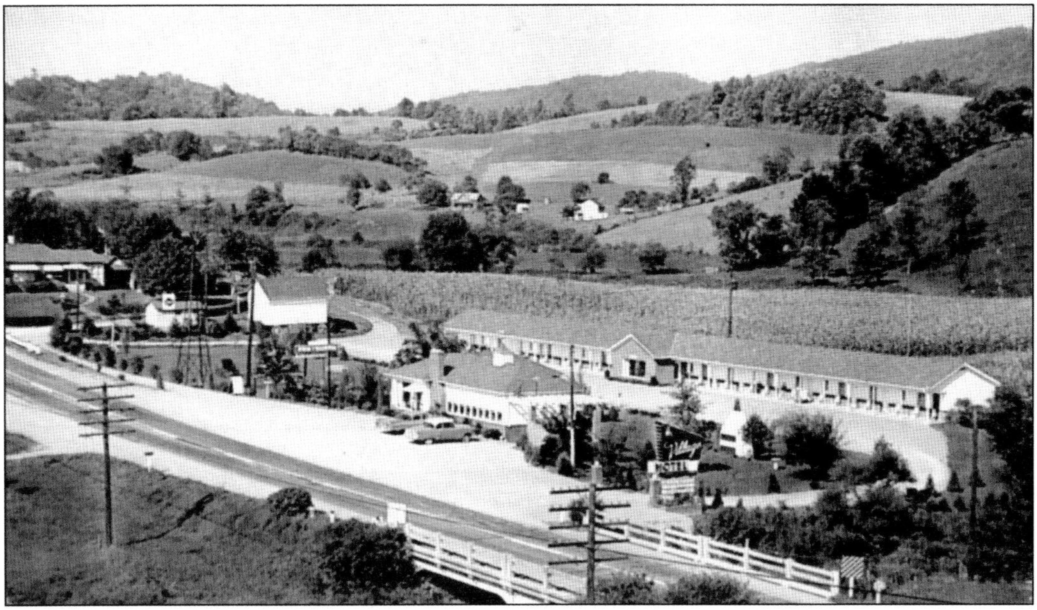

VILLAGE MOTEL AND RESTAURANT. The Village Motel and Restaurant advertised the best old-fashioned cooking around. This business was located along Highway 11 in Atkins. At the time this photograph was taken, there was only a field where Interstate 81 is now located. (Courtesy Dr. Paul Brown.)

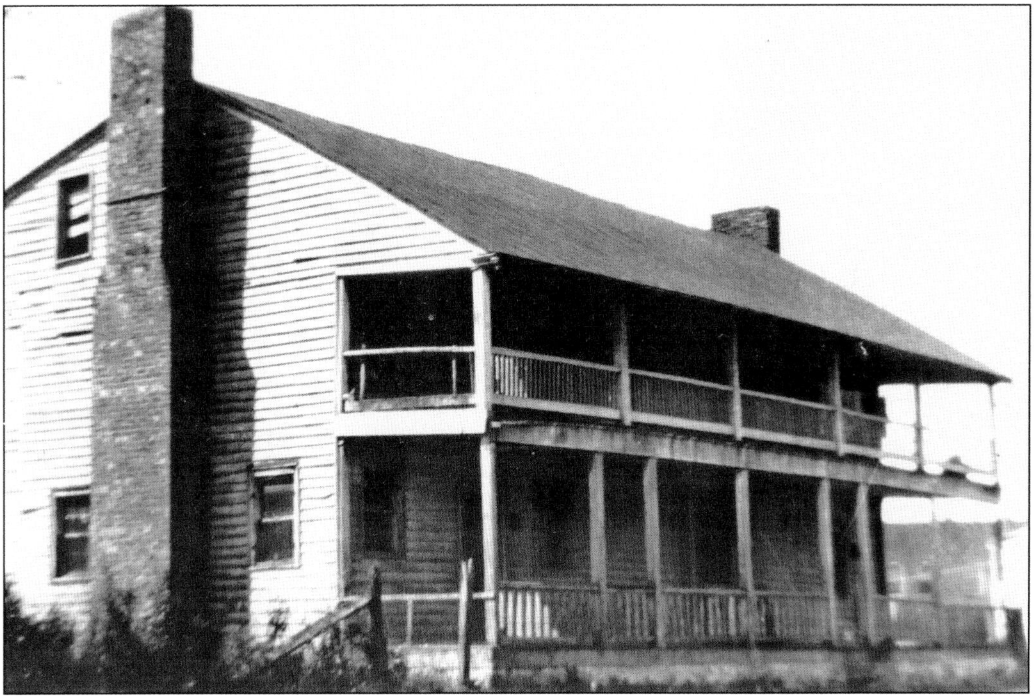

SHUGART TAVERN. Built *c.* 1815 by Henry Shugart, this log structure sat on Main Street at the current location of Dean's Bike Shop and Rector's Supply. The train station was then located across the river on Chilhowie Street. Those bringing products into town for shipping would sometimes lodge in one of the tavern's 14 rooms. (Courtesy Mack Sturgill Collection.)

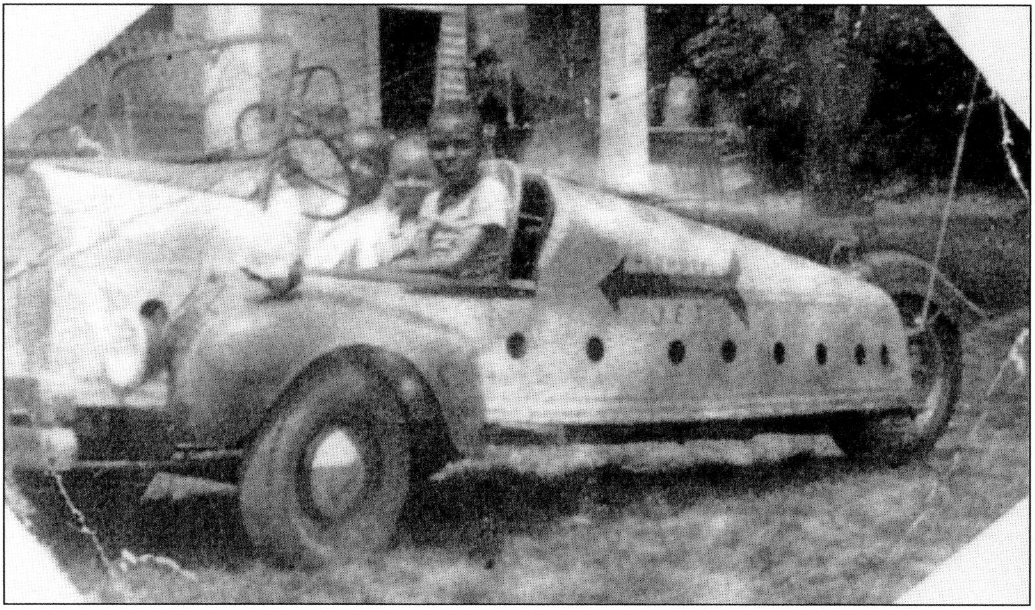

HARRY PLUMMER'S SCRAP CAR. Chilhowie Greever Drug Corporation's head chemist was a black man named Harry Plummer. He was an inventor who made three automobiles from scrap metal found around town. In the 1930s, Ford Motor Company offered Plummer a job in Detroit, which he declined. Harry and his father, William, were genius inventors. Some of Plummer's descendants still live in the area. (Courtesy Lillian P. Thompson.)

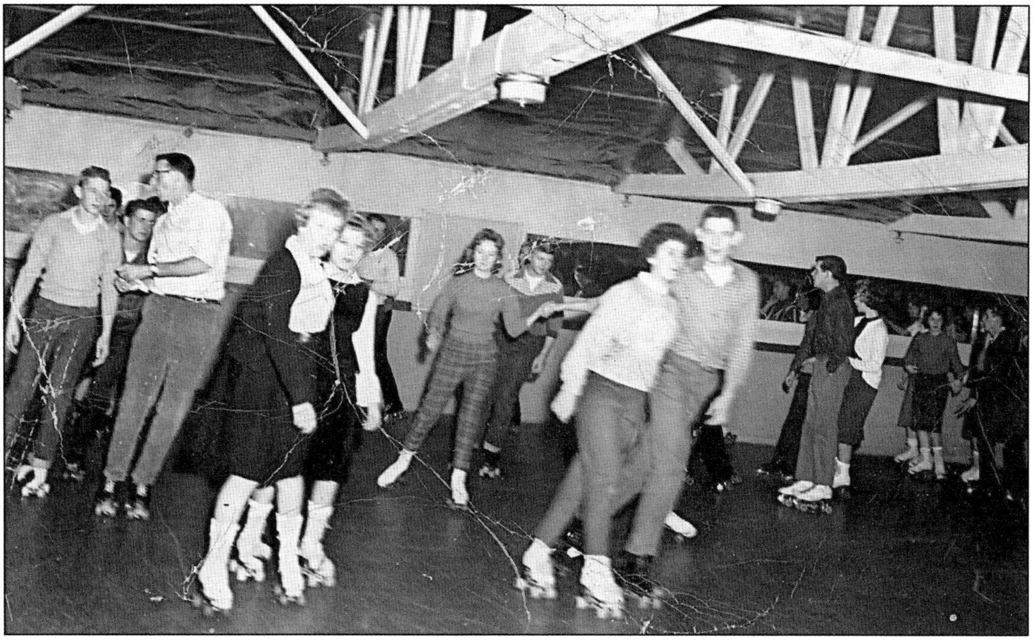

MURPHY'S SKATING RINK. Located on Highway 11, west of Chilhowie, this skating rink was very popular in its day. Murphy's operated a bus, which came into Marion to pick up skaters. Locals could catch the bus to the skating rink and back and skate the evening away for just 50¢. Through mirrors on the walls, skaters could view their performance. Many met their future spouses here. (Courtesy Patty Dennison.)

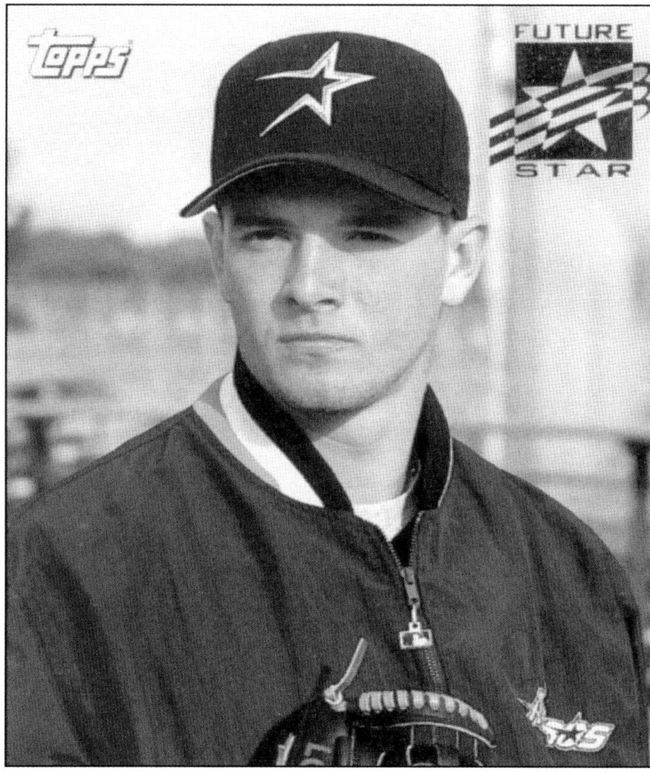

Billy Wagner, Marion Native. New York Mets' $43-million pitcher was born in Smyth County and attended grade school here. Later he attended school in Tazewell where he played ball. Wagner has a 100-mile-per-hour fast ball and is one of Major League Baseball's most feared pitchers. Though most are not nearly as famous, Wagner comes from a family of ballplayers. (Courtesy Sam Wagner.)

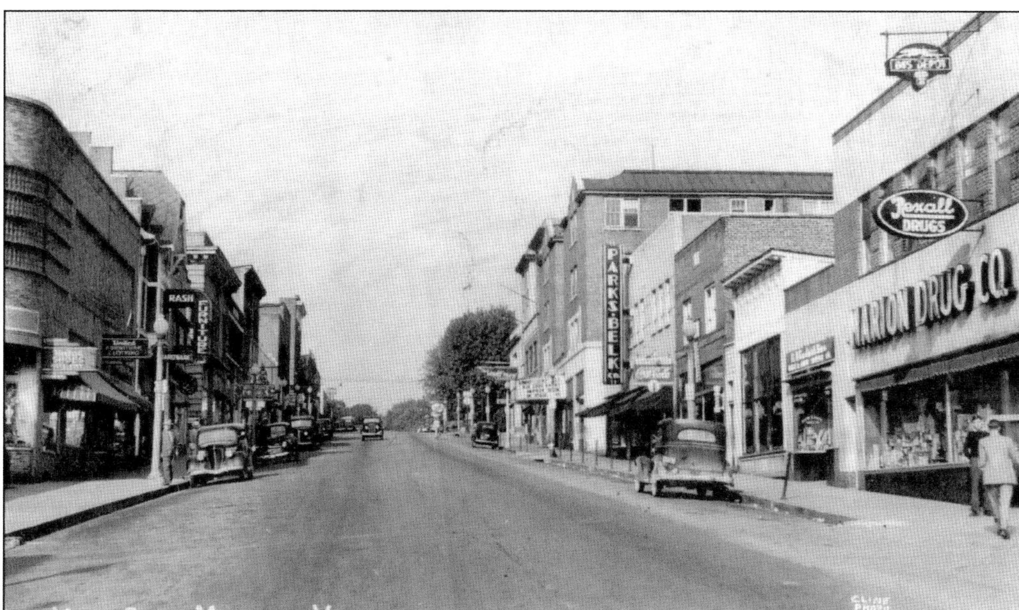

Naming the Greyhound. The transcontinental bus line began in 1914. Jerry Freeman, a resident of Marion, presented the name of Greyhound to the business in a contest. His name, Greyhound, was chosen as the winner, and he was given a lifetime ticket to ride for free to any area where Greyhound traveled. Note the Greyhound sign above the Marion Drug Company. (Courtesy Terry Hayden.)

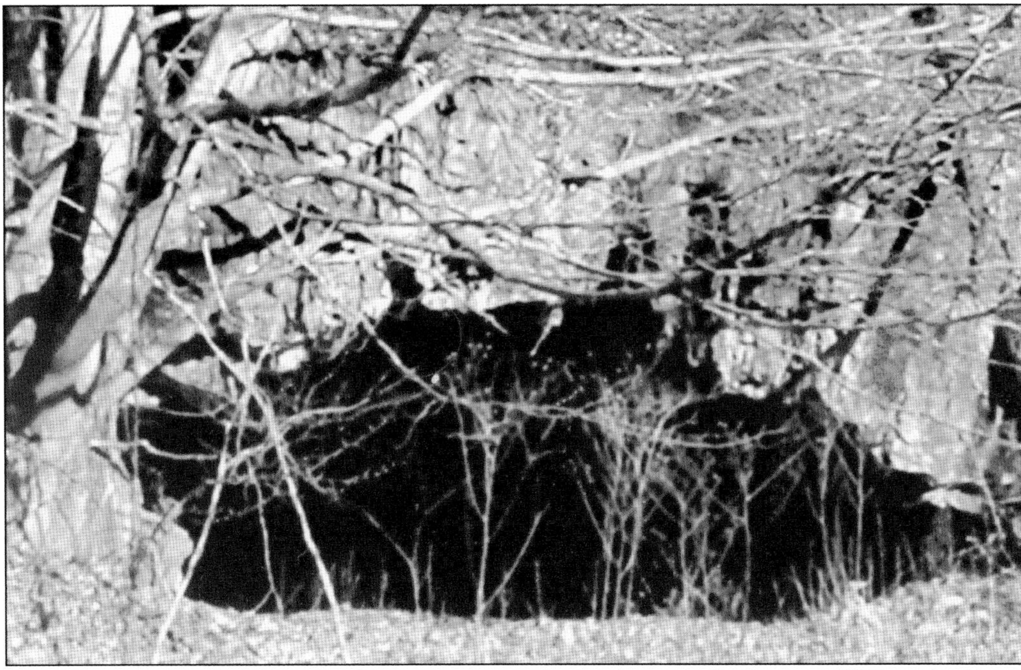

CAVE IN SUGAR GROVE. This large opening is located in a hillside just off Flatridge Road. Inside water drips from the top down the clay walls. Many stories about valuables that were hid in caves during the Civil War to keep them out of the hands of the enemy have circulated. Many children have used this cave as a clubhouse, but no hidden treasure was found. (Courtesy Debra Williams.)

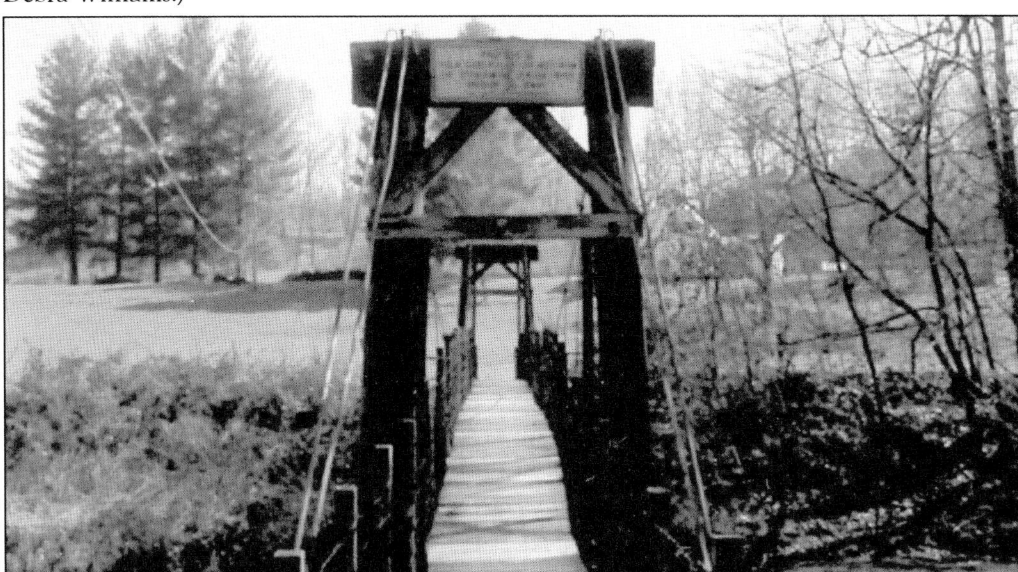

THE SWINGING BRIDGE. This rare, unique structure crosses the South Fork of the Holston River in the Love's Mill area. The bridge was once in a state of disrepair and in danger of being dismantled. The neighborhood rallied and was successful in getting the State of Virginia to maintain the bridge. A sign instructs patrons to walk slowly and carefully to prevent the bridge from swaying. (Courtesy Debra Williams.)

TAXI. Trains and automobiles became popular because they provided faster transportation, so horses and buggies went by the wayside. Few people owned cars before the 1960s, and after the Marion and Rye Valley Railroad went out of business, taxi cabs became the main method of transportation to town for staples. Here Carl Thomas poses on the taxi owned by his uncle, Henry Bise, who drove for Safeway Cabs. (Courtesy Garry Carrico.)

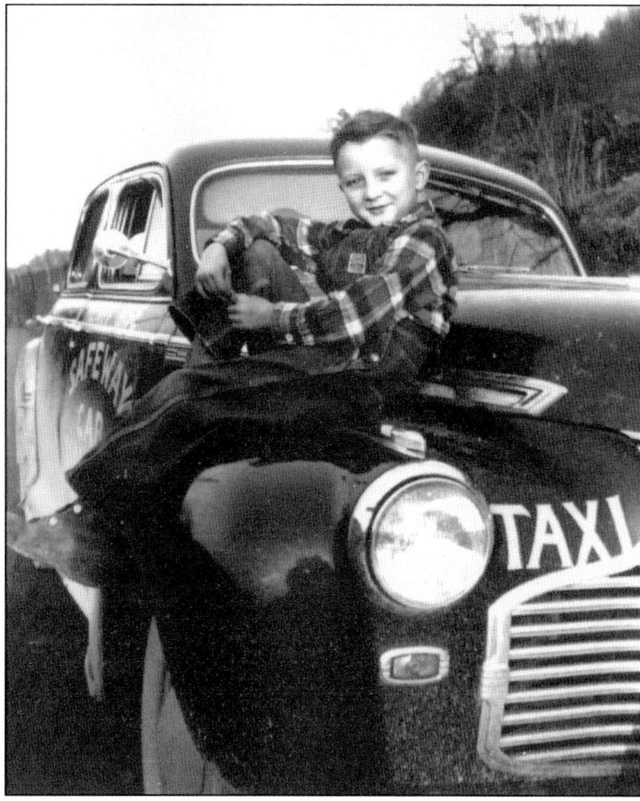

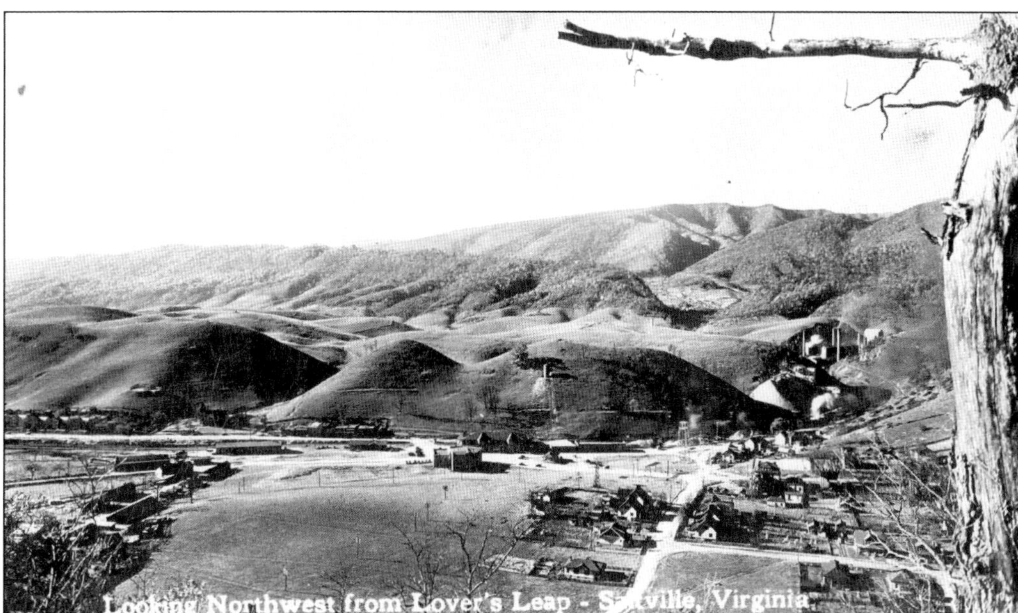

SCENE FROM LOVER'S LEAP. This pre-1930s view shows the new Saltville even before the post office (now the library) was built. Notice the freight station in the center and Olin to the back of the photograph. Though the town was small, you can clearly see the houses along West Main Street. (Courtesy James Schwartz.)

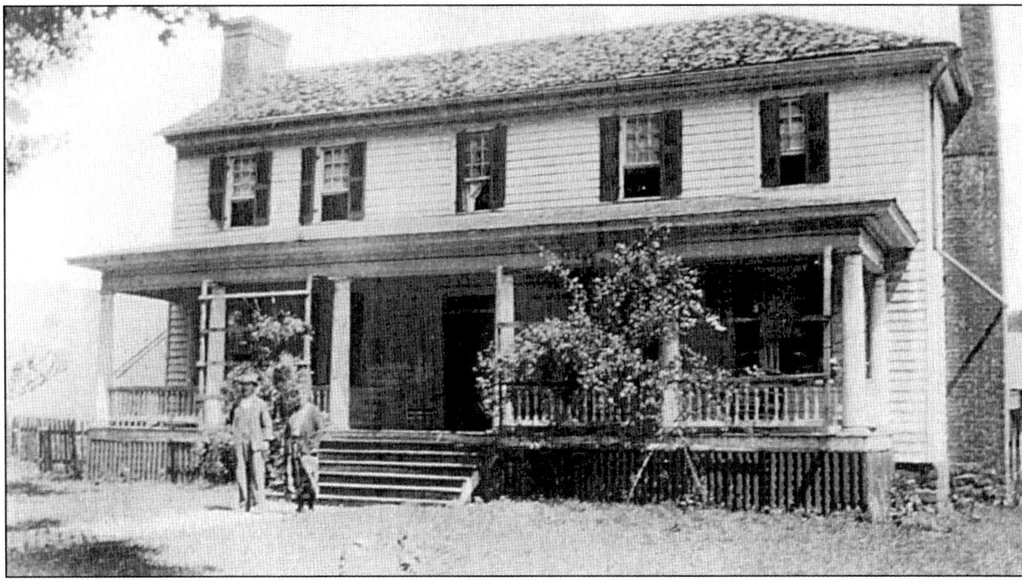

White Hall. White Hall is the home of James Sanders, who once ran the saltworks in Saltville. His widow, pregnant with their 11th child, became the first woman in Smyth County to obtain a business license in order to operate a boarding house for support. This home was later torn down to make room for the White Hall Apartments. (Courtesy Kitty Henniger.)

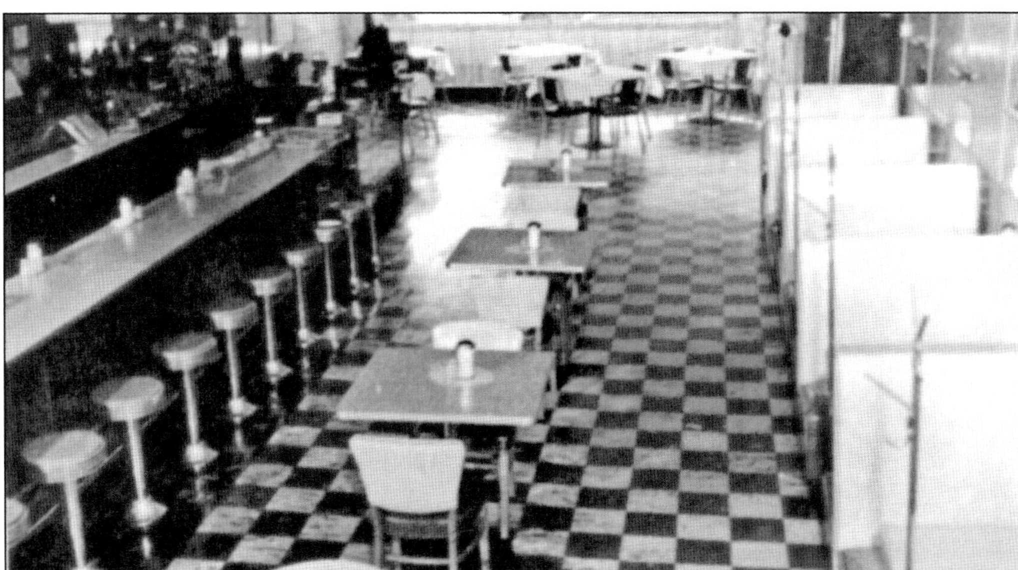

Carrier's Restaurant. Lester Carrier owned this popular restaurant in the early 1950s. The full-service menu listed items such as roast beef, mashed potatoes, green beans, homemade rolls, and choice of a drink for 25¢. A tuna fish sandwich, chips, and a pickle cost 15¢. This structure was later sold to Clarence and Imogene Coulthard, owners of Home and Auto True Value and the first cable service in Marion. (Courtesy Mack Sturgill Collection.)

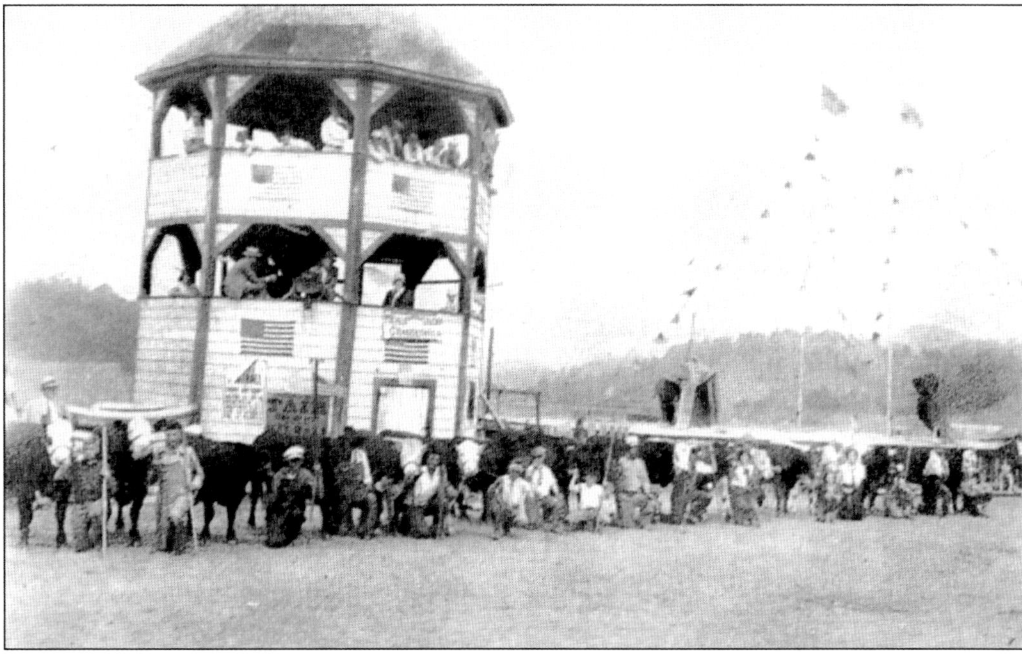

SMYTH COUNTY FAIR. In the early 1900s, the county fair was held on Fairground Hill in Marion. This was a big event in the area. Judges gathered in this two-story stand, which provided a better view. Notice the American flags and advertisements on the grandstand, one of which is for an Emory and Henry football game. Farmers pose in this photograph with their livestock during a contest. (Courtesy Mack Sturgill Collection.)

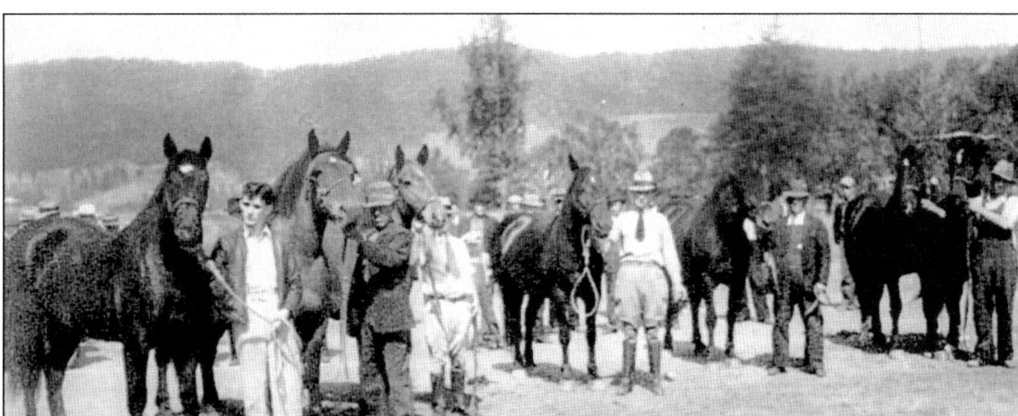

RICH VALLEY FAIR AND HORSE SHOW. The Rich Valley Fair began in 1926 as a project of the Future Farmers of Virginia. Pictured are draft horses entered in the horse show. Agriculture exhibits and home-economics exhibits have also been popular through the years, as are the country music concert and beauty pageant. The fair has drawn as many as 6,000 people in one night. (Courtesy Mack Sturgill Collection.)

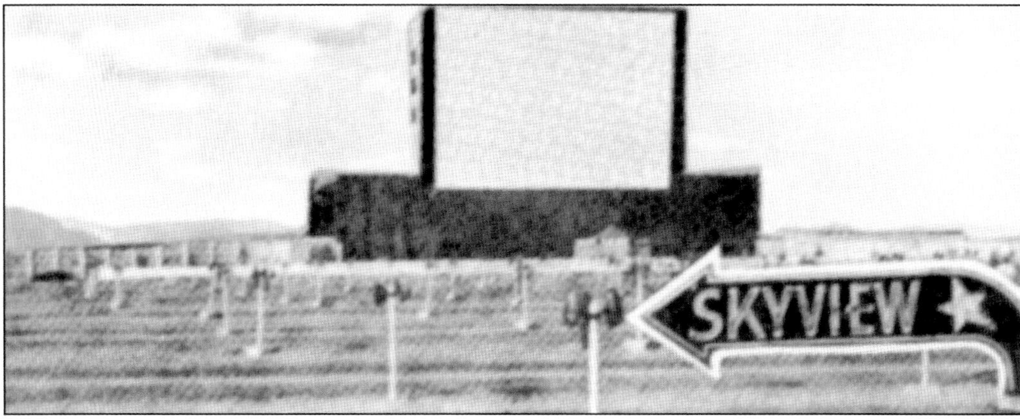

SKYVIEW DRIVE-IN. This theater was once located where Highway 11 crosses Interstate 81 in the Adwolfe area. It was moved to make way for the interstate. Howard Chitwood Sr. opened it *c.* 1948. A small building in the center housed the movie projectors and a snack bar. Sound came from speakers attached to a pole. The speakers could be placed in the car window for louder sound. (Courtesy Mack Sturgill Collection.)

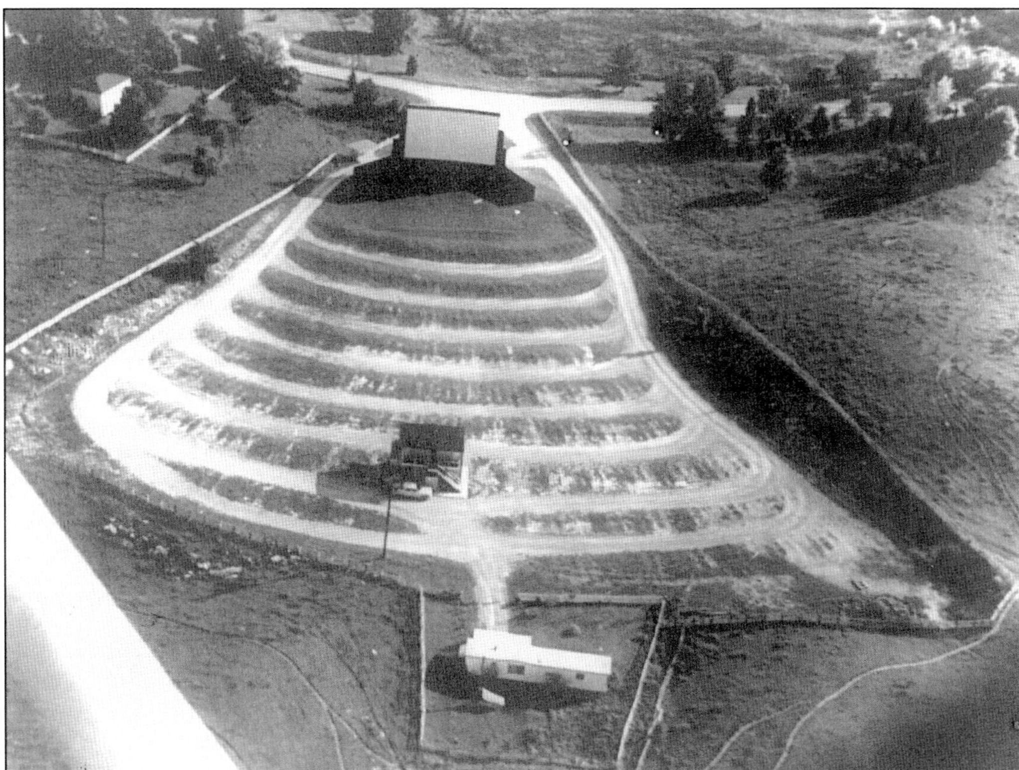

THE PARK DRIVE-IN. Located in Marion on Park Boulevard, the Park Drive-In was a popular place for local movie goers. William and Amelia Gwyn McKenzie built and later sold the drive-in to Jackie Barker. Ervin Johnson ran the movie projector during Barker's ownership. The drive-in was closed for years until Jerry Harmon bought and expanded it to include various other activities. (Courtesy Jackie Barker.)

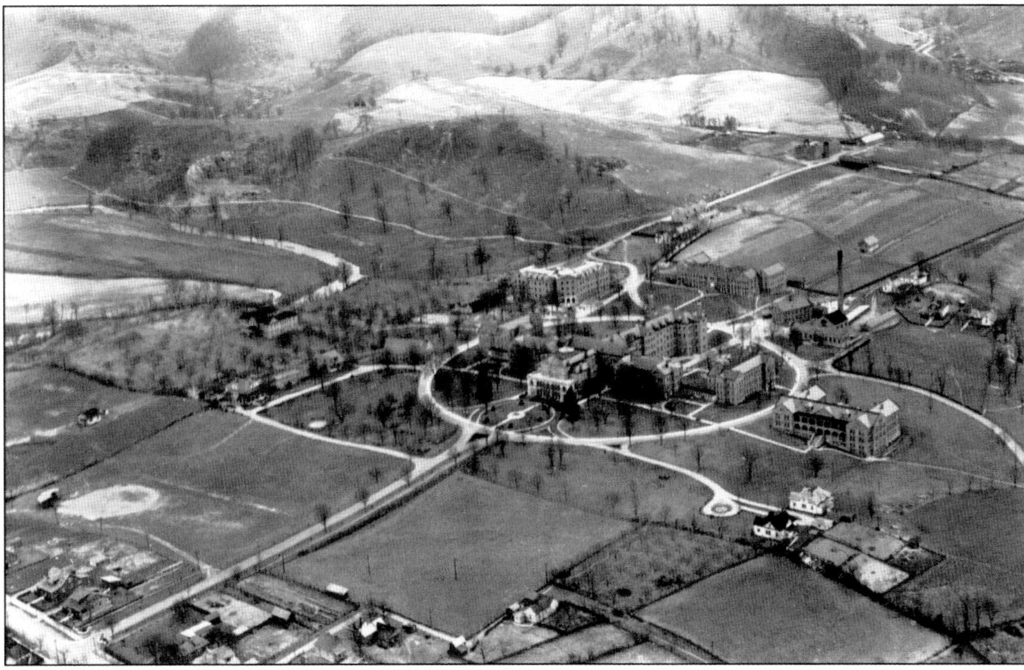

TOURING SOUTHWESTERN LUNATIC ASYLUM. The attractive British-style Southwestern Lunatic Asylum building, which was surrounded by floral gardens and farmland, opened in 1887. The rumors throughout Virginia of out-of-control mental patients brought tourist from all over the state. The road formed a circle around the hospital, where tourists viewed the patients like wild animals in a zoo. (Courtesy Kenny Sturgill.)

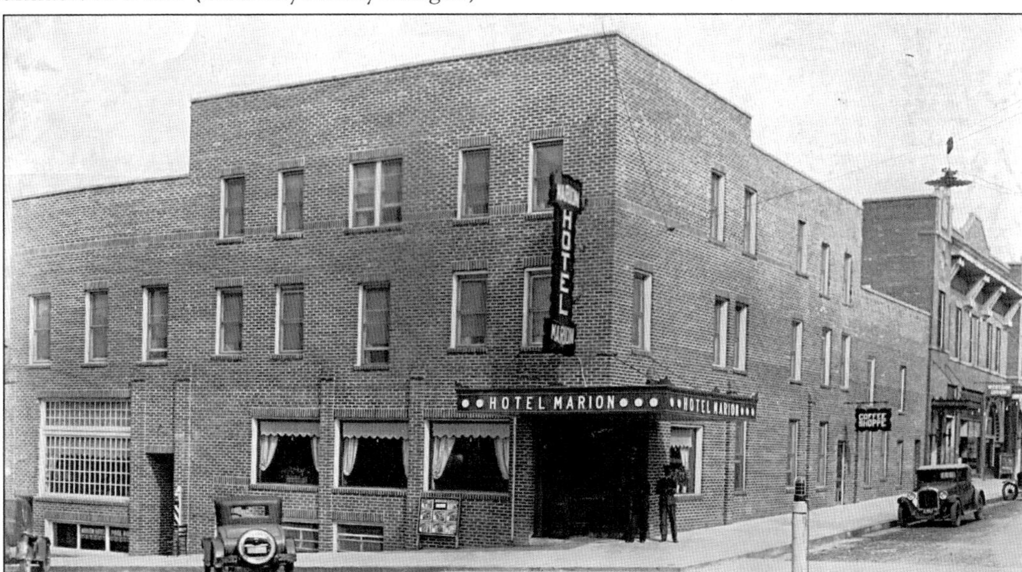

HOTEL MARION. Located across Main Street from the Lincoln Hotel, the three-story Hotel Marion housed a coffee shop, 80 guest rooms, a pool hall, and a barber shop. Marion Theatre, one of Marion's first moving picture houses, was located on the first floor of the hotel annex. The building was demolished in 1971. (Courtesy Clegg Williams.)

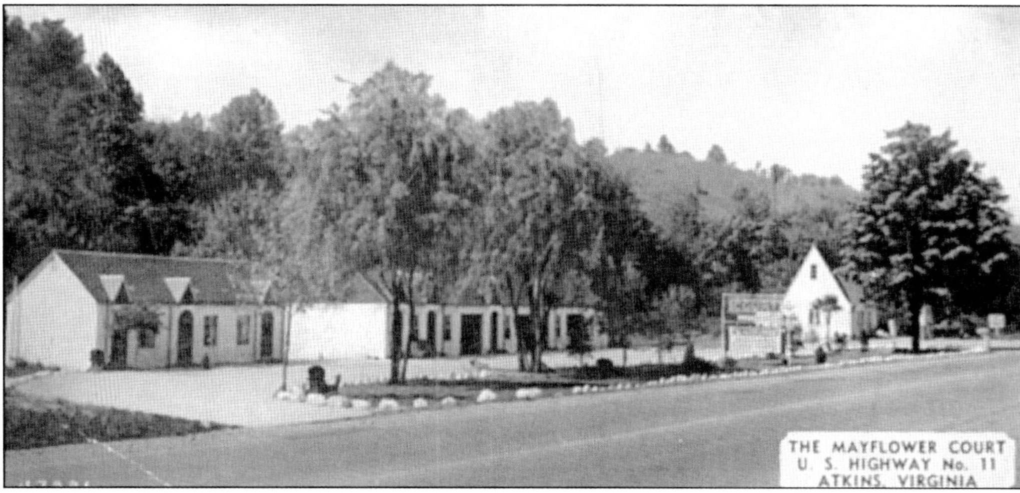

THE MAYFLOWER COURT. Harry Richardson started his venture in a service station next door, and in *c.* 1950, he expanded into the motel business—Mayflower Court. Located on Highway 11 in Atkins, this motel was in high demand as this was a busy roadway until the interstate came through in the 1960s. Different owners tried to revive this structure by converting it into apartments with no success. (Courtesy Dr. Paul Brown.)

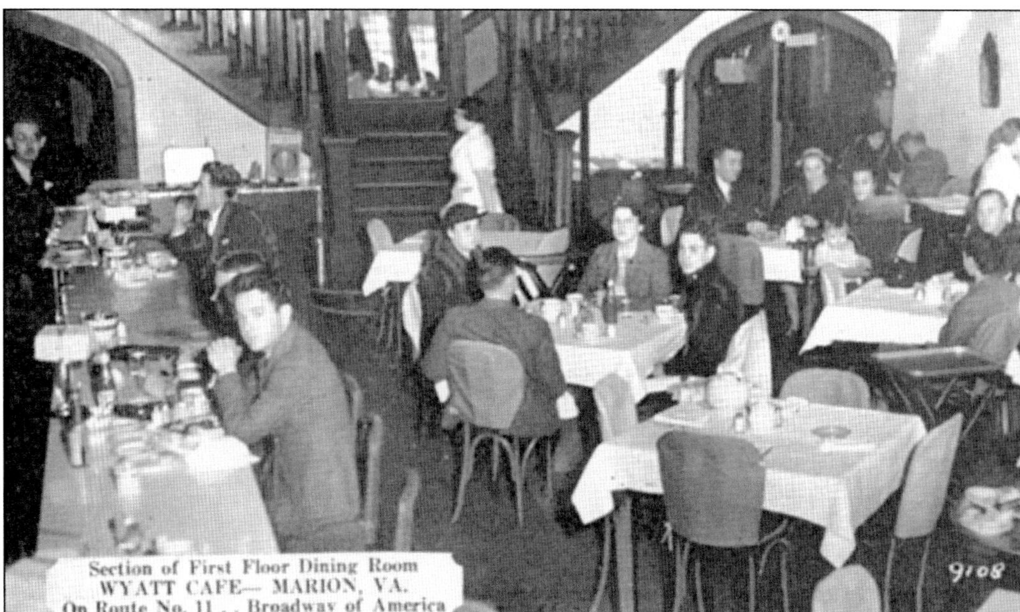

WYATT'S CAFÉ. Inside the old Greer's Tea Room, on Main Street, Walter Wyatt owned this modern-day restaurant during the late 1930s. This was a booming place during its time; notice the first floor is nearly full of customers. The beautiful Y-shaped stairs lead to the second floor, which housed the ballroom. This building has recently been remodeled by Joe and Susie Ellis. (Courtesy Dr. Paul Brown.)

Three

LOCAL ADVERTISING

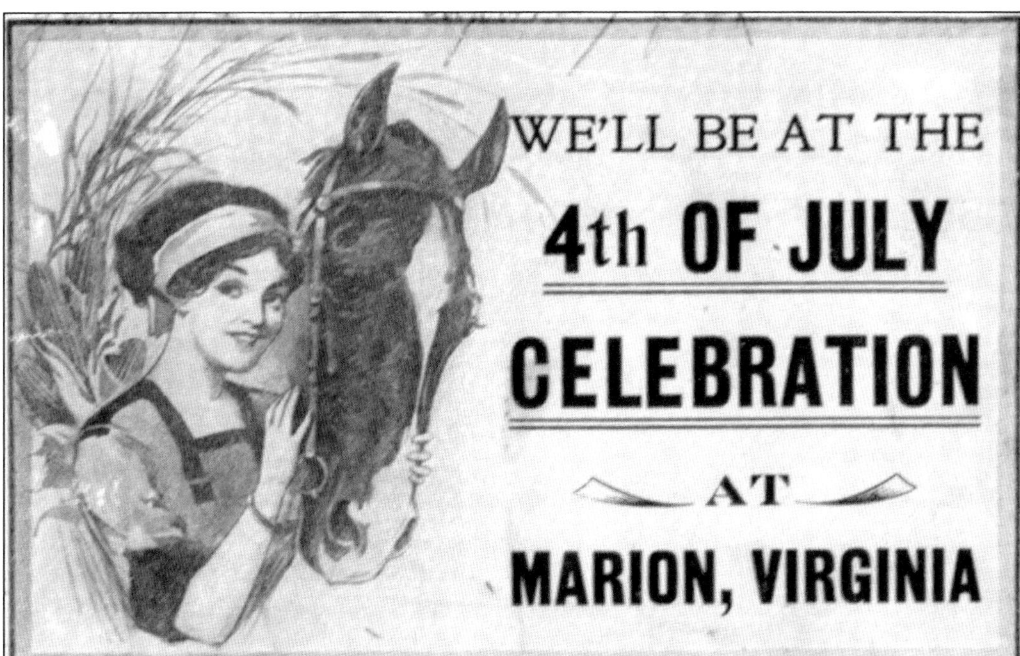

FOURTH OF JULY ADVERTISEMENT. This Fourth of July advertisement reminded citizens to gather at the Fourth of July Celebration in Marion. For generations, Smyth Countians have celebrated the Fourth at a fireworks display behind the Marion Senior High School. These fireworks can be seen from many locations around town. (Courtesy Clegg Williams.)

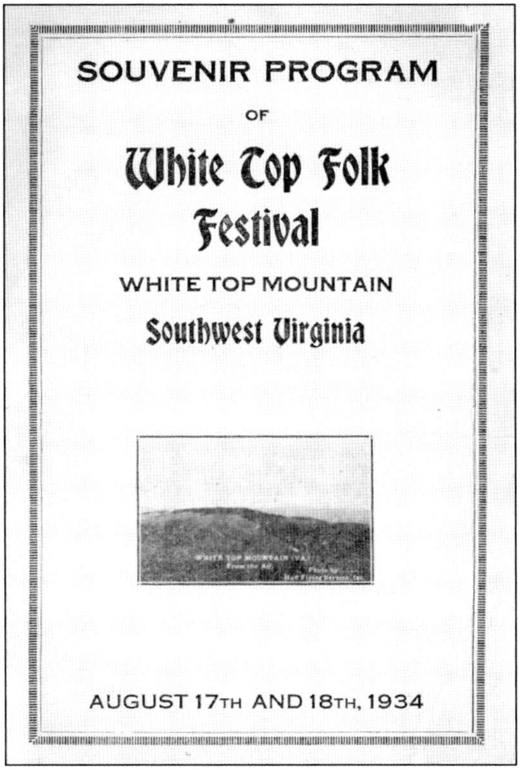

WHITE TOP FOLK FESTIVAL PROGRAM. This tattered old program was given to spectators who attended the White Top Folk Festival, held on August 17 and 18, 1934. The photograph on the cover is a shot of White Top Mountain from the air taken in a plane owned by Oliver Huff of Huff Flying Service, Inc. (Courtesy Atwood J. Huff.)

BANK OF MARION RECIPE. This Bank of Marion recipe came from an old cookbook. It reveals that after almost 45 years in business, the bank had a capital of $61,650 and surplus and profits of $80,000. The bank of Marion was established in 1874 and first located in the Jackson building. It was the first bank to serve Smyth, Tazewell, and Grayson Counties. (Courtesy Helen Byrd.)

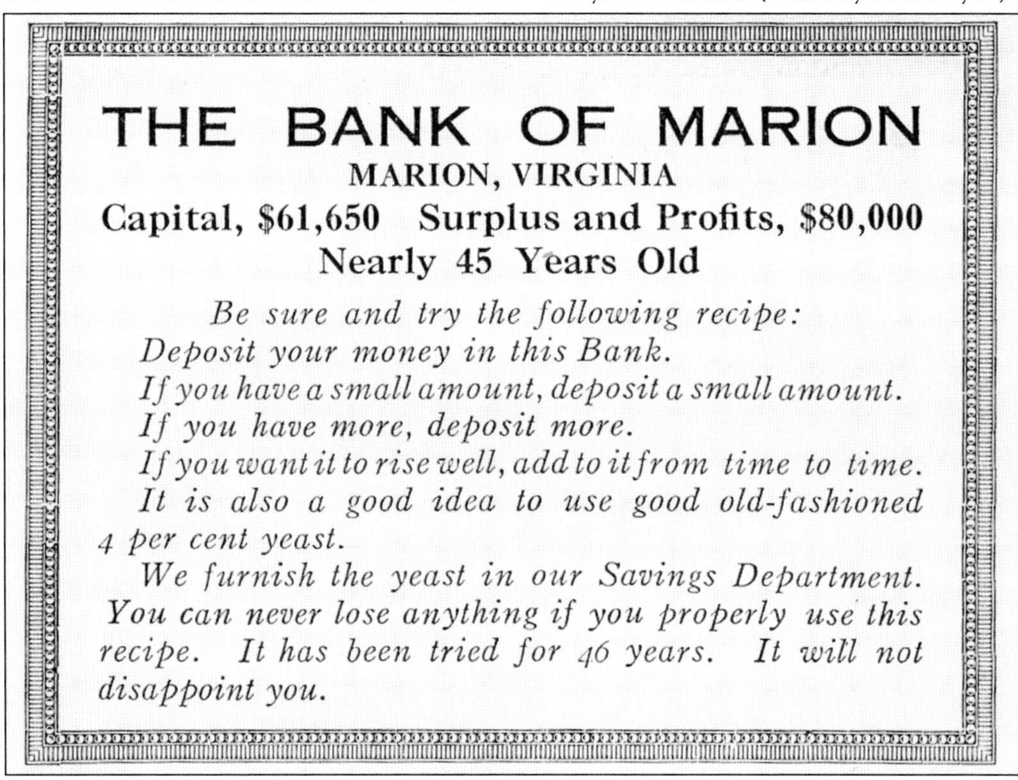

VIRGINIA TABLE COMPANY ADVERTISEMENT. The Virginia Table Company, located in Marion, was a division of the Virginia-Lincoln Furniture Corporation. Willard Lincoln was instrumental in organizing the Virginia Table Works in 1906, which was the parent plant of the Virginia Lincoln Corporation. This company was reorganized in 1912, after W. L. Lincoln sold out to Charles Lincoln, who became president. This advertisement is for dining room and library tables. (Courtesy Helen Byrd.)

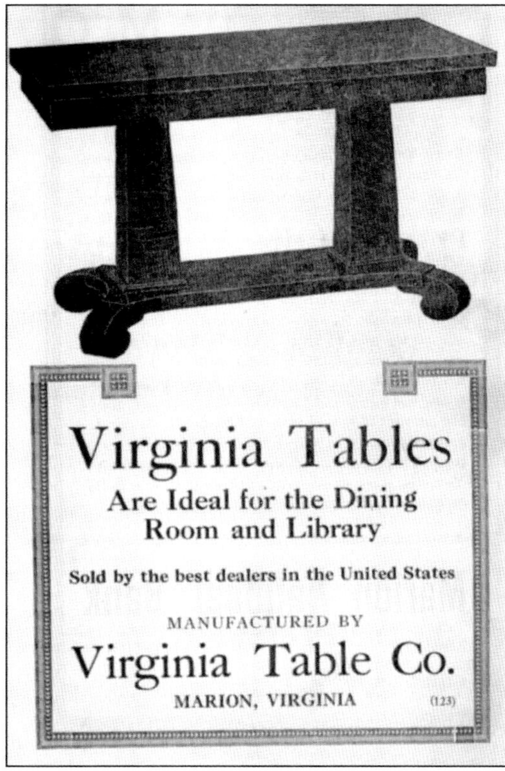

BONHAM BROTHERS. This apple crate label was made for Hill Crest Orchards, which was owned by the H. L. Bonham estate. The apple empire began in 1911 when Hezekiah Love Bonham replenished land that he had cleared of hardwood trees with apple orchards. The Bonham Brothers grew and distributed apples from 1912 to 1989. Notice that the label also advertises White Top Mountain, seen in the background. (Courtesy Frank Detweiler.)

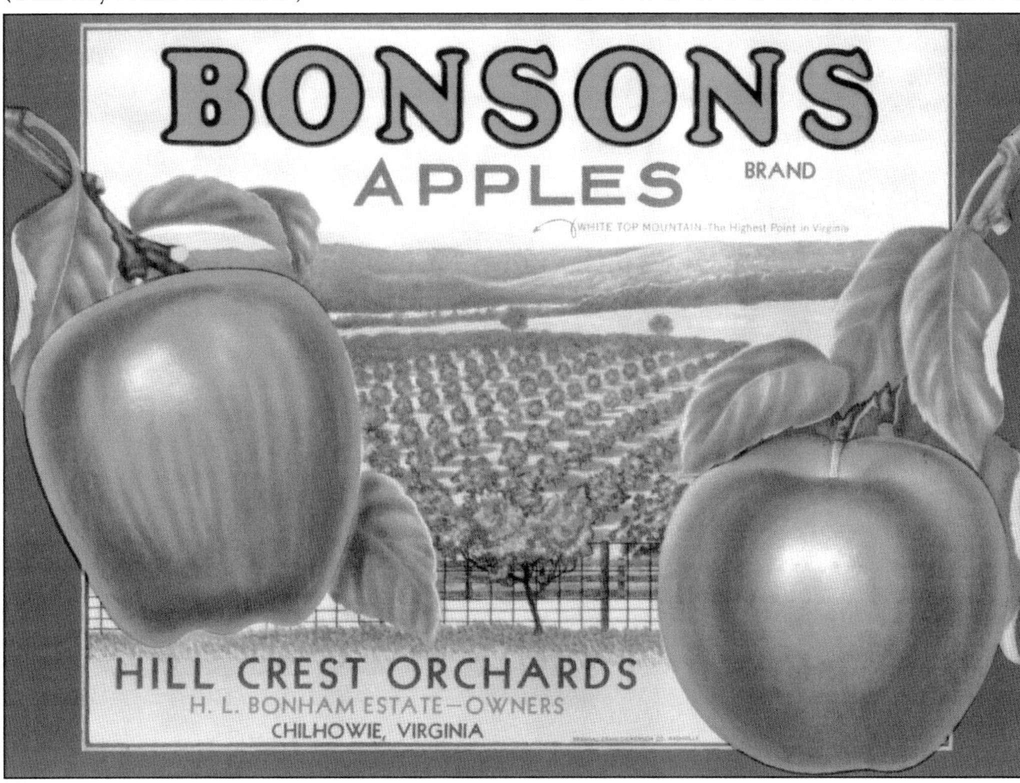

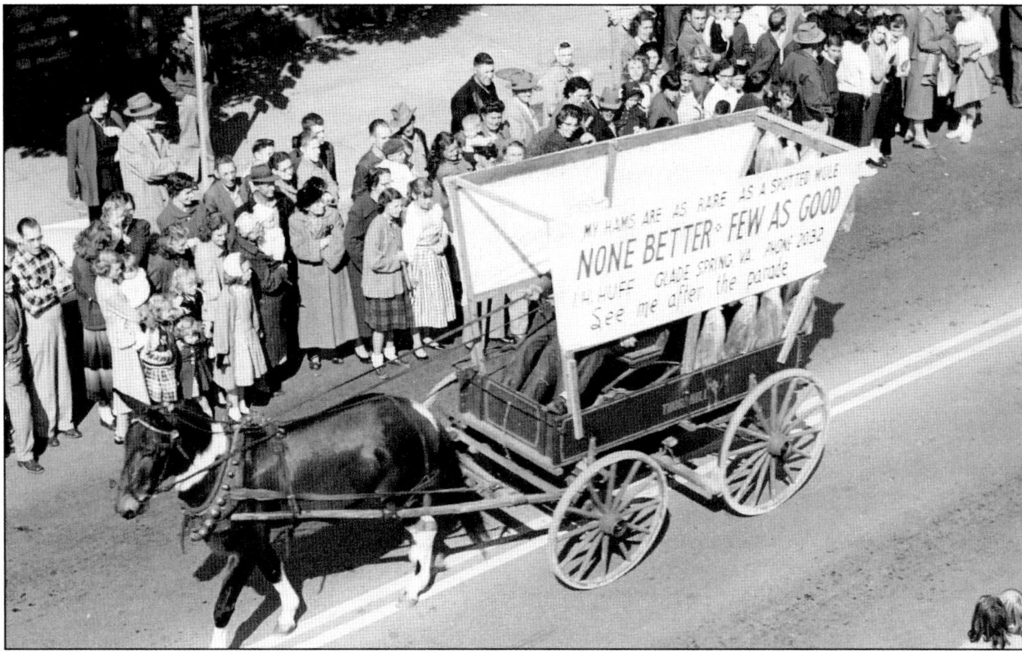

HUFF HAMS PARADE ADVERTISEMENT. Local venders and politicians attended parades as an opportunity to advertise to hundreds of people at one time. Huff Farms used a covered wagon in this parade to promote their hams. The slogan reads, "My hams are as rare as a spotted mule. None better. Few as good. See me after the parade." (Courtesy Atwood J. Huff.)

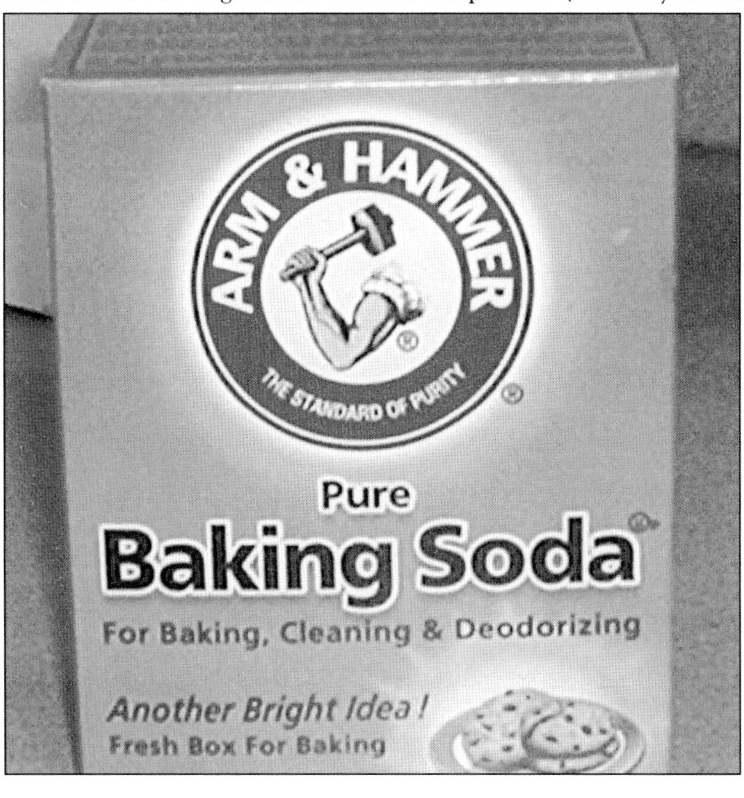

THE FAMOUS ARM. Rex H. Wolfe, born in Glade Spring in 1905, was widely known for his boxing abilities. Sherwood Anderson said Wolfe's arm muscle was the biggest he had ever seen. Pictures of Wolfe's biceps were sold to Arm and Hammer Baking Soda and *Atlas Magazine*. These two companies used these pictures for advertising and trademarks, which are still used today. (Courtesy Debra Williams.)

DR. PEPPER ADVERTISEMENT. The famous soft drink Dr. Pepper was named in honor of Wytheville physician Charles T. Pepper because of an infatuation with his daughter. At the time of its creation in 1885, it was popular to give products a name preceded by Dr. in hopes of making them appear more healthy. Dr. Pepper was promoted as "liquid food" that should be consumed at 10:00 a.m., 2:00 p.m., and 4:00 p.m. (Courtesy Mack Sturgill Collection.)

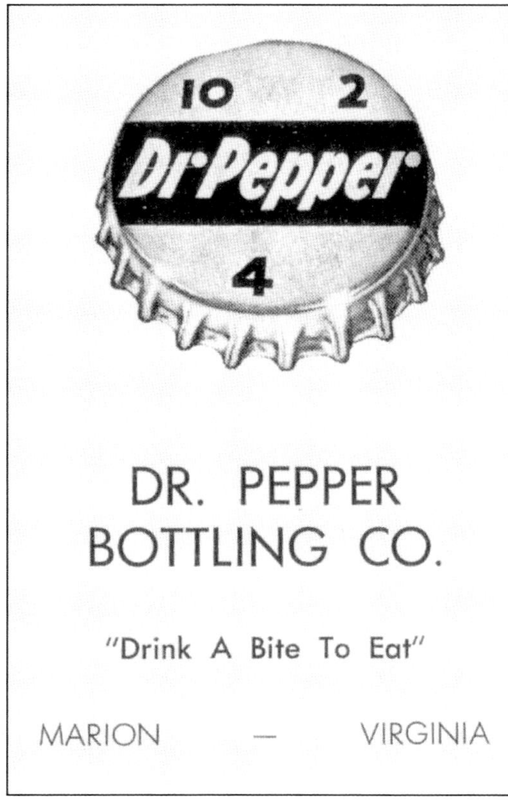

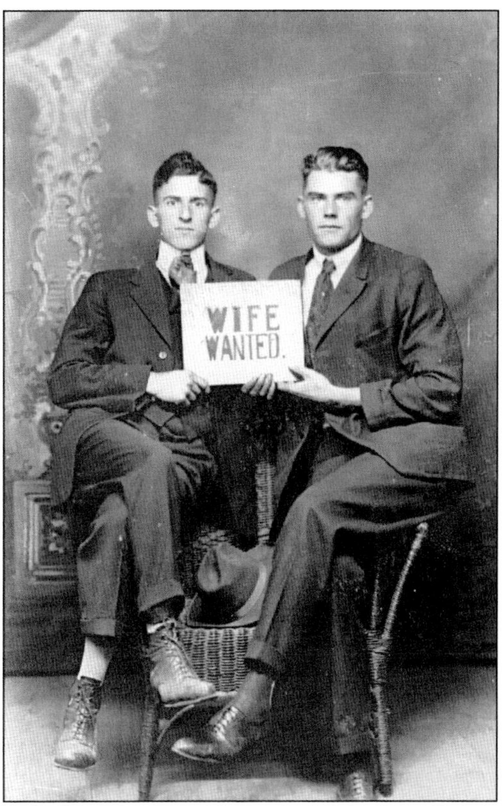

WIFE WANTED. The subjects of this charming postcard are two young bachelors who are advertising for a wife. These two dressed in their Sunday best for the occasion. The photograph was most likely taken by a traveling photographer who moved from town to town, snapping photographs in exchange for payment from locals. (Courtesy Dr. Paul Brown.)

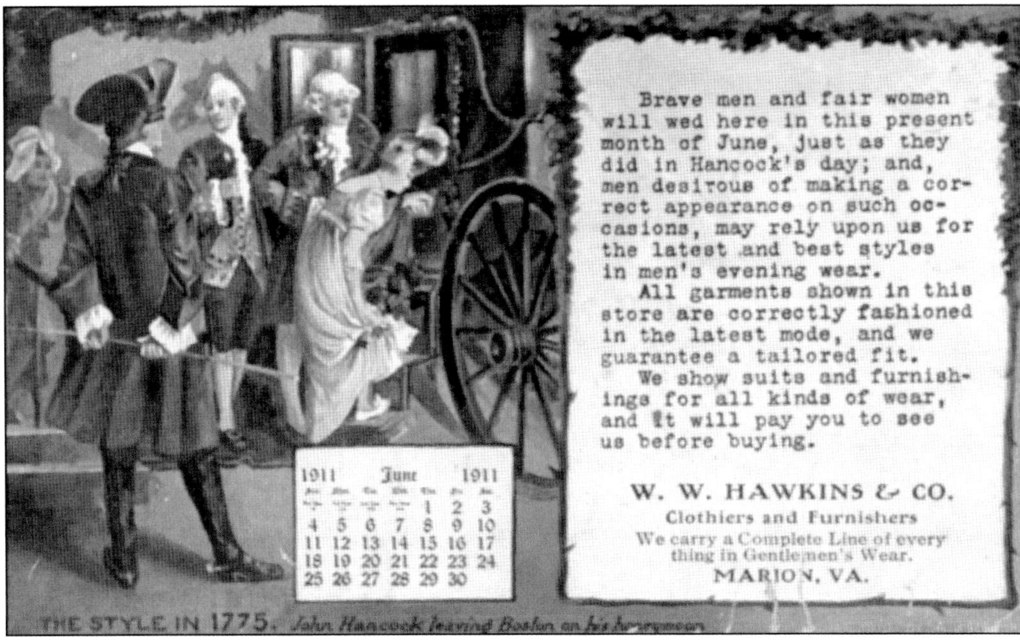

W. W. Hawkins Clothing Advertisement. This calendar was an advertisement for W. W. Hawkins and Company for June 1911. The photograph shows the clothing style in the year 1775 and reminds consumers that June is wedding month and that W. W. Hawkins is the place to buy formal wear for men. They guaranteed a tailored fit and the latest style. (Courtesy Clegg Williams.)

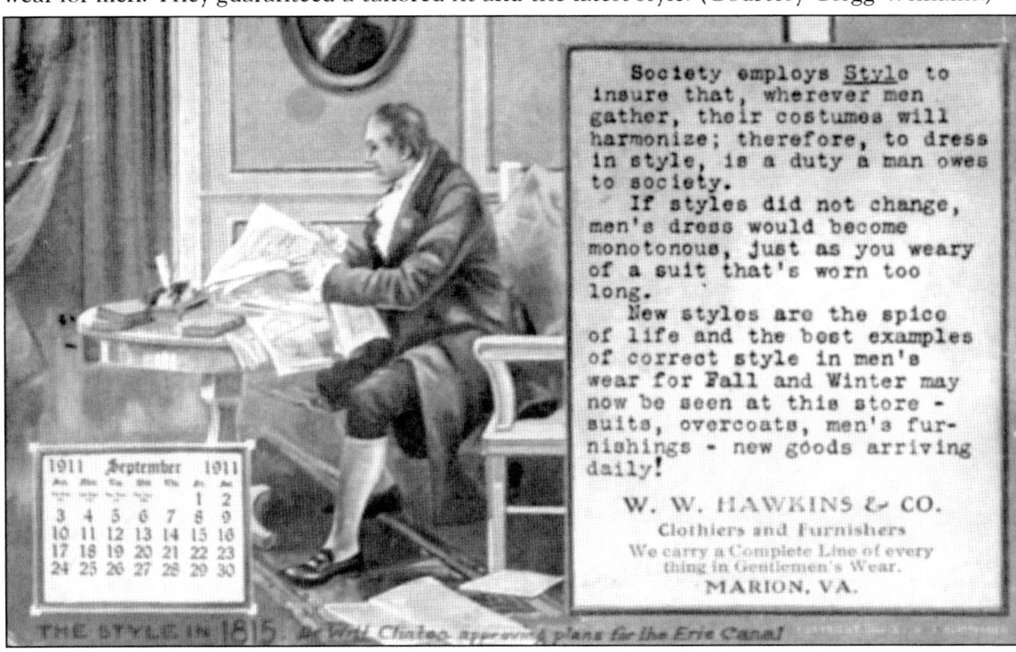

W. W. Hawkins Calendar. This calendar advertises the gentlemen's clothing sold by the W. W. Hawkins and Company. The advertisement shows a man dressed in style in the year 1815 and states that "to dress in style is a duty that man owes to society." This calendar advertises suits and overcoats for the coming winter. W. W. Hawkins and Company was located on the current drive-through lot at the Bank of Marion on Main Street. (Courtesy Clegg Williams.)

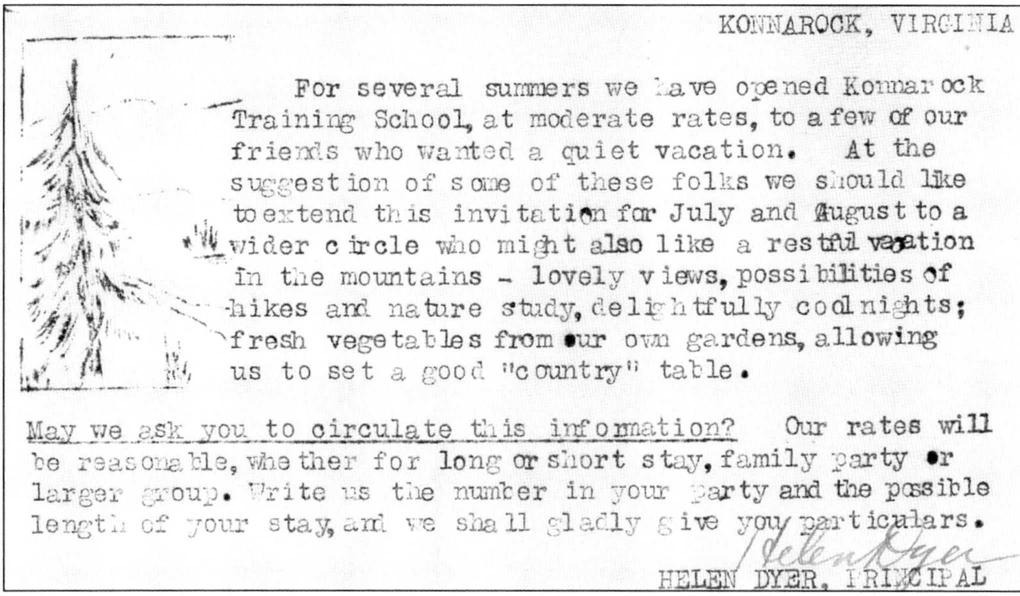

KONNAROCK, VIRGINIA

For several summers we have opened Konnarock Training School, at moderate rates, to a few of our friends who wanted a quiet vacation. At the suggestion of some of these folks we should like to extend this invitation for July and August to a wider circle who might also like a restful vacation in the mountains - lovely views, possibilities of hikes and nature study, delightfully cool nights; fresh vegetables from our own gardens, allowing us to set a good "country" table.

May we ask you to circulate this information? Our rates will be reasonable, whether for long or short stay, family party or larger group. Write us the number in your party and the possible length of your stay, and we shall gladly give you particulars.

Helen Dyer
HELEN DYER, PRINCIPAL

KONNAROCK TRAINING SCHOOL ADVERTISEMENT. This postcard was used to advertise the Konnarock Training School as a summer spot for vacationers who might enjoy a stay in the mountains. Lovely views, hikes, and nature studies were offered to lodgers during the months of July and August. At the time, Helen Dyer was the president. (Courtesy Clegg Williams.)

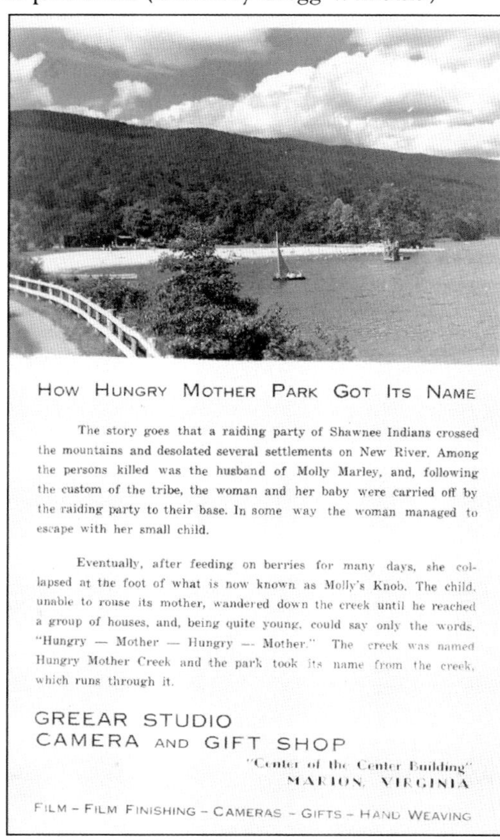

HUNGRY MOTHER POSTCARD. This postcard was designed by Greear Studios to advertise Hungry Mother State Park. It tells the story of how the park was named after Hungry Mother Creek, which runs through it. This postcard also advertises film, film-finishing, gifts, cameras, and hand weaving for Greear's Studio, which was located in the middle of the Center Building. (Courtesy Clegg Williams.)

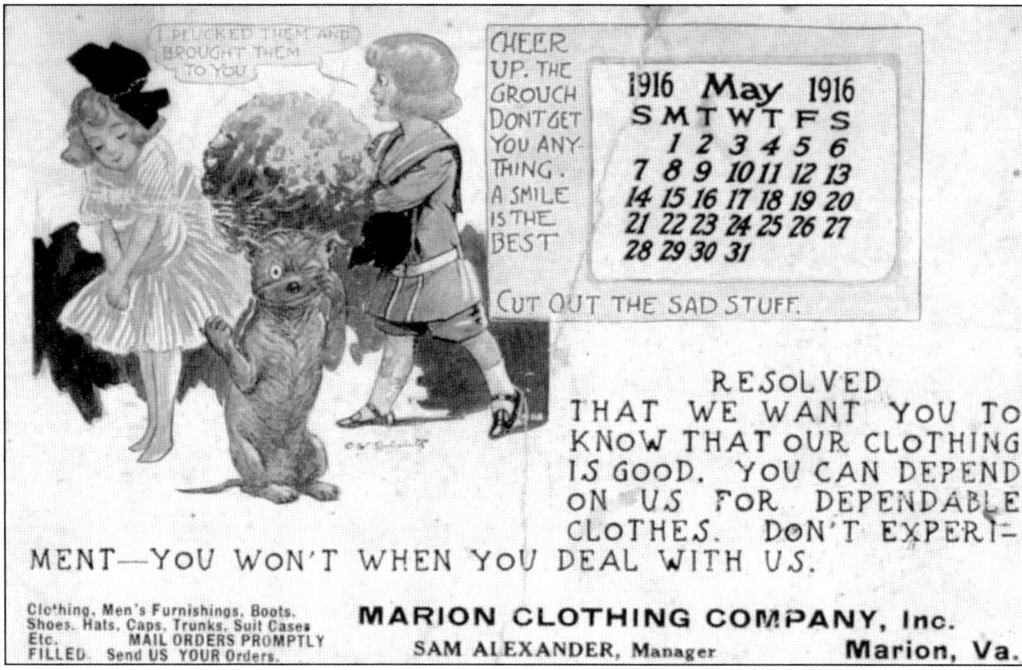

MARION CLOTHING COMPANY. This 1916 calendar advertisement is for Marion Clothing Company, which was Marion's second oldest clothing establishment other than the Weiler-Wolfe Store. Sam Alexander was the store manager in 1916. The calendar advertises clothing, men's furnishings, boots, shoes, hats, caps, trunks, and suitcases. Marion Clothing Company also filled mail orders. This business was located on Main Street in Marion. (Courtesy Dr. Paul Brown.)

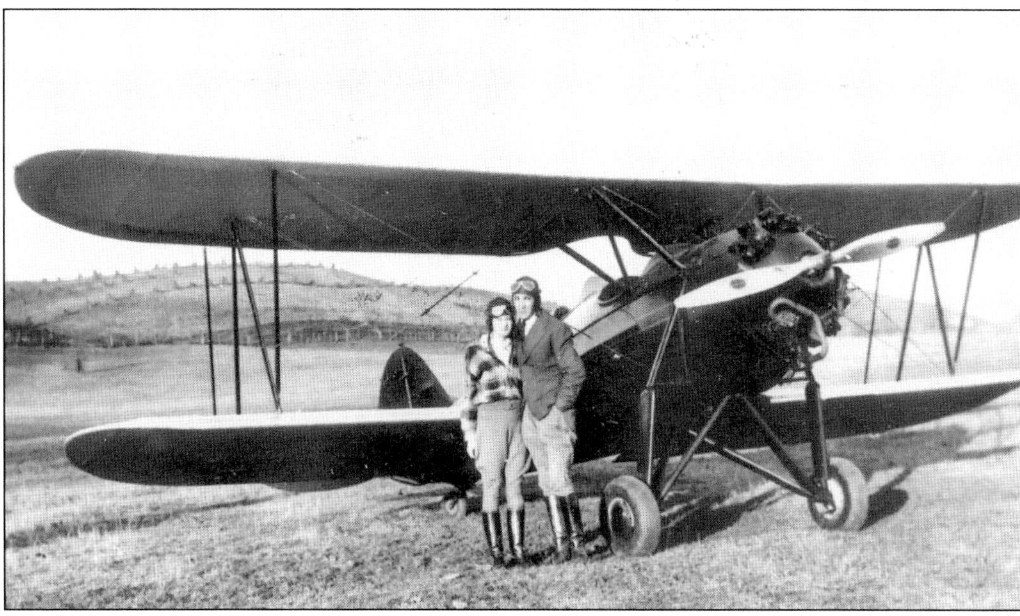

HUFF FLYING SERVICE, INC. Oliver and Nellie Huff are pictured with the plane owned by Oliver, which he used to fly photographer Dave Greear to take pictures of the area for Greear's Studio. On special occasions, for a $5 fee, Huff would take people up to see the sights from the airport at St. Clair's Creek. Huff also flew for Brandif Airlines for 25 years. (Courtesy Atwood J. Huff.)

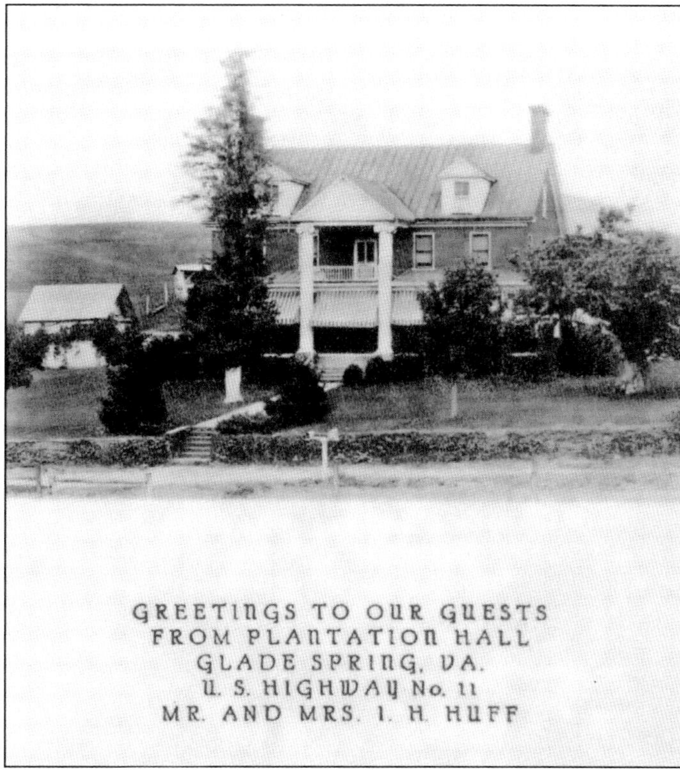

PLANTATION HALL. George Huff built this huge brick home located just east of exit 32 of Interstate 81 around 1900. Openings were built into the chimneys so one could look straight through the window, chimneys, and out the other window. Advertisements were made up for travelers who stopped in for the night because hotels were not that common in this area. (Courtesy Atwood J. Huff.)

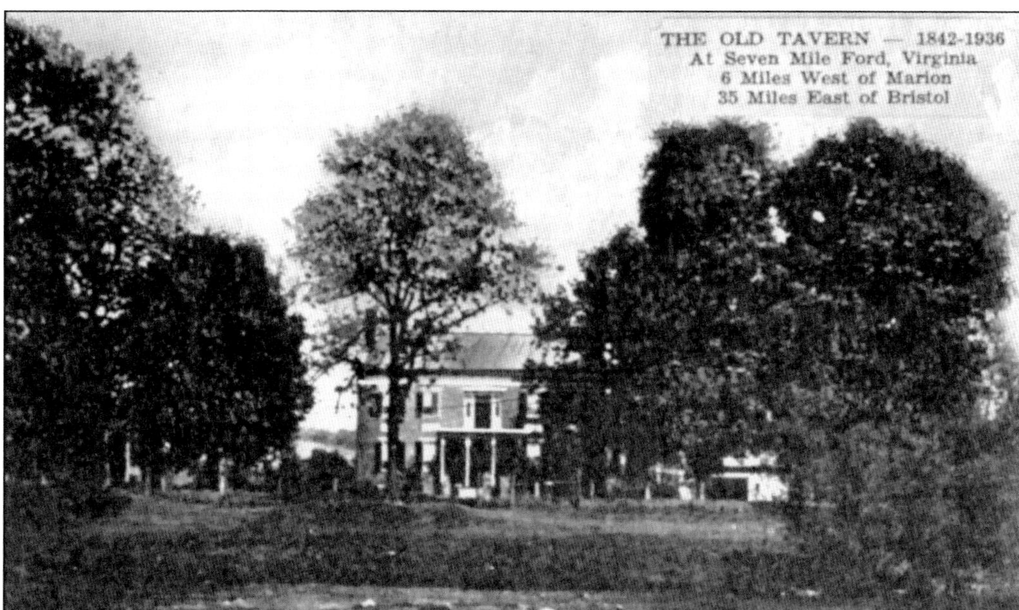

PRESTON HOUSE ADVERTISEMENT. This postcard was an advertisement for the Preston House, located just off the Seven Mile Ford Interstate 81 exit ramp. It was built by John M. Preston as a stagecoach stop and inn along the Wilderness Road. The house is listed as a Virginia Registered Landmark and is also listed on the National Register of Historic Places. (Courtesy Dr. Paul Brown.)

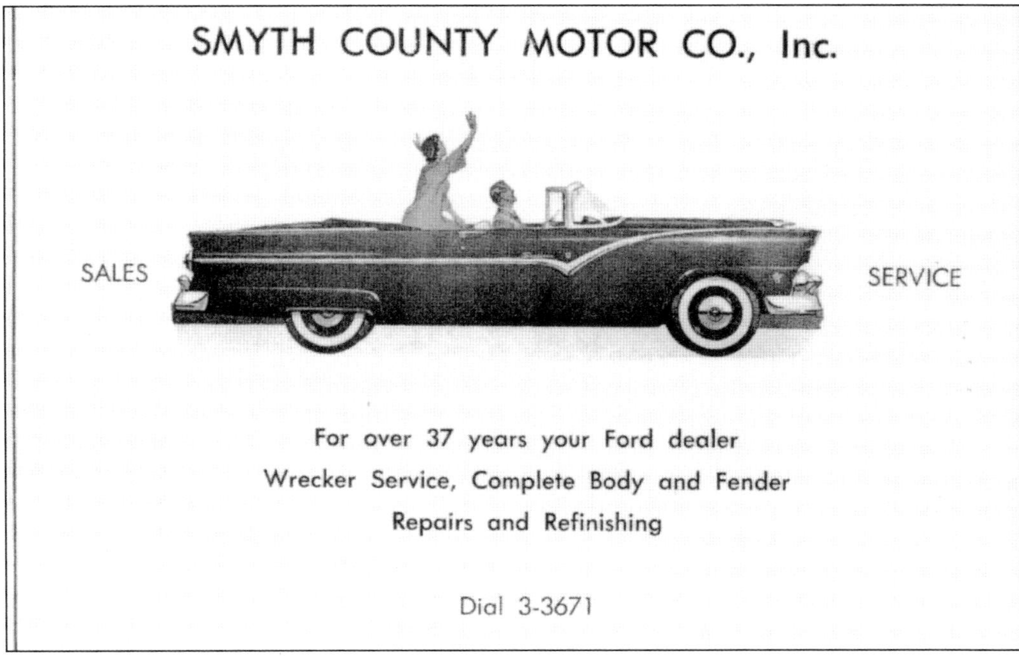

SMYTH COUNTY MOTORS. Col. James Tate founded Smyth County Motors in 1930 as a Ford sales company. This advertisement offers full-service sales, wrecker service, auto body repair, and painting. The business, located on Pendleton Street, was later bought out by the Snider family, who continued to be Ford representatives. Automobiles are no longer sold at this location. (Courtesy Mack Sturgill Collection.)

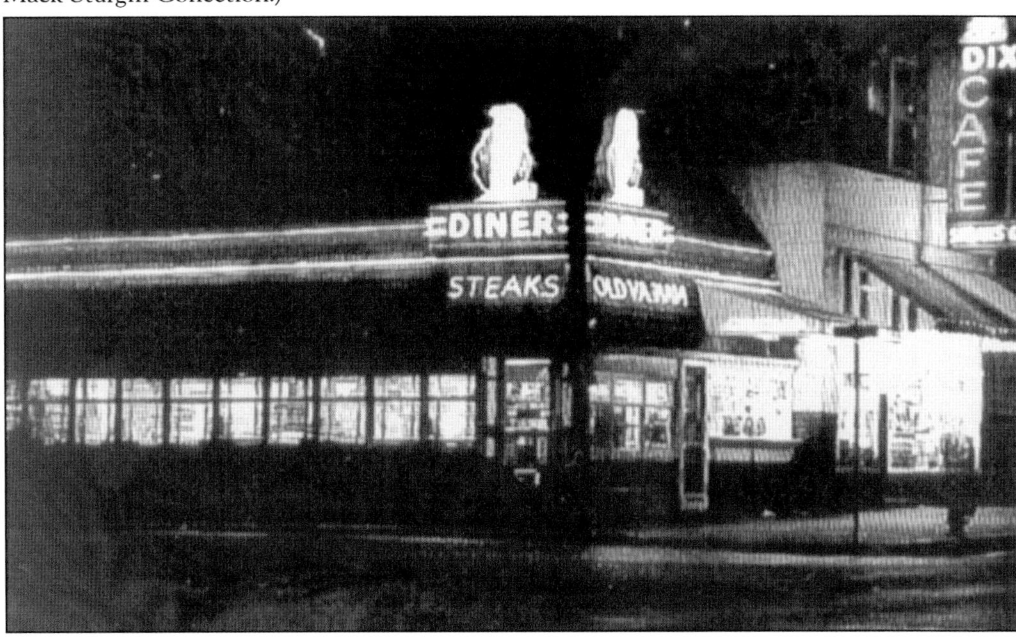

DIXIE CAFÉ. This was a popular spot for locals to gather for breakfast and share the latest gossip over a cup of coffee. Those employed nearby would stop in for a quick lunch. A hot beef or pork sandwich and two vegetables could be purchased for 45¢. Deward Miller owned this restaurant along with the Twin and Marion Diners in Marion. (Courtesy Mack Sturgill Collection.)

Four

INDUSTRY AND TRADE

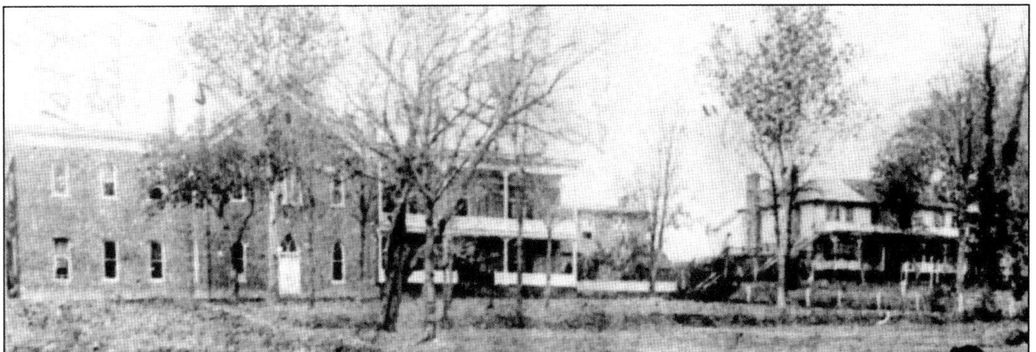

LAURA COPENHAVER INDUSTRIES. Located on the Marion College Campus, Rosemont (right), was the home base of Laura Copenhaver Industries, designed to keep alive the old-time art of hand weaving. On July 5, 1933, Eleanor Gladys Copenhaver, daughter of Bascom and Laura Lu Scherer Copenhaver, married author Sherwood Anderson at Rosemont. When not traveling, the couple made their home at Rosemont and also Anderson's Ripshin in Troutdale. (Courtesy Mack Sturgill Collection.)

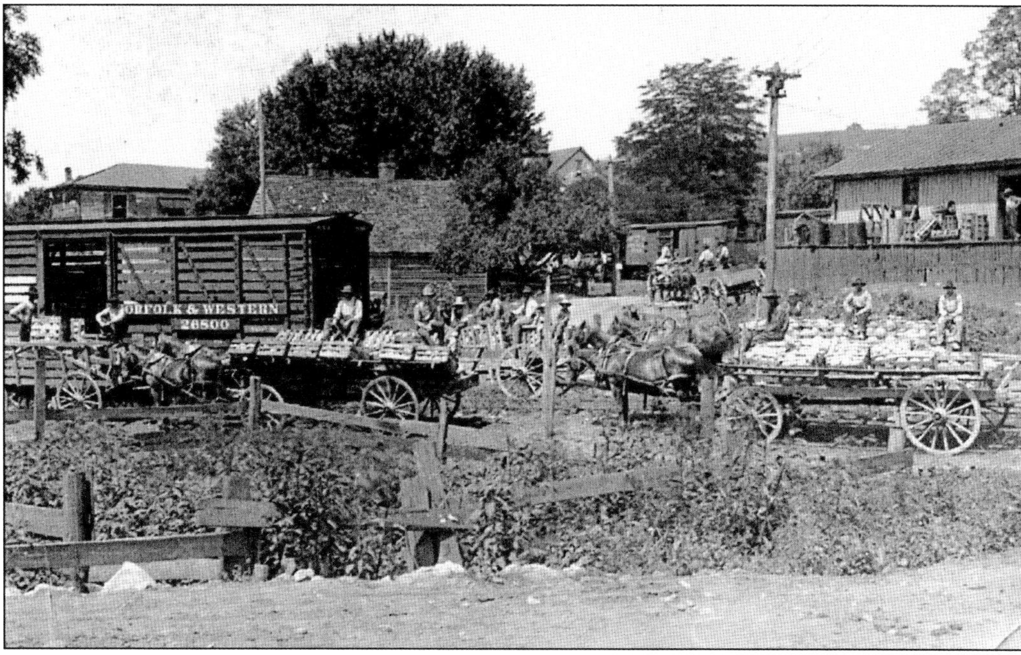

NORFOLK AND WESTERN FREIGHT YARD. Marion and Rye Valley freight cars were received or shipped out at the Norfolk and Western freight yards near the present-day town pool. Notice the boxcars in the background that are being loaded with crates of fresh cabbage. This cabbage most likely came from Atkins, "the cabbage capitol of Southwest Virginia." (Courtesy Mack Sturgill Collection.)

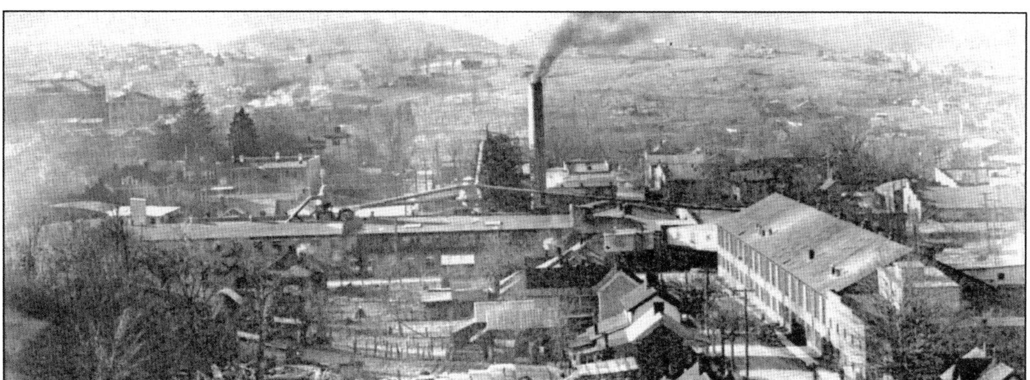

VIRGINIA-LINCOLN FURNITURE CORPORATION. Established in 1913, the Virginia-Lincoln Furniture Corporation was the largest plant and the first factory in the South to install complete conveyer equipment. Permanent exhibits were on display in New York, Chicago, and San Francisco for its dining room and bedroom furniture. In 1937, the plant employed 1,100 people with an annual payroll of over $600,000. (Courtesy Mack Sturgill Collection.)

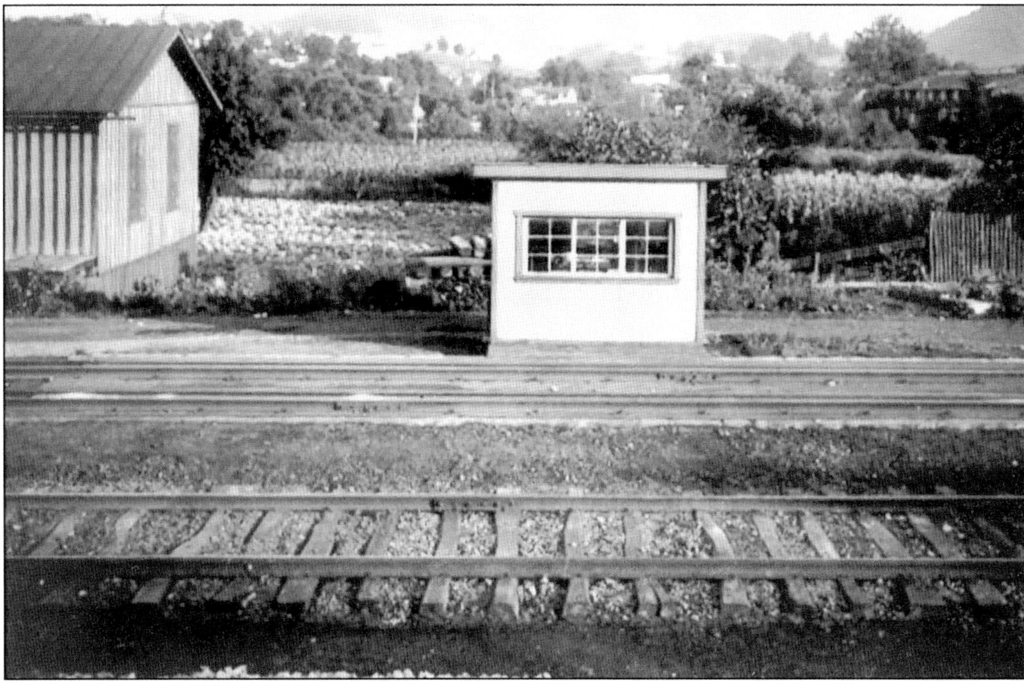

Railroad Scales. These scales were located about where the Marion Recreation Department is now. The freight depot sat where the parking lot is located. The scales measured the weight of each train car as they were pulled across this measuring device. The weight of empty compartments were written on each car for easy figuring of the added load for payment of shipment. (Courtesy Jeff Weaver.)

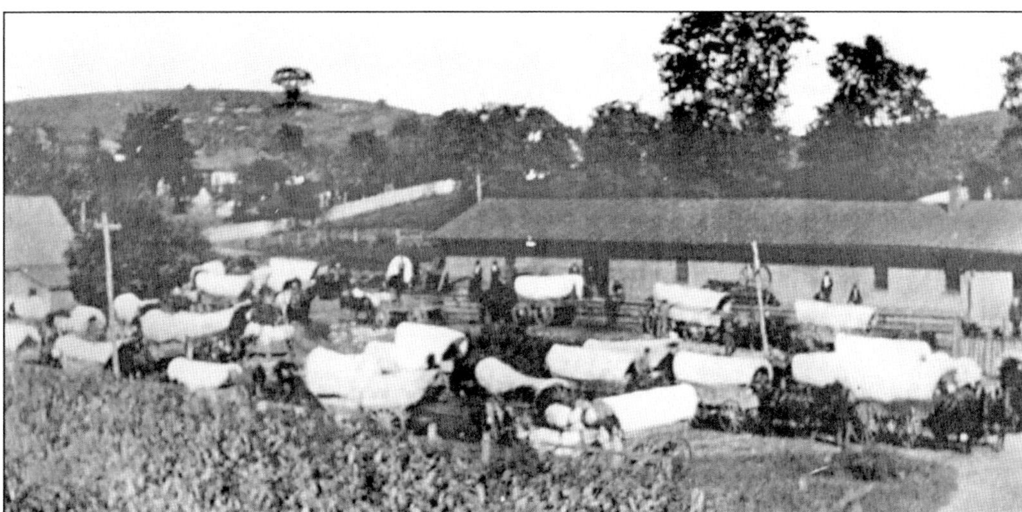

Old Norfolk and Western Station. This photograph, taken in the late 1800s, shows the covered wagons from Grayson County and North Carolina that transported produce to Marion for shipment to other markets. These wagons left loaded with supplies for personal use and stock for country stores along the way. This building was also used as a passenger depot until the new, brick depot opened in 1904. (Courtesy Mack Sturgill Collection.)

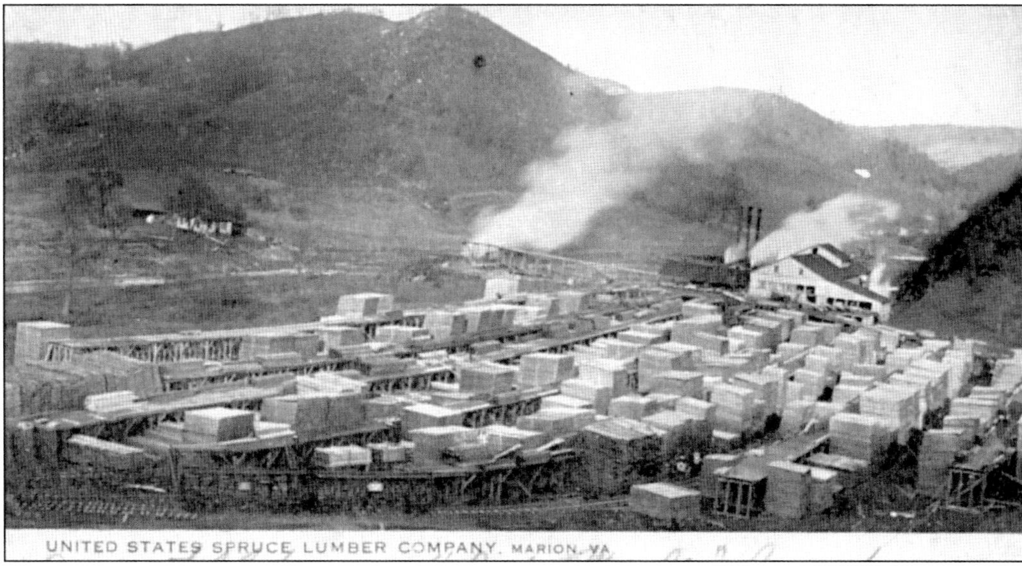

U.S. SPRUCE LUMBER COMPANY. The Spruce Lumber Company purchased 30,000 acres from the Douglas Robinson estate and built a mill at Marion in 1905. They purchased the Fairwood property in 1906 and then merged their two companies to form the U.S. Lumber Company. Timber was cut on the South Fork of the Holston, Comer's Creek, and Roland Creek for the Marion mill. (Courtesy Dr. Paul Brown.)

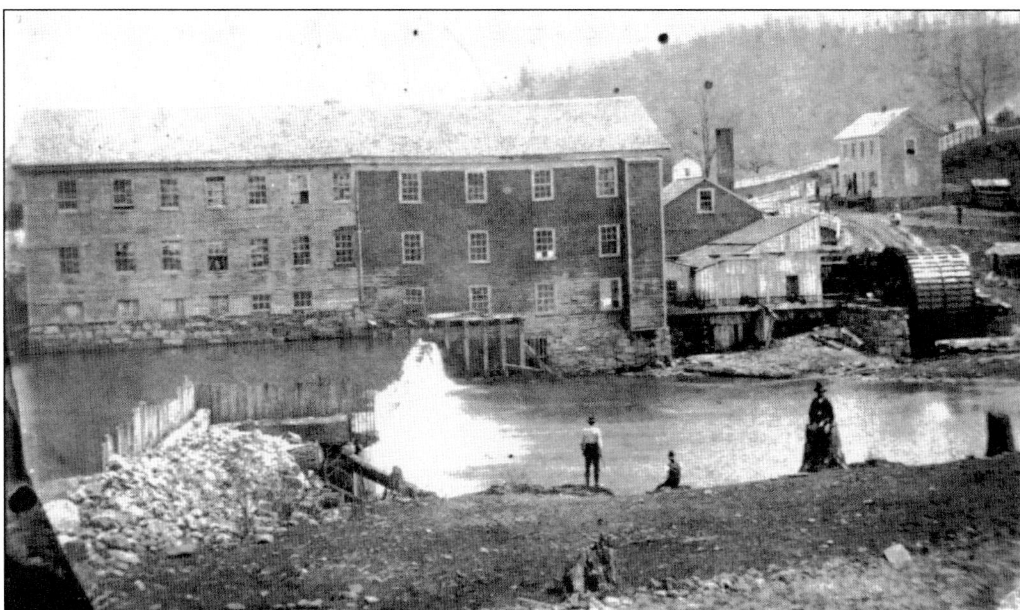

HOLSTON MILLS. Known as "the Factory," Holston Mills was the most prosperous and largest plant in Smyth County. Farmers from miles around sold their fleece to Holston Mills, which was used to make suits for men, shawls, petticoats, and also Civil War uniforms for the Confederacy. Upon purchasing the mill in 1880, George W. Palmer changed its name to Holstein Mills and constructed a flour and corn mill. (Courtesy Mack Sturgill Collection.)

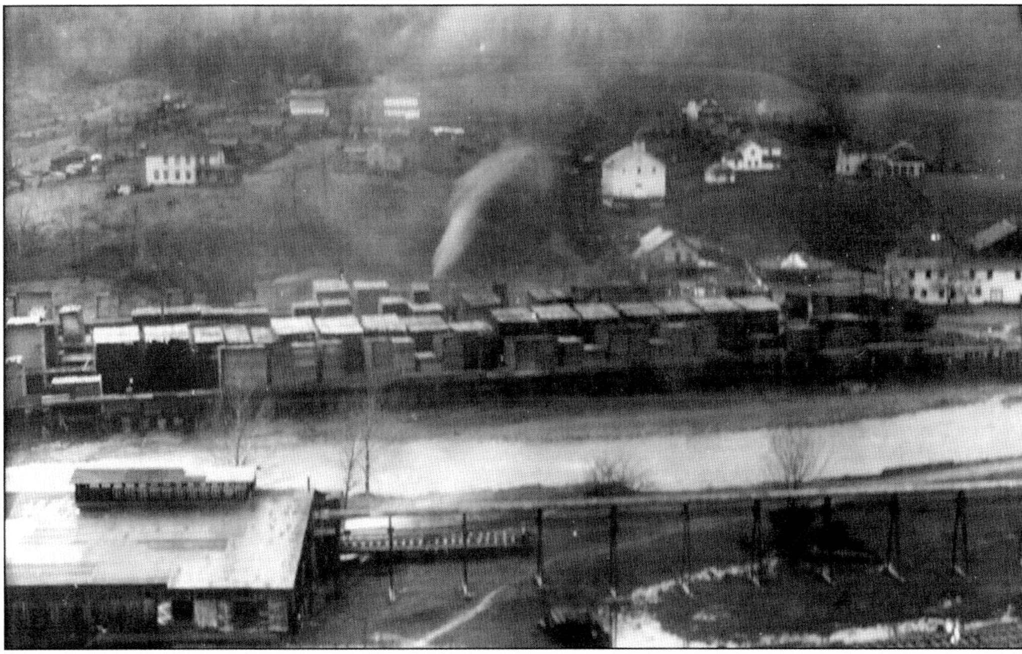

HASSINGER LUMBER COMPANY. The lumber operations of Hassinger Lumber Company, which began in 1906, lasted 22 years until the mill closed on Christmas Eve in 1928. The hemlock, white pine, yellow poplar, spruce, chestnut, and oak tress cut here were sold through the Lumber Company of Pittsburgh, Pennsylvania, Luther Hassinger's former employer. (Courtesy Clegg Williams.)

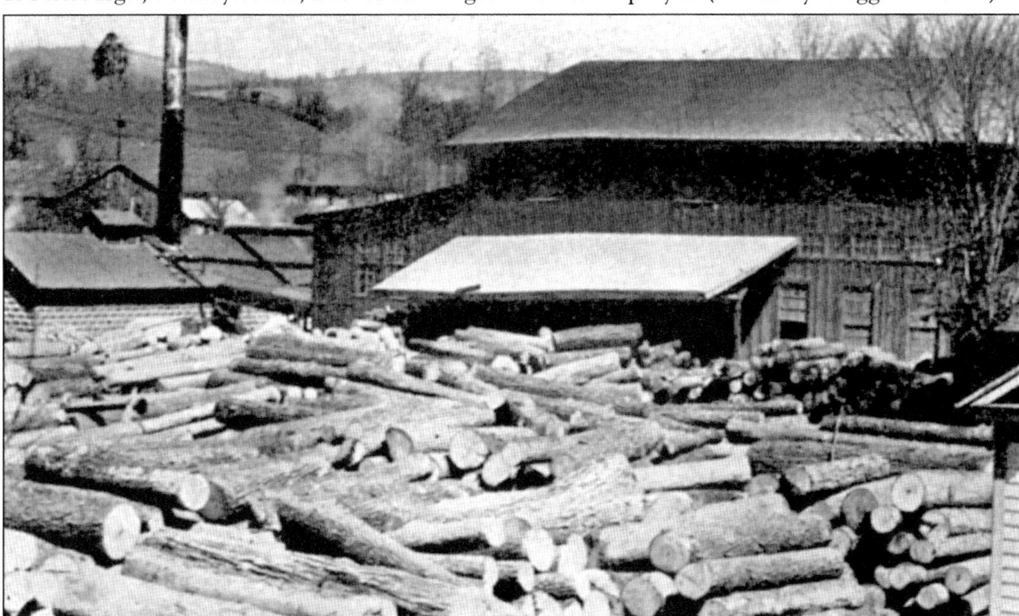

LOOK AND LINCOLN. In 1862, Nathan Loomis Look and Charles Francis Lincoln purchased 50 acres of land with improvements in Marion on the middle fork of the Holston River for $6,000. This would become the permanent site of Marion Handle Mills, a company that was formerly located in Rich Valley. In 1914, this manufacturer employed 50 men and produced 600,000 plow handles and 400 wagons. (Courtesy Mack Sturgill Collection.)

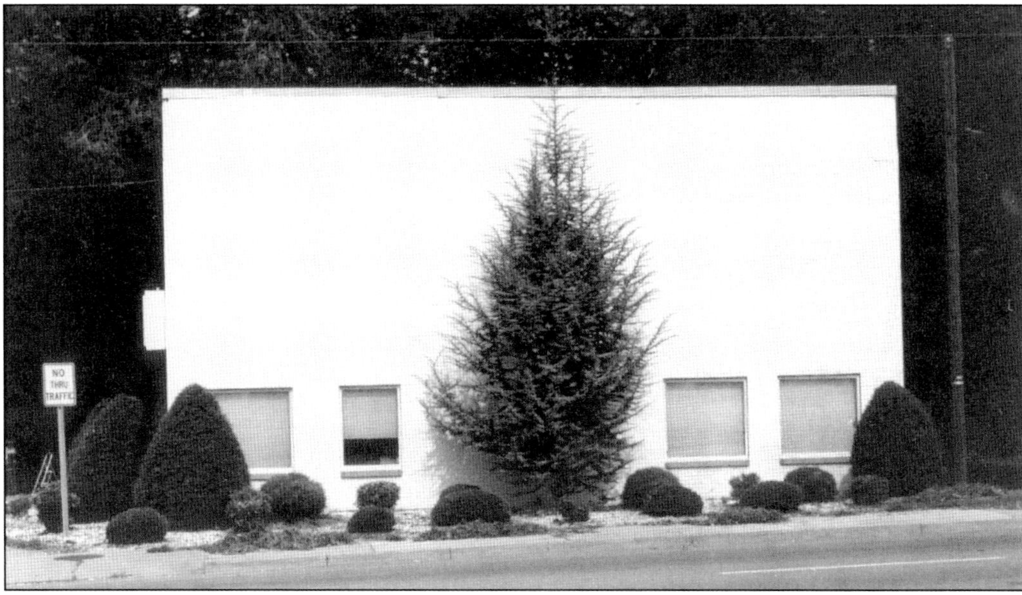

WHERE MOUNTAIN DEW WAS BORN. A stockholder of the Tip Corporation, Allie Hartman, and his brother offered their trademark for a lemon-lime drink they called Mountain Dew. It was only used for their personal entertaining. In 1962, W. H. Jones, manager of the Tip Corporation, used the trademark, old bottles, and his own lemon-lime concoction to form the world-renowned drink we know today. Hungate Business Services is currently located here. (Courtesy Ron Harrington.)

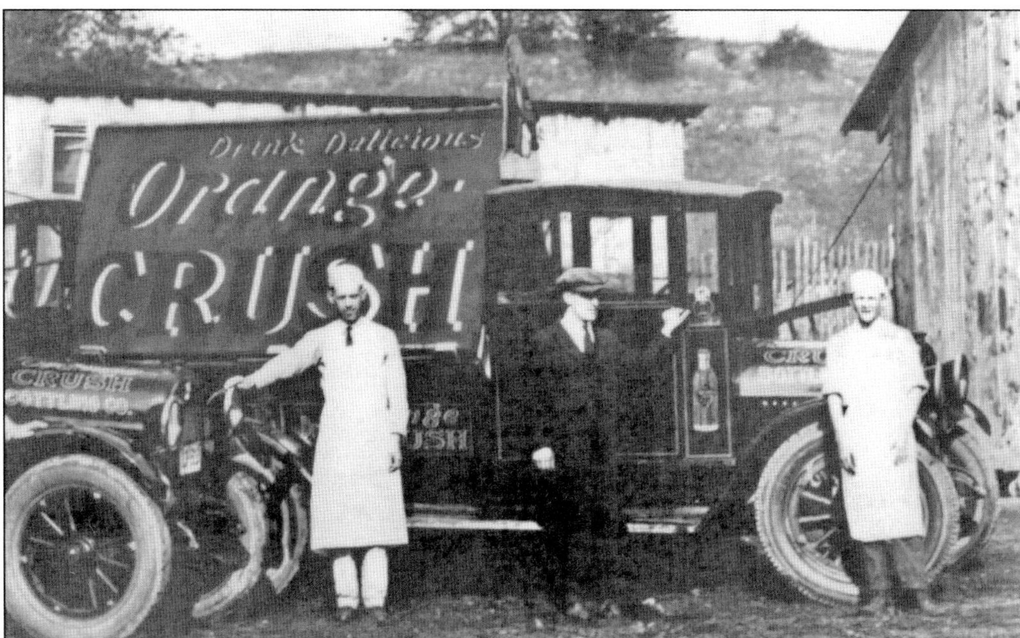

ORANGE CRUSH BOTTLING. B. Scott Sprinkle and N. E. Robinson owned the Crush Bottling Company when this photograph was taken in 1925, after the company moved from Main Street to the Marion and Rye Valley Rail Depot. Notice the sign that hails "Drink Delicious Orange-Crush." (Courtesy Mack Sturgill Collection.)

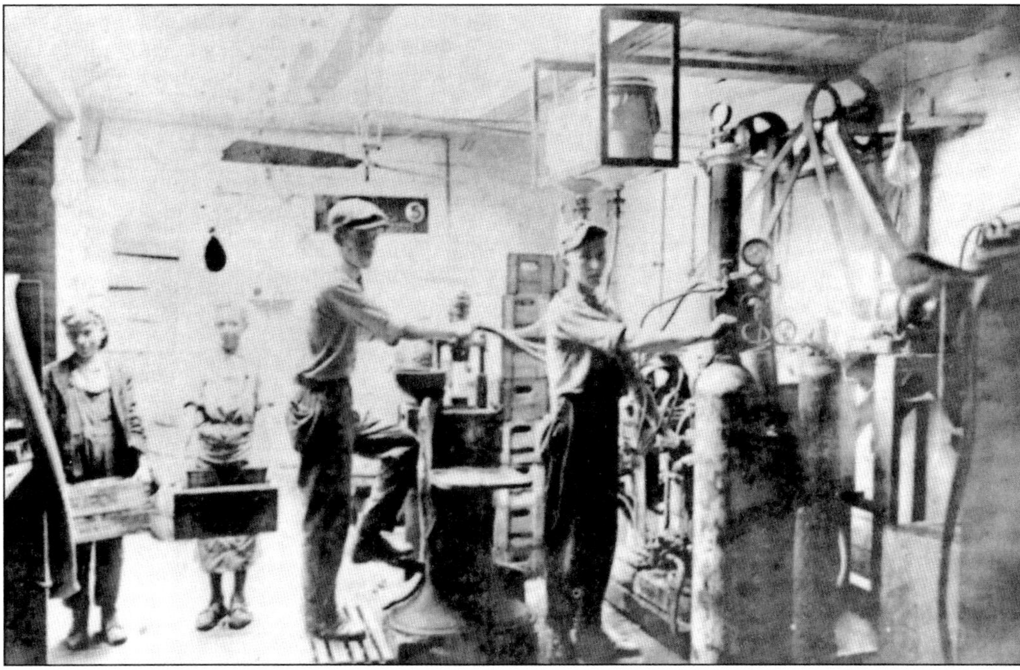

MARION'S FIRST SODA BOTTLING PLANT. This plant was established in 1905 by J. L. Thornton on Main Street, in the building where Home and Auto True Value Hardware later was located. Here the employees, all youth, are shown preparing the soda pop. W. S. Johnson is the one at the bottling machine. Notice the deep crates and the 5¢ sign on the back wall. (Courtesy Bill Huber.)

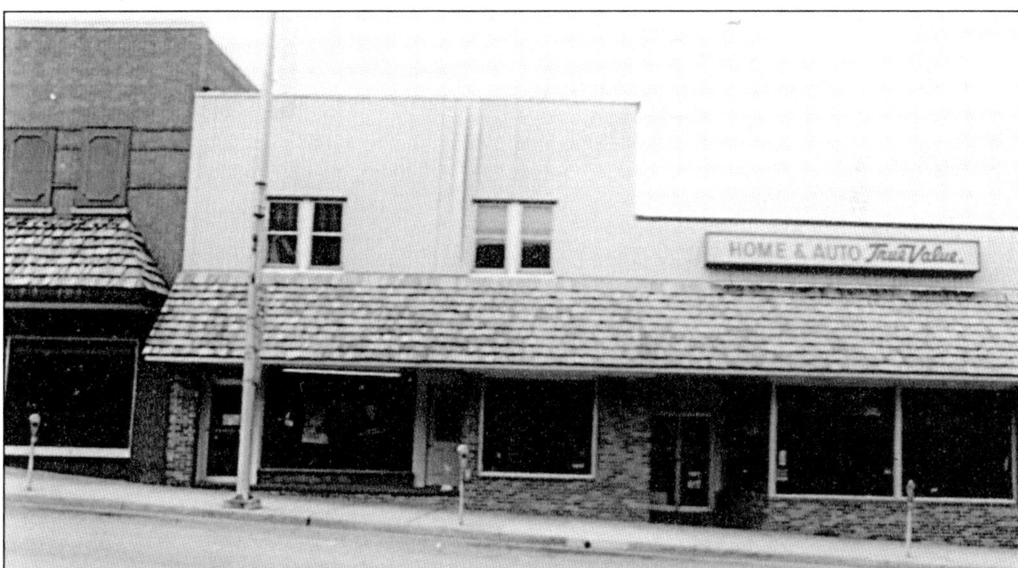

HOME AND AUTO TRUE VALUE. In 1944, Clarence and Imogene Coulthard started their business in the smaller building to the right. As this company grew, they purchased the Greenwood Building to the left for expansion. During the 1960s, the Coulthards started the first television cable system in Marion. Though the cable service was sold and the other business consolidated, this business still operates in Marion today. (Courtesy Bill Huber.)

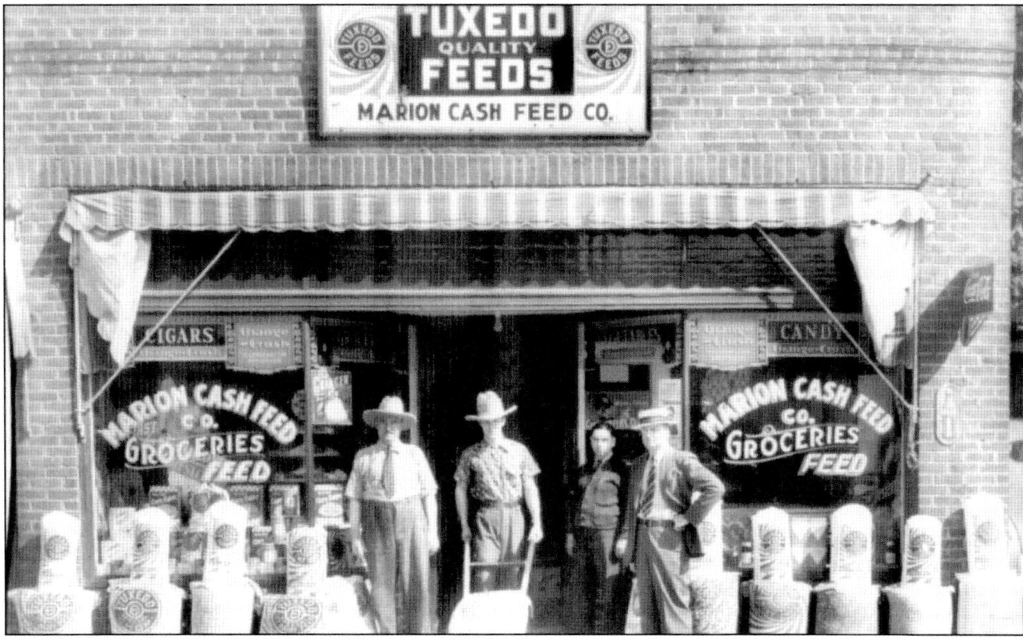

MARION FEED AND SEED. Locals stopped here for lunch and sat around the pot-bellied stove to share their tall tales. From 1939 to 1952, this store was located in the Seaver Building. Customers could get a sandwich and soda pop for a dime. People traded eggs for bulk sugar, beans, coffee, and such. Shown here from left to right are E. J. and Bob Hutton, owner William "Shorty" Eads, and a salesman. (Courtesy Evelyn Eads Yarber.)

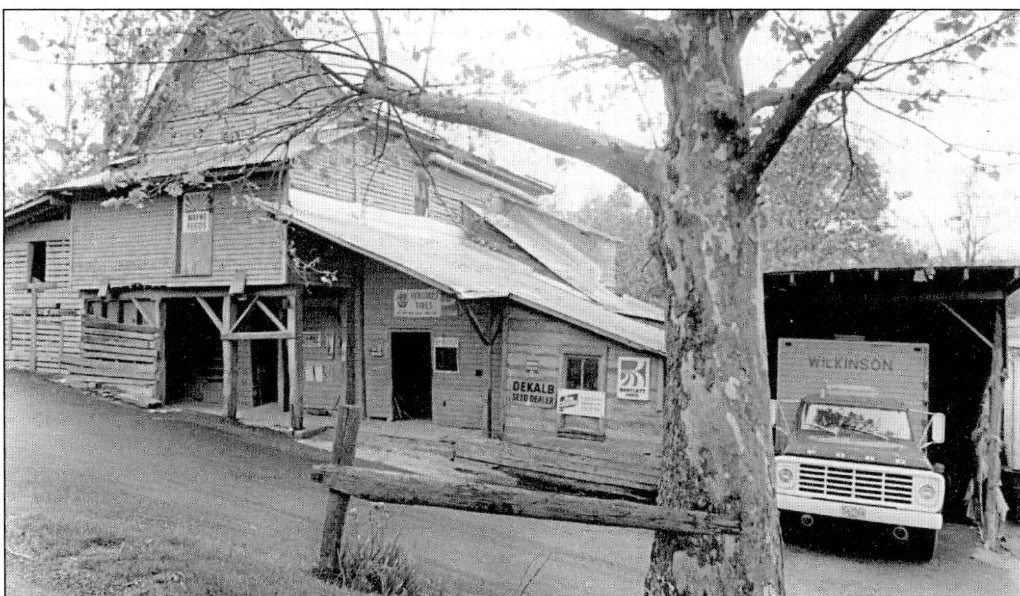

J. T. WILKINSON AND SON MILL. Located along the South Fork of the Holston River, just over the Washington County line, this gristmill was known to be operating during the early 1800s. Before it began specializing in feed in the 1940s, the mill once ground flour, buckwheat, cornmeal, oats, and such. The original waterwheel still remains, though it stopped operating in July 2000. (Courtesy Debbie Wilkinson Tuell.)

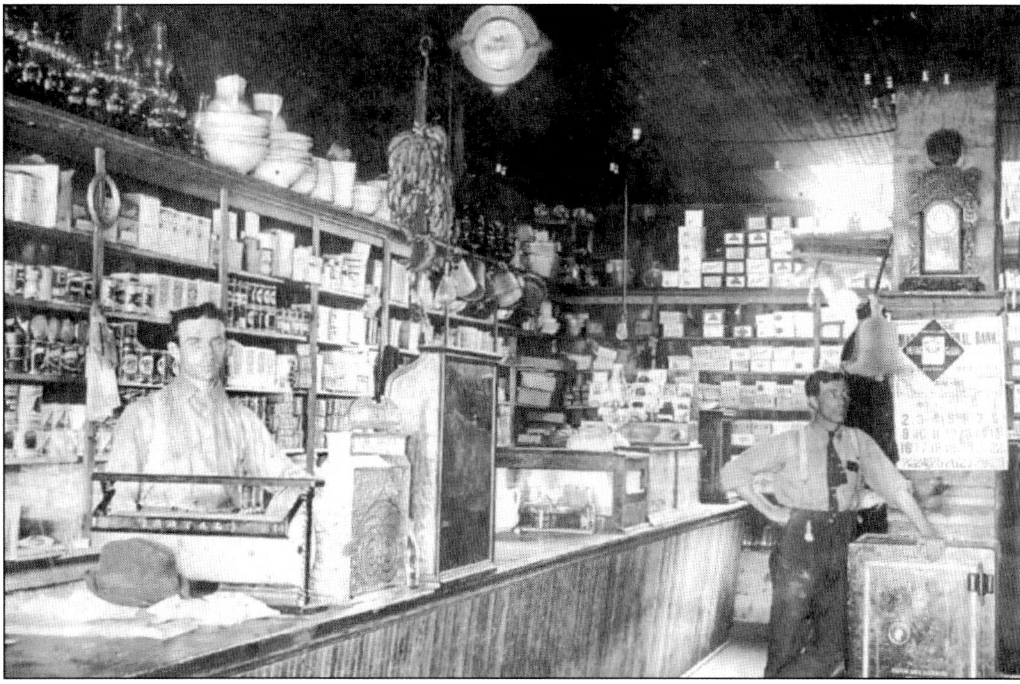

Teas' Company Store. During the early 1900s, Teas was a booming community because of the Teas Extract Plant. Most of those who lived here worked at the plant. Robert Haulsee (behind the counter) and Charles Keesling posed for this photograph inside the company store that carried fabrics, clothes, shoes, cooking supplies, and food items. (Courtesy Mack Sturgill Collection.)

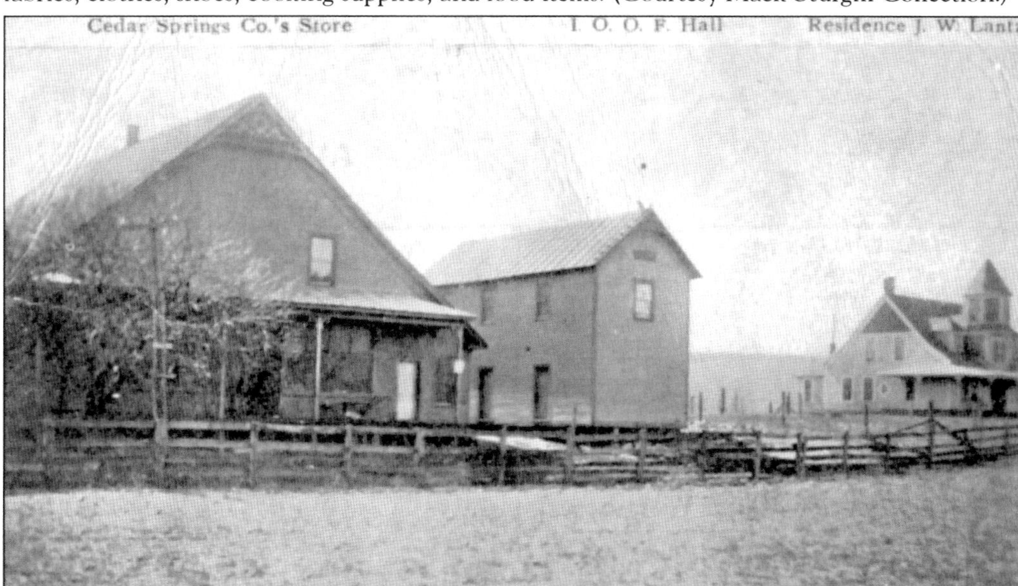

Cedar Springs Company Store. The Cedar Springs community sprang up thanks to the nearby iron mines in Wythe County. The company store carried all kinds of foods, hardware, cloths, and such, as well as the area post office. The Independent Order of Odd Fellows held their meetings in the building next door. On the far right was the home of J. W. Lewis, president of the iron mines. (Courtesy Dr. Paul Brown.)

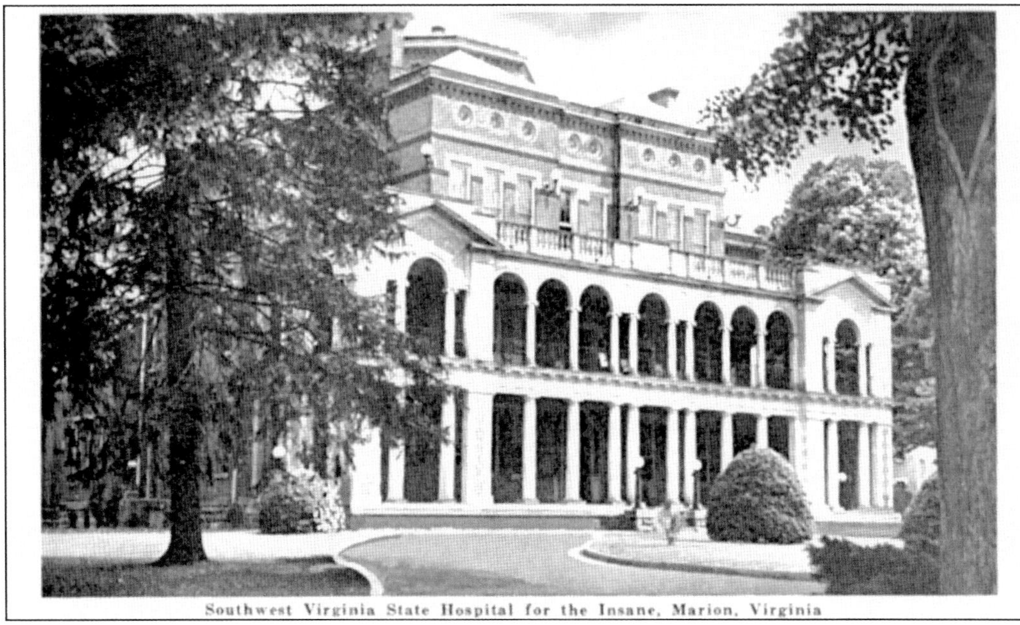

ECONOMIC SECURITY FOR SMYTH COUNTY. After the Civil War, the community was struggling with poverty and unemployment. When it was learned that the state planned to build a state hospital, citizens of the community rallied for the Southwestern Lunatic Asylum to be located here. In 1887, one of largest public institutions in Virginia was opened in Marion. The considerable payroll and purchases from the asylum boosted the economy. (Courtesy Dr. Paul Brown.)

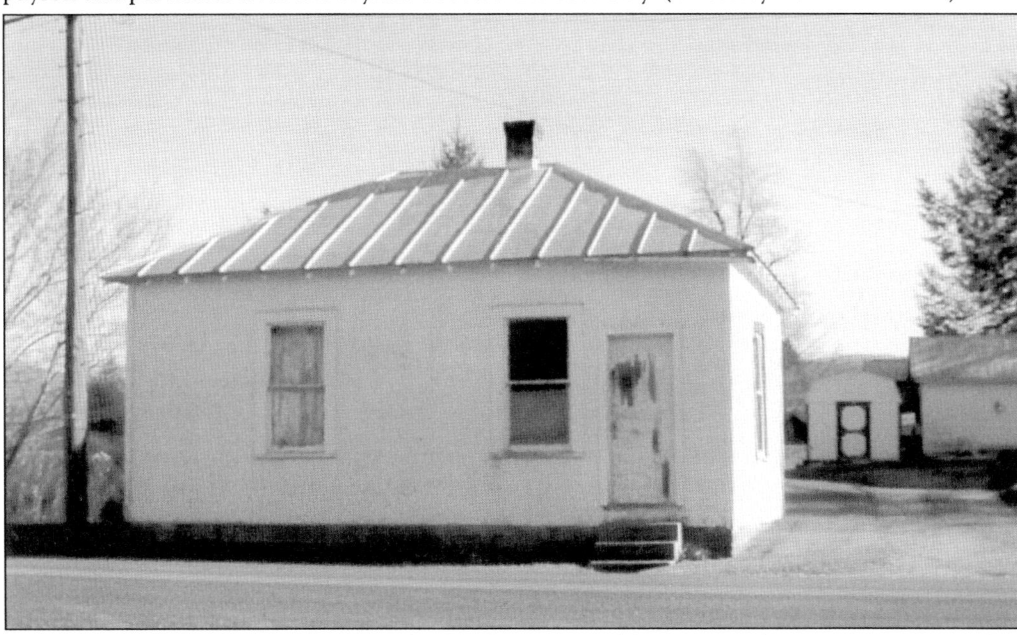

SUGAR GROVE CANNERY. This cinder-block cannery, like many others, was put into place during the Depression by the government to help the citizens provide for themselves during such hard times. Area families took their fruits, vegetables, and meats to have them steam pressure canned for safety. The building, which is located along Teas Road, is currently vacant. (Courtesy Debra Williams.)

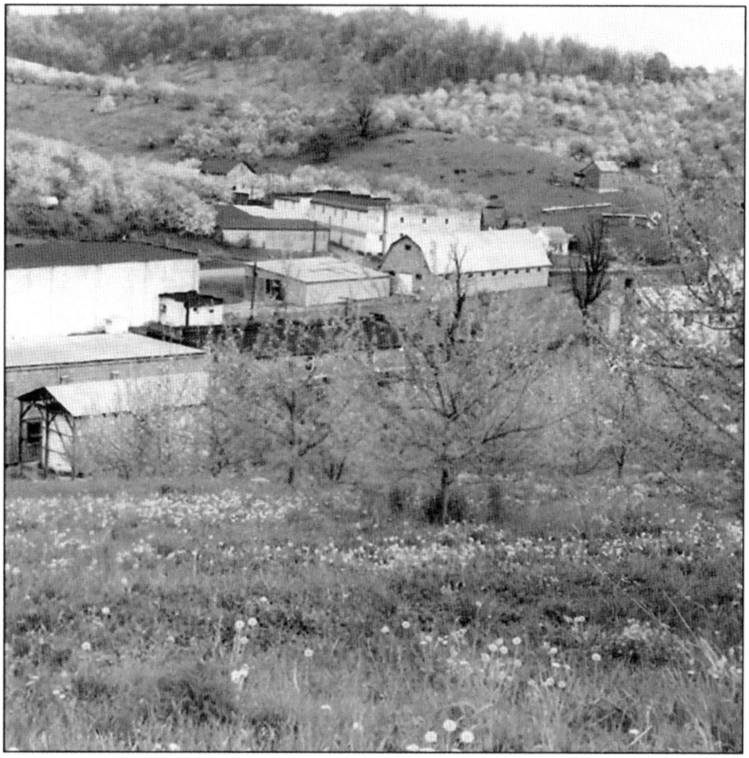

BONHAM EMPIRE. H. L. Bonham started his apple orchard *c.* 1911 in the Chilhowie area and bought up available lands for orchards throughout the area. His descendants carried on the empire after his death in 1934 until 1983, when they decided to sell out because of losses. Pictured here are the cannery, packing house, storage, and other parts of Bonham's empire. Bonham received many honors for his legendary farming techniques. (Courtesy Mack Sturgill Collection.)

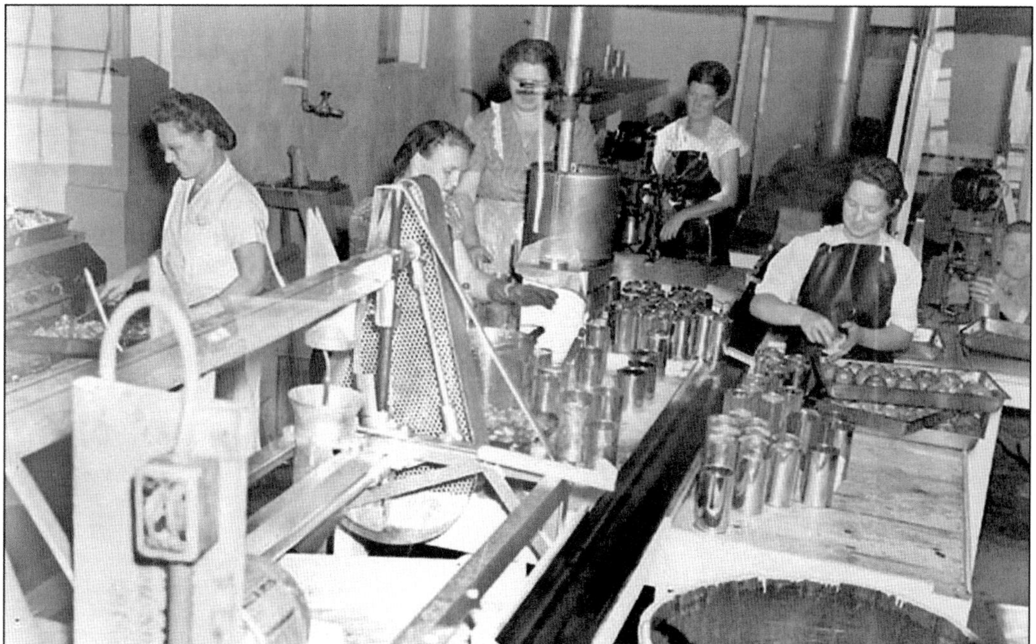

AN APPLE A DAY. Here at the Bonham Cannery, these women are hard at work processing the apples into fried apples and cider. The apples were grown by Bonham Brothers in nearby orchards. The cannery opened in 1940 along the Old Packing House Road and closed in the 1980s when the business was sold. (Courtesy Mack Sturgill Collection.)

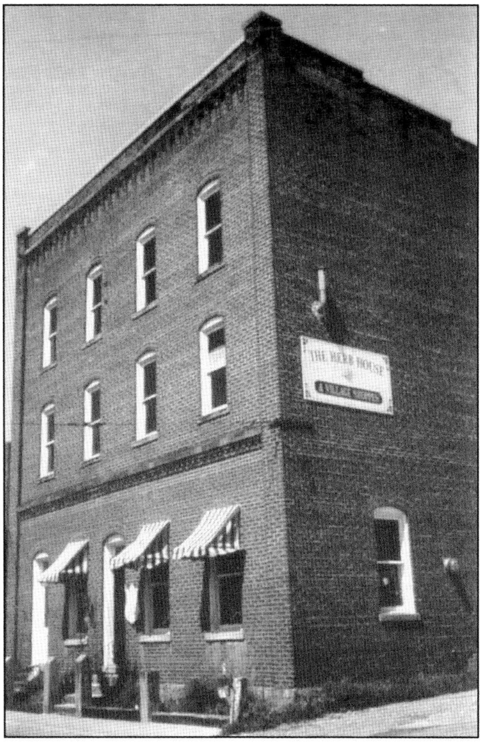

R. T. Greer Crude Drug Company. In 1905, because of Marion's rail shipping ability and this being the largest producing area of roots, herbs, berries, and other medicinal products, R. T. Greer chose Marion for the location of his company. This was the second largest business of its kind in the world. Greer was the first person to ever collect and sell pollen for medicinal purposes. (Courtesy Dr. Paul Brown.)

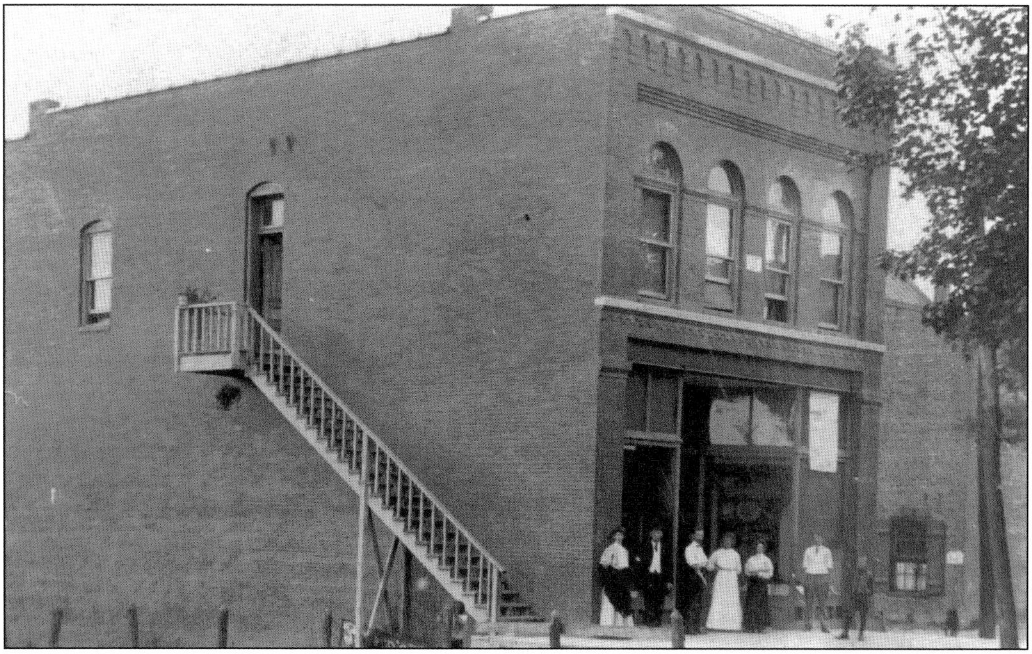

J. B. Rhea Building. Built in 1905 for J. B. Rhea on the corner of Main and Chilhowie Streets, this structure held F. F. Francis Hardware, Standard Oil, 3C Nectar, and Marion Bottling Company. Apartments were located on the second floor. Many businesses here failed because it was too far from town to draw customers. In the 1970s, Happy's Restaurant was successful here, owned by Jerry Hounshell. (Courtesy Mack Sturgill Collection.)

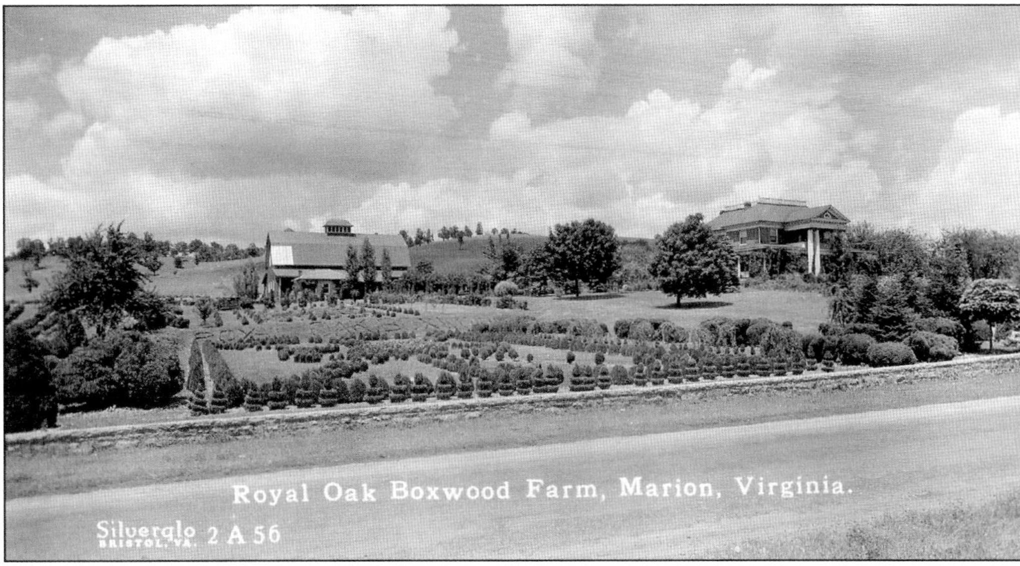

ROYAL OAK BOXWOOD FARMS. Charles Wassum Sr. started his tree farming business prior to the 1920s. He planted estates around Vermont, Connecticut, and New York. When John D. Rockefeller approached him for a portfolio, Wassum pulled out the only picture he had—a $5 bill, which displayed his very own boxwoods around the Lincoln Memorial. Needless to say, Wassum had no problem making a sale. (Courtesy Atwood J. Huff.)

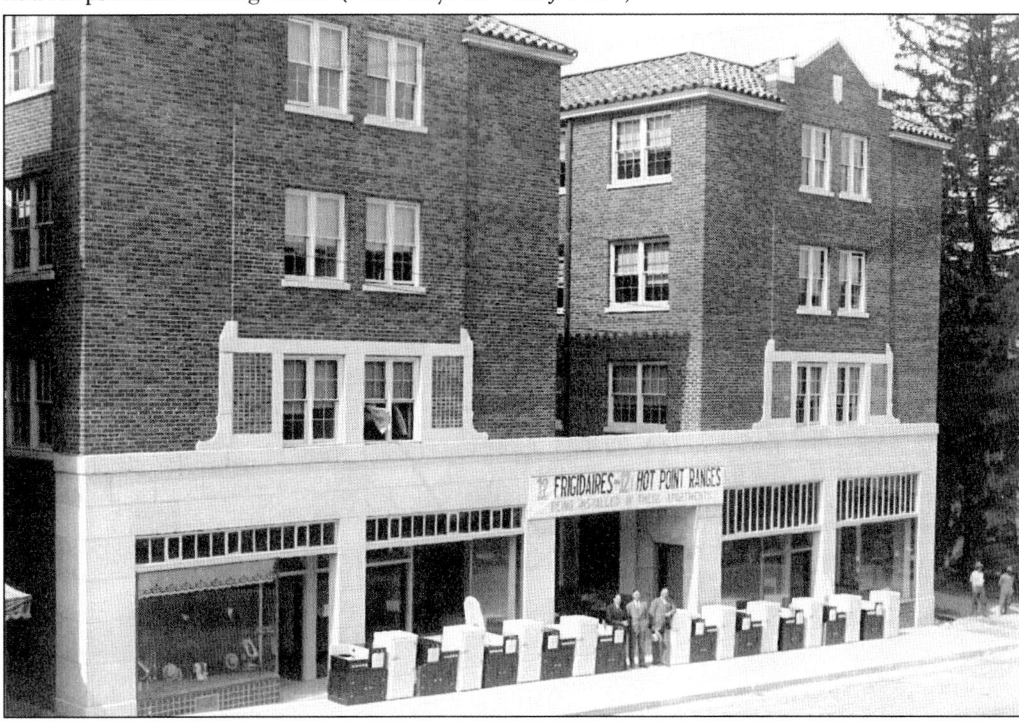

ROYAL OAK APARTMENTS. Charles Wassum Sr. built these 12 apartments and 4 stores *c.* 1929. This building surrounded the opening of the Lincoln Theatre. Note the sign for the theater isn't up in this picture. Displayed on the street are High Point stoves and Frigidaire refrigerators, which were being placed into each new apartment. (Courtesy Atwood J. Huff.)

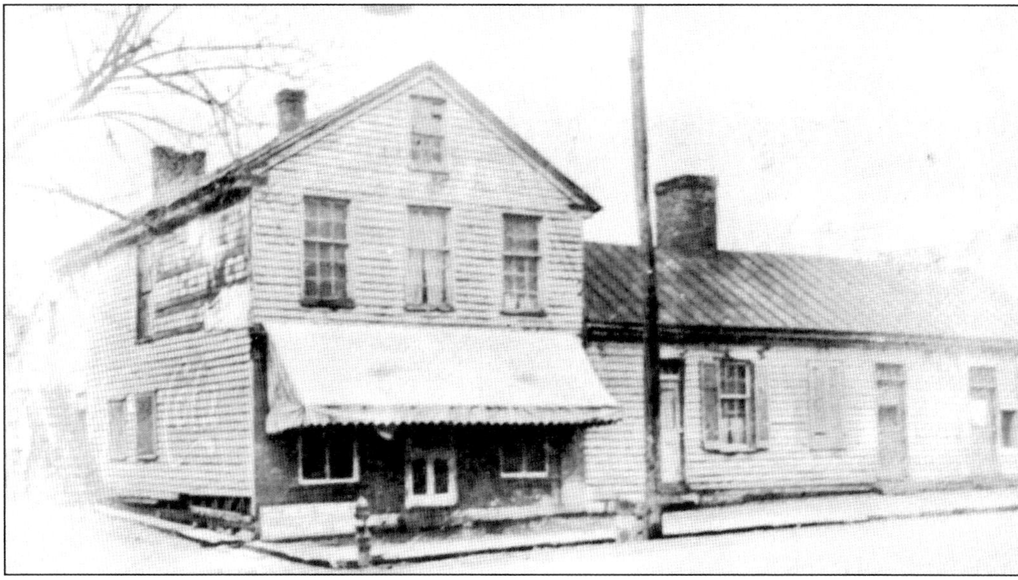

Marion Democrat Office. This building was the home of the *Marion Democrat* in 1884. Smyth County's first newspaper, the *Marion Visitor*, started operation in 1858 under the leadership of George J. Curtis and James W. Kennedy. It may have been destroyed by Stoneman's Raiders since its last issue was published in December 1864. Sherwood Anderson bought the *Marion Democrat* and the *Smyth County News* in 1927. (Courtesy Mack Sturgill Collection.)

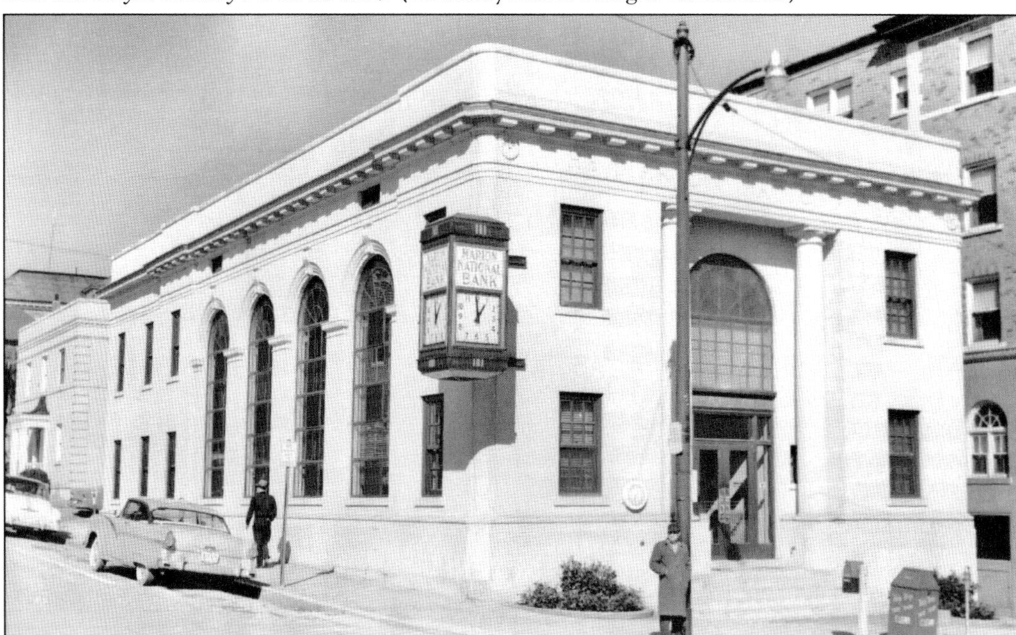

Marion National Bank. The Marion National Bank was made of granite and limestone. Massive arched windows give way for the evening sun. Opening in 1927, the bank moved to its new location across the street in 1972. The building was later renovated for offices. Note the four-sided clock, which is no longer there. The Bank of Marion now uses this building. (Courtesy Gary and Bonnita Frazier.)

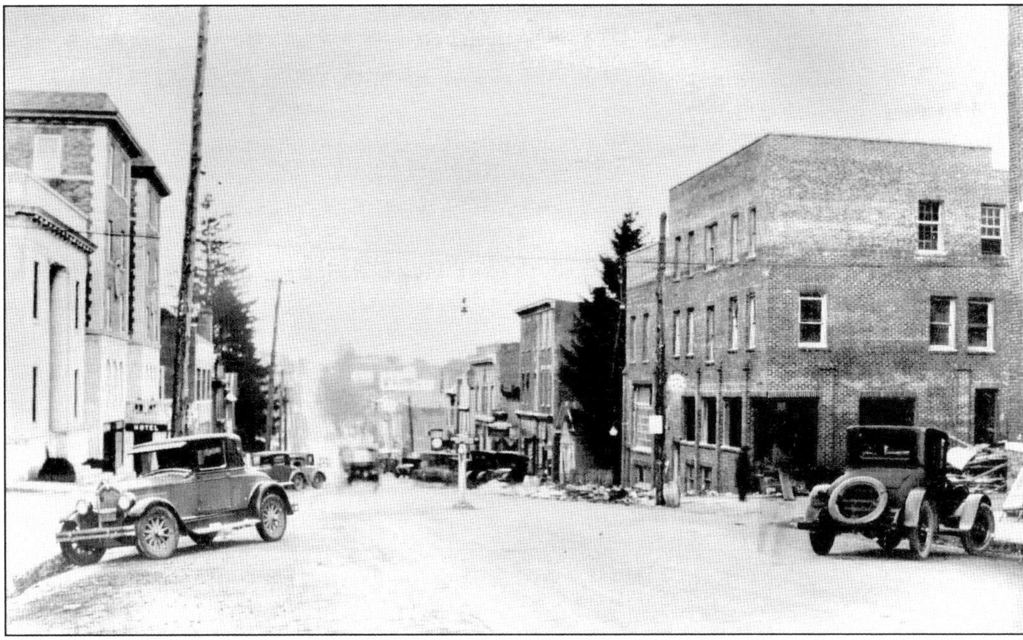

MAIN STREET, 1928. This photograph is of Main Street in Marion in 1928. There is not much in this photograph that looks familiar today. The pile of rubble to the right is due to the Marion Hotel renovation. The cars were parked diagonally at that time, and the stoplight was in the middle of the street. (Courtesy Mack Sturgill Collection.)

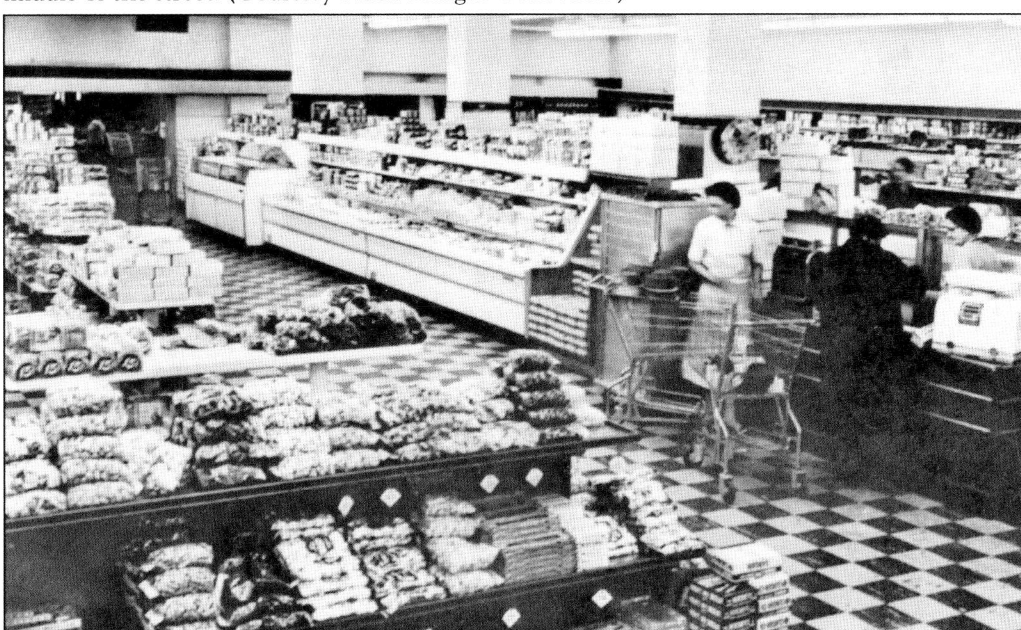

PIGGLY WIGGLY GROCERY STORE. O. C. Sprinkle and J. D. Buchanan opened this fine grocery store in 1922 on Main Street in Marion where Framing Unlimited is now located. Groceries came into the store through the back on a roller conveyor. The store had automatic doors in the back that led out to Alley Street. The tile floors, open coolers, and grocery buggies haven't changed much from today's stores. (Courtesy Mack Sturgill Collection.)

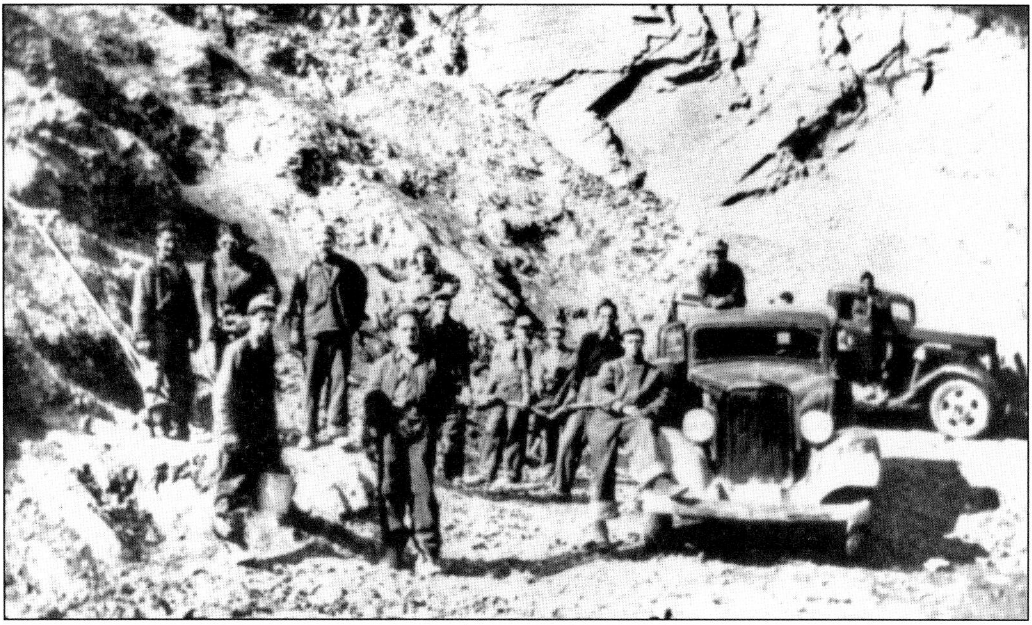

MINERS IN SMYTH COUNTY. Iron mining began in this area before the 1770s. The first ore was dug on the Williams property, just north of Sugar Grove. Tradition has it the cannons used during the Revolutionary War were made at the old forge in this area, but it was most likely the bullets. Some serious attempts were made to mine on a large scale but with no success. (Mack Sturgill Collection.)

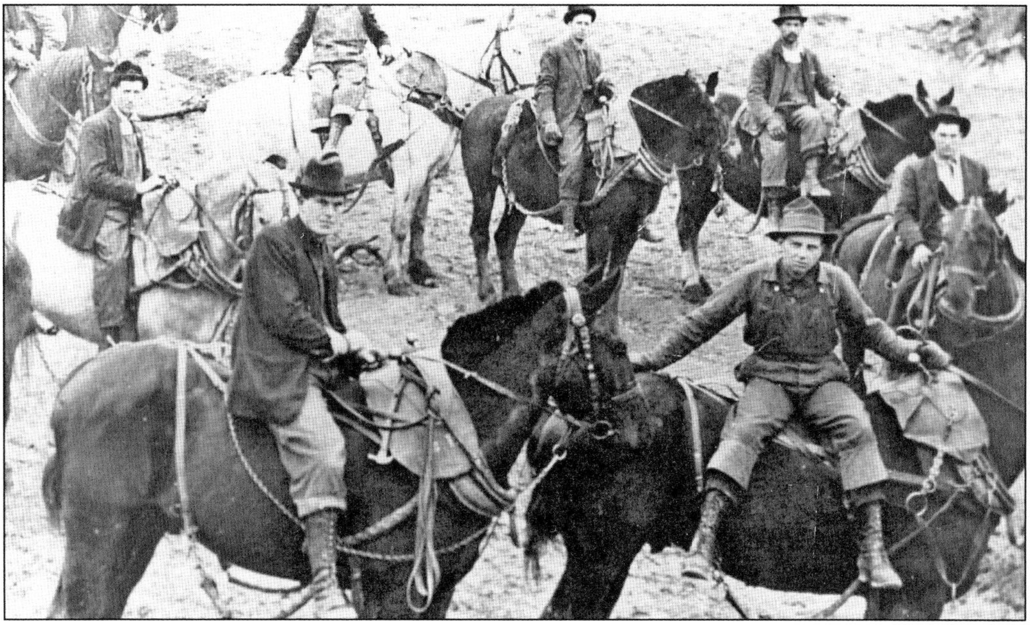

LOGGERS IN HURRICANE. Before the Hurricane became a national recreation area, the logging companies in the area hired loggers to cut the virgin timber. Loggers used chains to pull the downed logs to where the Marion and Rye Valley Railroad would collect the wood and transport it to the companies. The men lived in logging camps. Pruner Walter Weaver is the first one on the left. (Courtesy Tommy Weaver.)

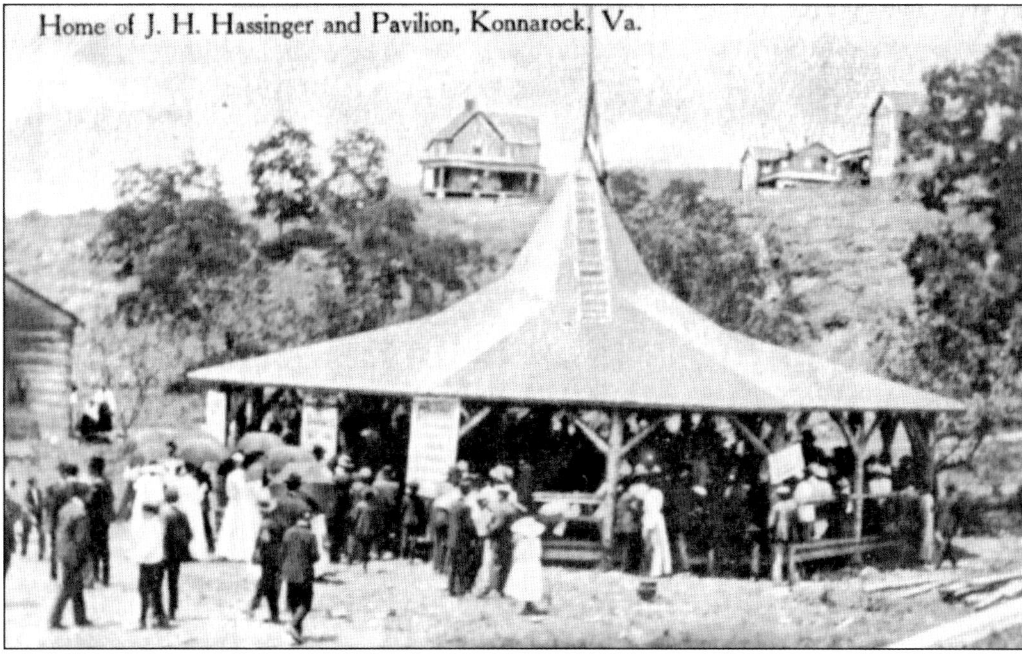

KONNAROCK. Konnarock became a thriving community when Luther Hassinger built a band mill near Whitetop Mountain in 1906. Due to growth, many buildings were constructed, including a commissary, a boarding house, a school for grades 1 through 11, a post office, and a blacksmith shop. Because of expansion, company houses were constructed at Big Hill for employees and doctors were hired to provide medical care. (Courtesy Dr. Paul Brown.)

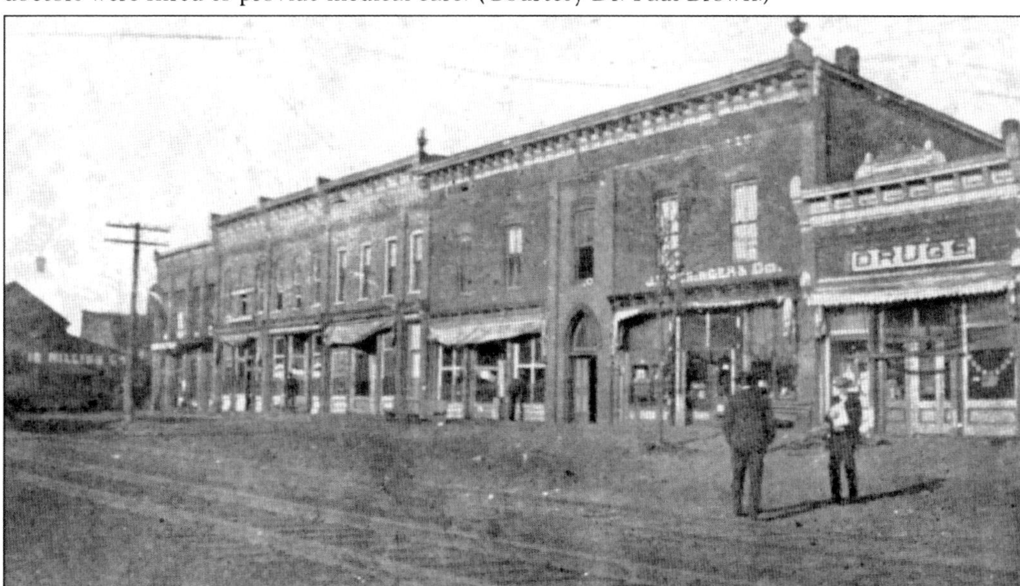

CHILHOWIE MAIN STREET. Notice how Chilhowie's Main Street faced the railroad tracks over a century ago. In 1904, the entire block was destroyed by fire and was rebuilt to face what is Main Street today. Located in the background is Chilhowie Milling Company, which was built in 1882 by James D. Tate. It produced flour under the names of "Our Pride," "Purity," and "Peerless Flour." (Courtesy Clegg Williams.)

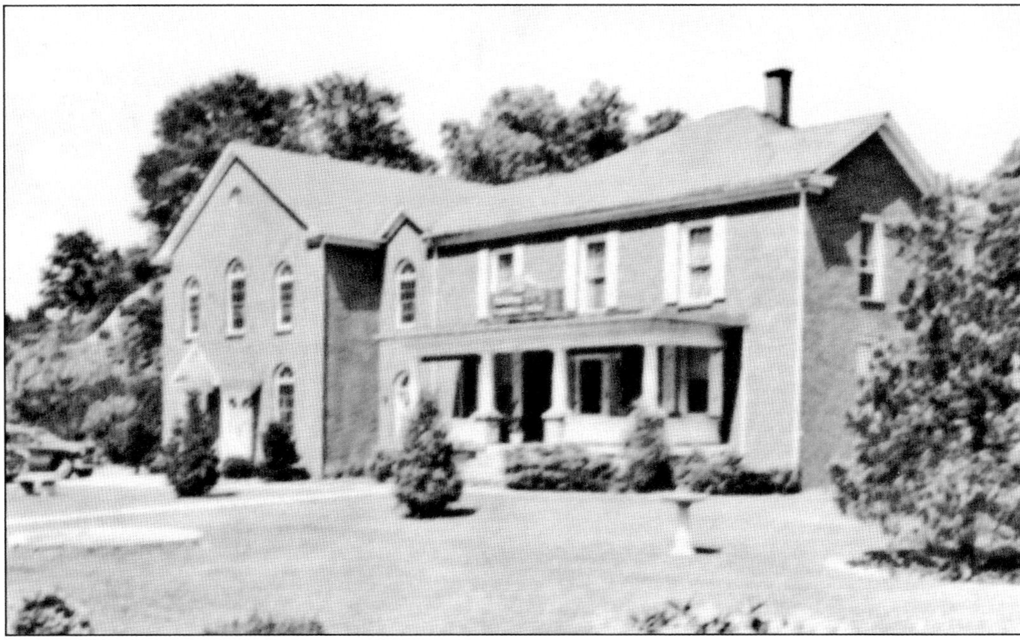

BARNETT'S FUNERAL HOME. This beautiful house became Barnett's Funeral Home in 1946. As years passed, additions were made to include more room for services and for a bigger chapel. Peyton Barnett inherited the business from his father and ran this business until his death in the mid-1990s. The building was razed in 2006 for office space. (Mack Sturgill Collection.)

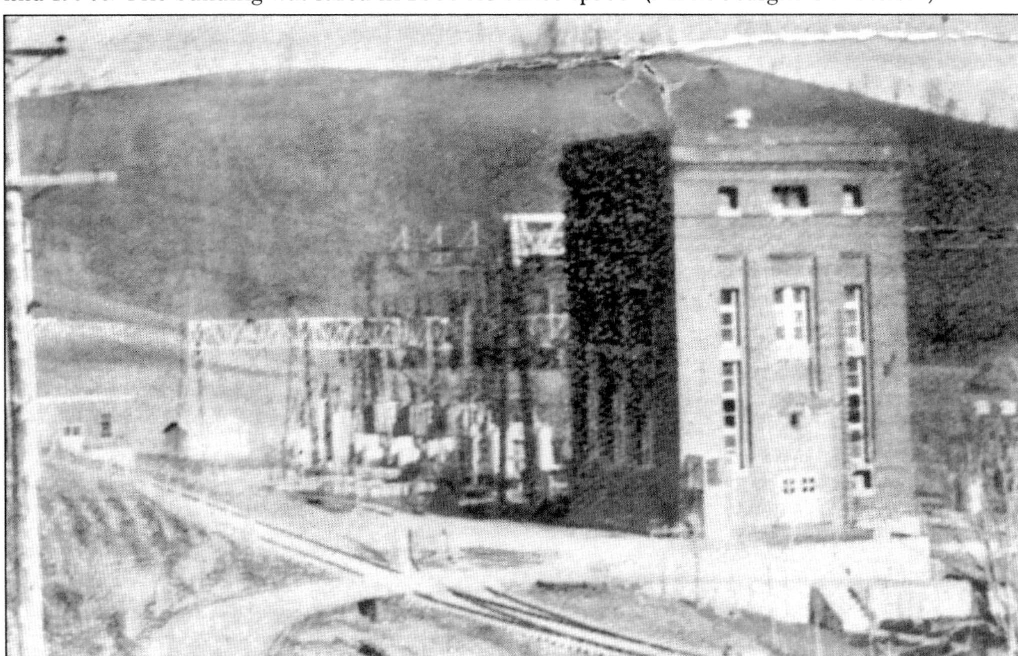

APPALACHIAN ELECTRIC POWER SUB STATION. Located in Saltville, this 132,000-volt sub station had a capacity of 40,000 horsepower. It served as a connecting link between the north and south power transmission systems. This building still stands today. (Courtesy Mack Sturgill Collection.)

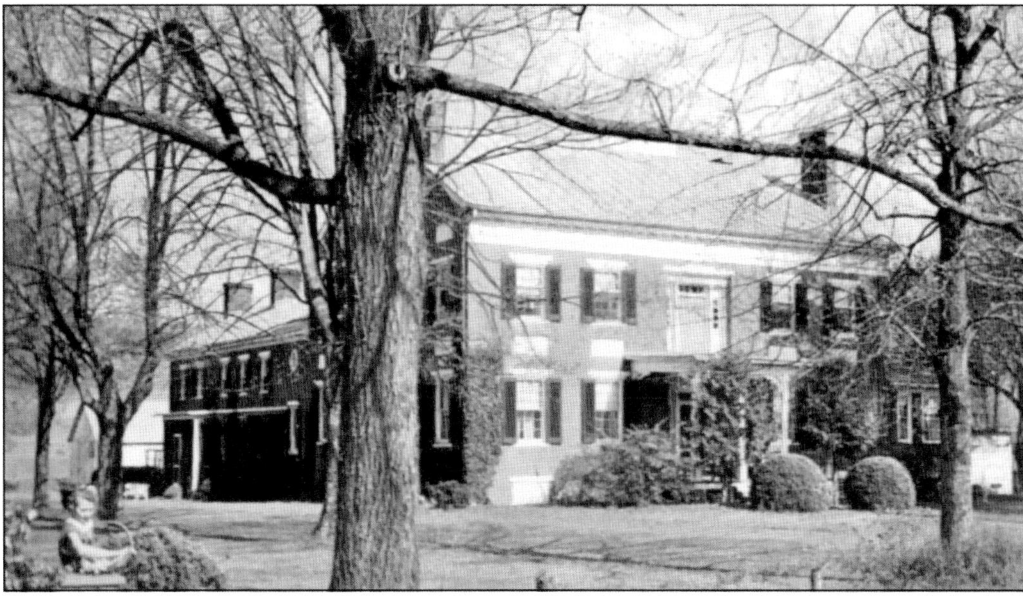

WILDERNESS ROAD TRADING POST. Herondon, named by owner Lucy Herndon Crockett, was located at Seven Mile Ford and was the location of the Wilderness Road Trading Post. Here Crockett sold items such as autographed copies of her book and artwork and hooked rugs made by local women. From 1882 to 1886, a private school was conducted in the building. Nellie Preston operated a tea room here. (Courtesy Mack Sturgill Collection.)

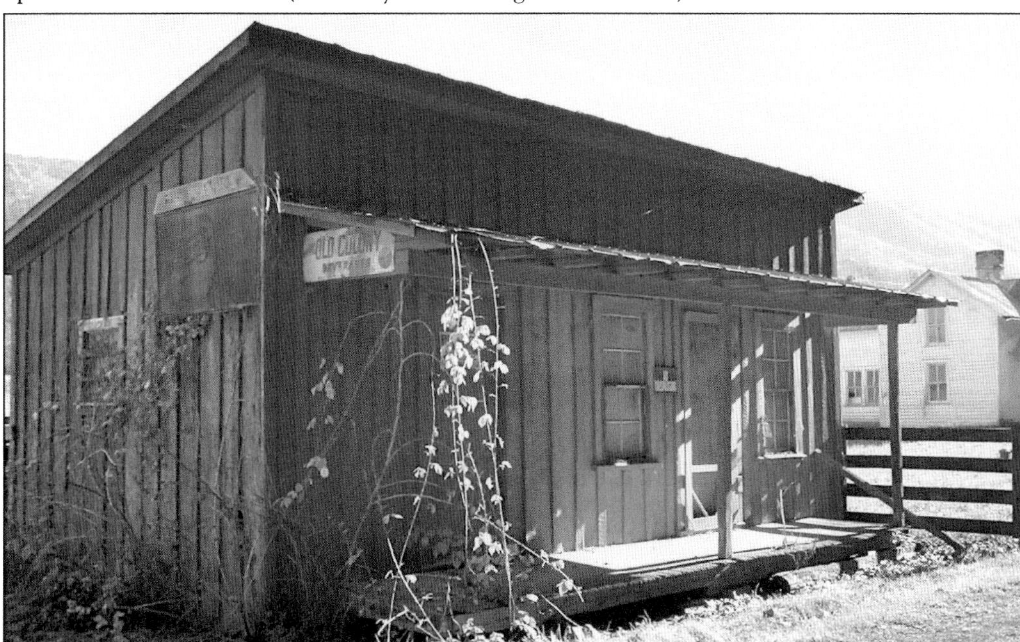

C. B. BLEVINS'S STORE. With the exception of the faded signs, this vacant building, just off Mill Creek, looks as though the owner just locked up for the day. Old farmers stopped in for a soda pop and a Moon Pie and to discuss the daily events of farming. Notice the advertisement on the side of the old store: "Old Colony Beverage. Bigger bottle. Better value. Five cents." (Courtesy Debra Williams.)

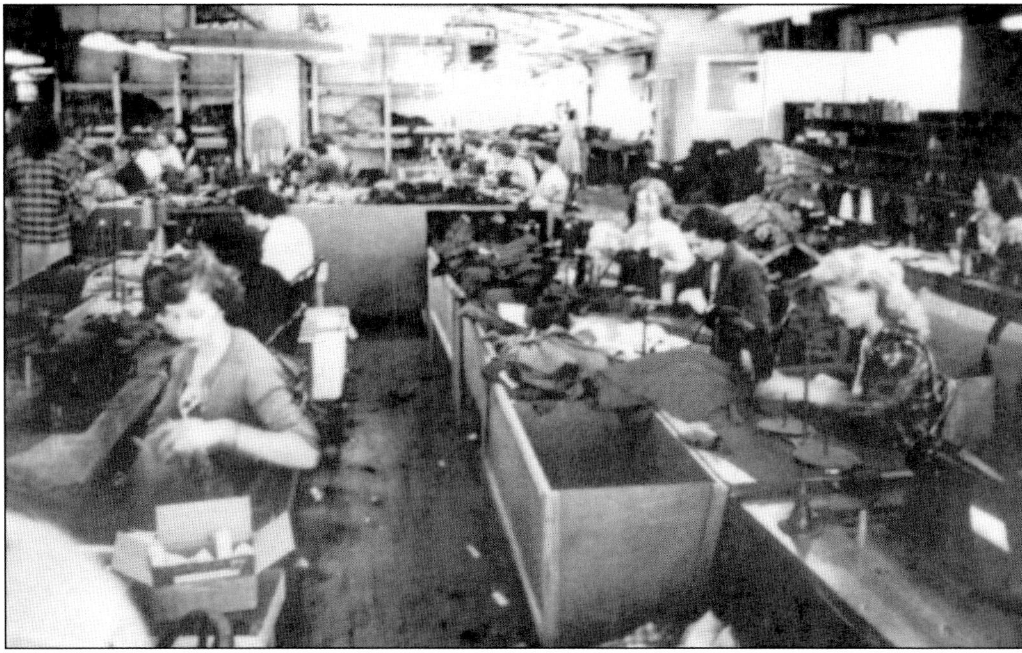

A Day's Work. This *c.* 1950 photograph shows the factory workers busy sewing garments at the old Harwood Manufacturing Company. This company employed several hundred people and produced pajamas, undergarments, and shirts. Harwood had two locations: one on Matson Drive and one on Cherry Street. After the closing of these two factories, employees held reunions to keep in touch. (Courtesy Mack Sturgill Collection.)

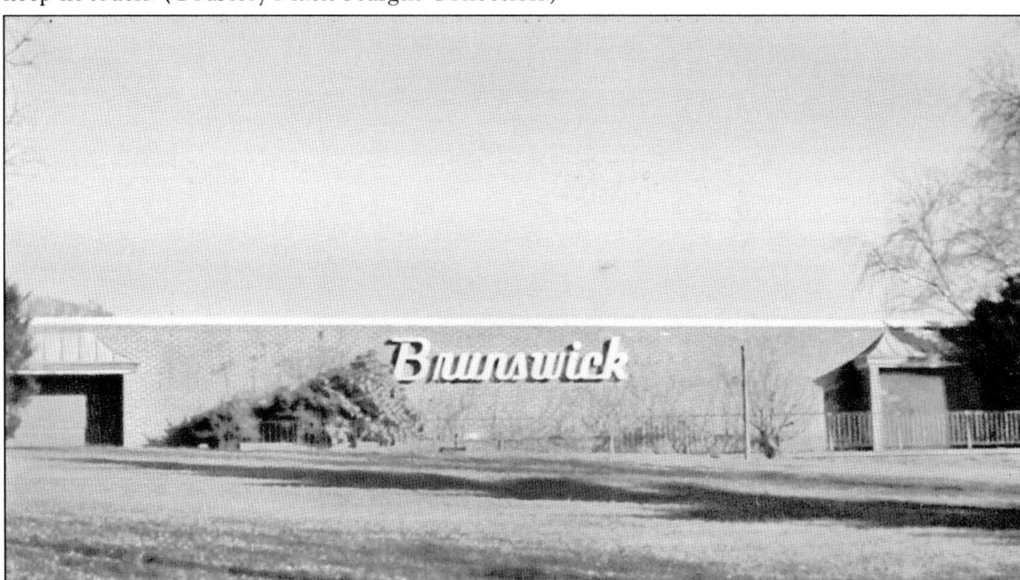

Brunswick in Sugar Grove. This branch of Brunswick opened during the 1960s to manufacture bombs used during the Vietnam War. Buildings were spaced hundreds of yards apart so if one building blew up, the others would still remain. Many employees lost their lives working here. The area was heavily guarded. After the war, manufacturing halted and many were laid off. This property is now privately owned. (Courtesy Debra Williams.)

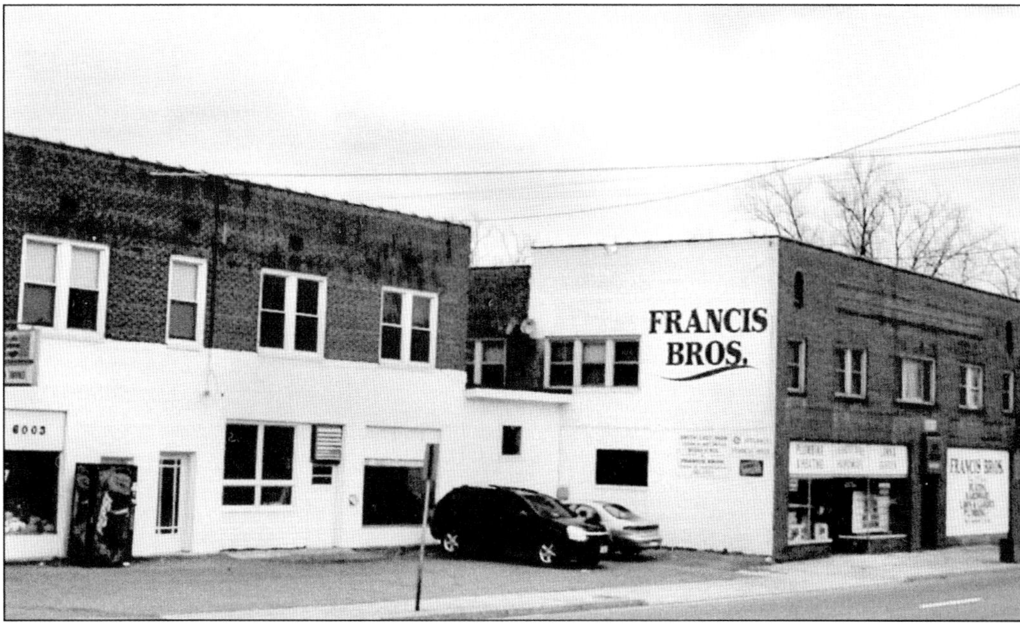

SITE OF FIRST INDUSTRY. Arthur Campbell and siblings, Margaret and John, settled the Royal Oak area of the county in 1766. Four years later, Arthur established a gristmill, the first this side of the New River and the first industry in this area. The mill was located along Staley's Creek, behind Francis Brothers' Hardware. (Courtesy Debra Williams.)

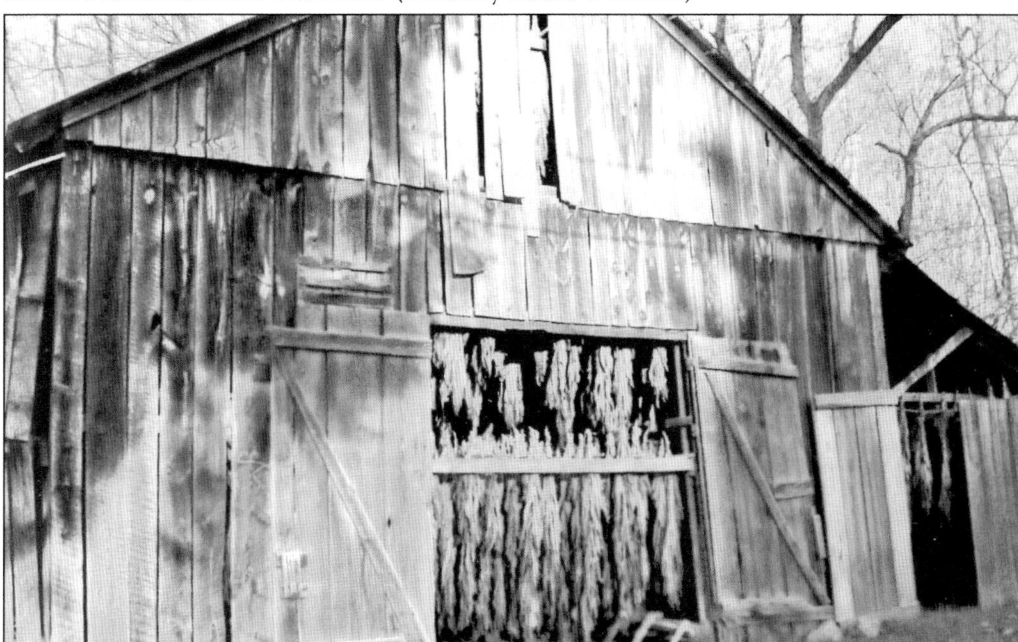

EVIDENCE OF HARD WORK. Native Americans introduced tobacco to the settlers in Jamestown. It became a staple as well as the principal currency. To grow the cash crop, small stems are first planted into a bed and then transplanted into the field. Plants are fertilized and suckered throughout the growing season. They are then topped, cut, speared, and hung to dry, as seen here. Later the crop is stripped, graded, bundled, and sold. (Courtesy Debra Williams.)

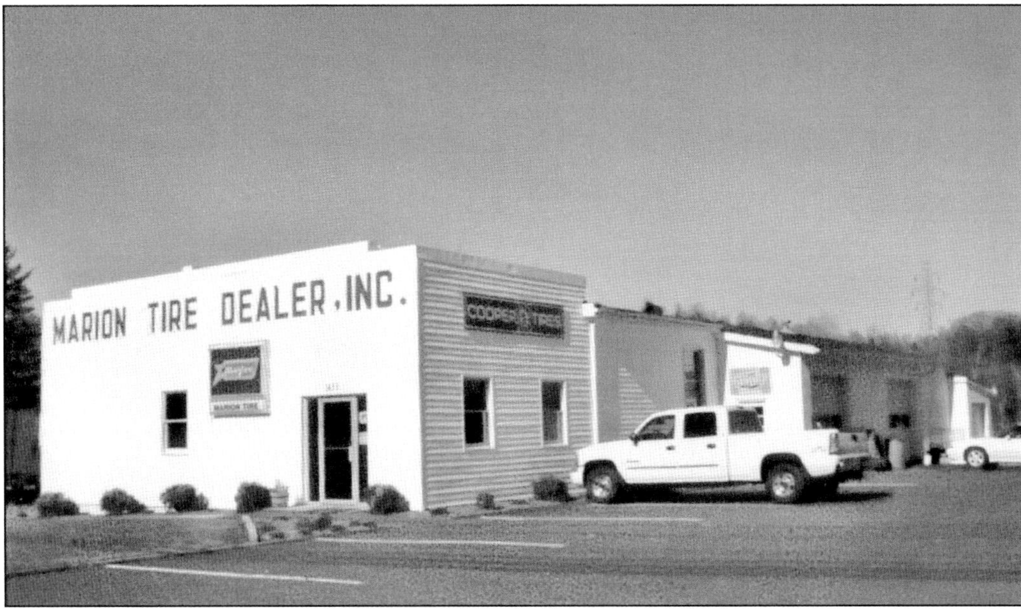

SHANKLIN DAIRY PROCESSING CENTER. John Shanklin brought his family from West Virginia to start Shanklin's Dairy Farm. This cinder-block structure was erected in 1946 for processing milk into products such as butter, sour cream, cottage cheese, ice cream, and such. These products were sold door to door. The dairy closed, and the building was later sold and is now Marion Tire Center. (Courtesy Debra Williams.)

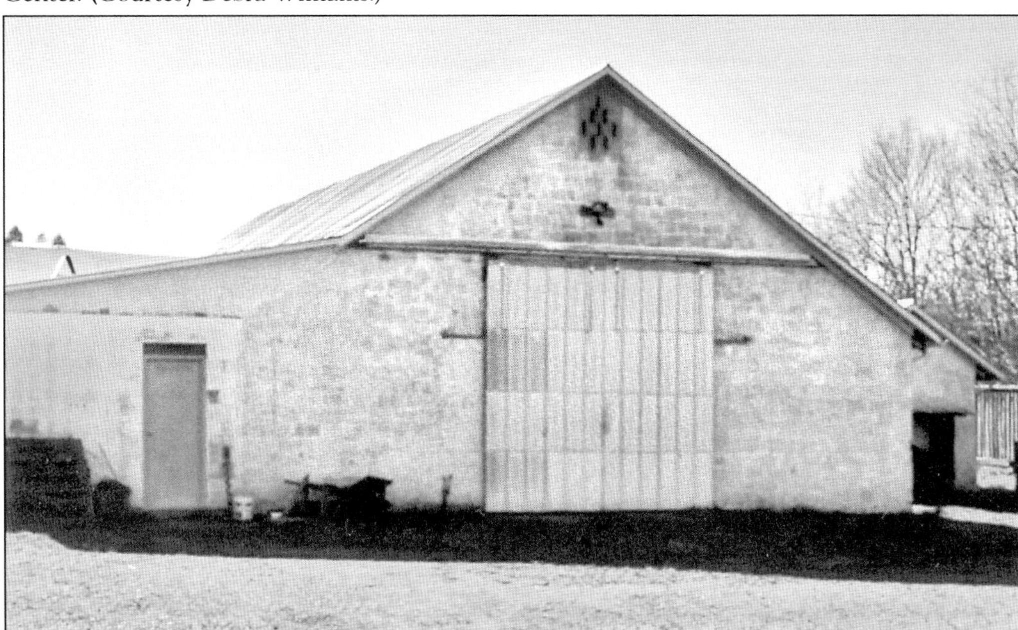

FIRST FREE SPAN MILKING BARN. Over 100 years ago, Frances Joseph Copenhaver Sr. bought the Crab Orchard Farm, which had once belonged in the family. Here near Adwolfe Road, Copenhaver built the first free-span barn in Virginia. Being very intrigued by this new venture, the secretary of agriculture came from Richmond to see the barn before completion and helped trowel the concrete. (Courtesy Debra Williams.)

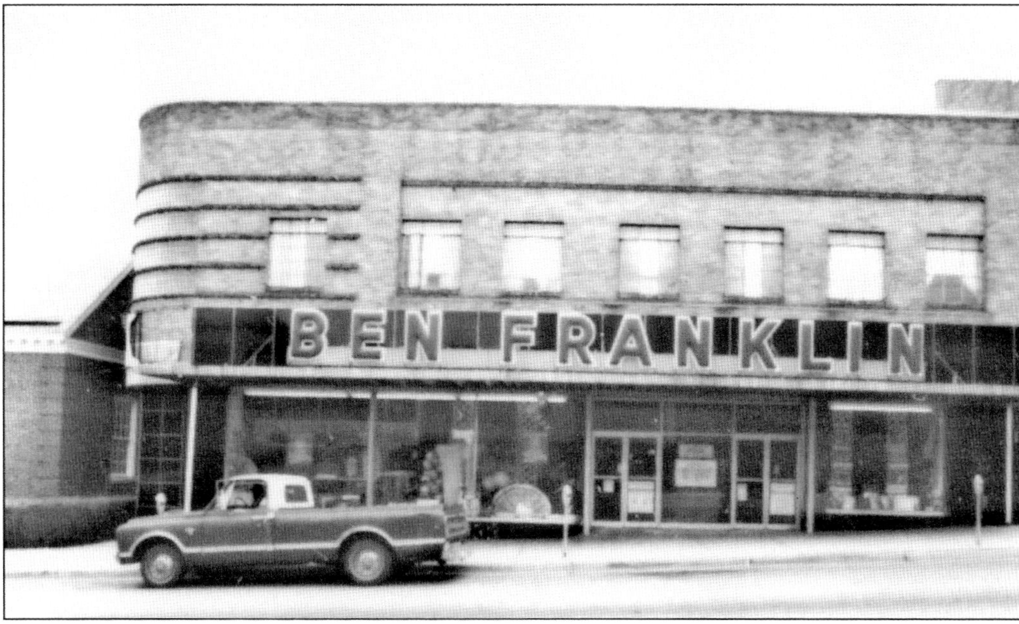

BEN FRANKLIN STORE. Built by the Lincoln Investment Corporation in 1936, this structure was called the United Building. Constructed to house several businesses at once, this may have been Marion's first mini-mall. The first floor contained the United Store, Lanson's Luncheonette, and a Kroger Grocery Store. Furniture was sold on the second floor. The Ben Franklin store was located here from the 1960s to the early 1980s. (Courtesy Bill Huber.)

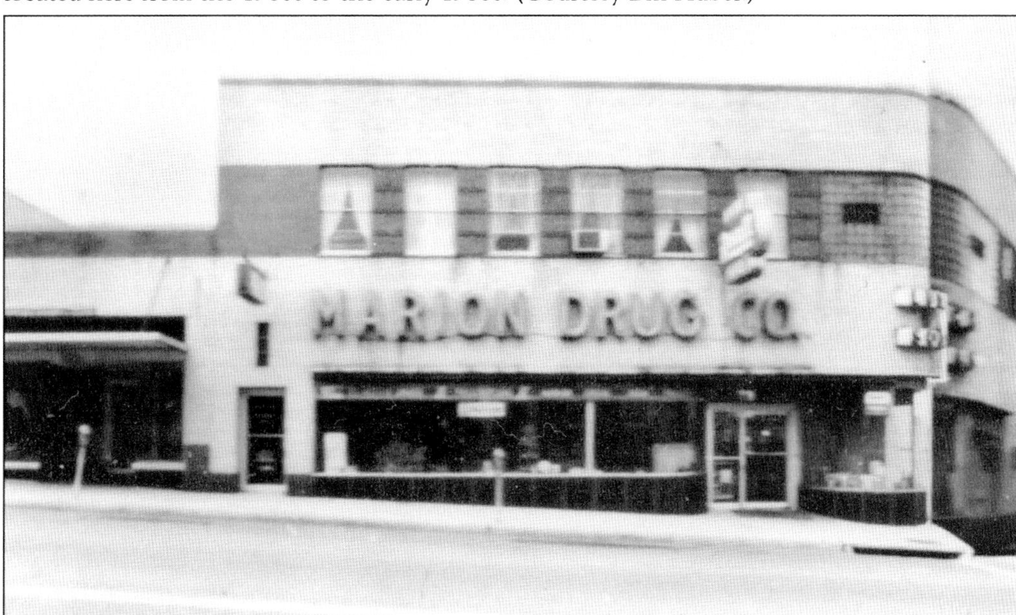

MARION DRUG COMPANY. Dr. O. C. Sprinkle, Dr. J. D. Buchanan, and C. Lee Richardson founded the Marion Drug Company *c.* 1913. W. M. Sclater Sr. bought the business in 1922 and housed it in this building in 1940. This business continued to operate under other owners until 1992. Locals caught up on gossip at the soda fountain located inside the store. The building later was sold to Brad Hayden. (Courtesy Bill Huber.)

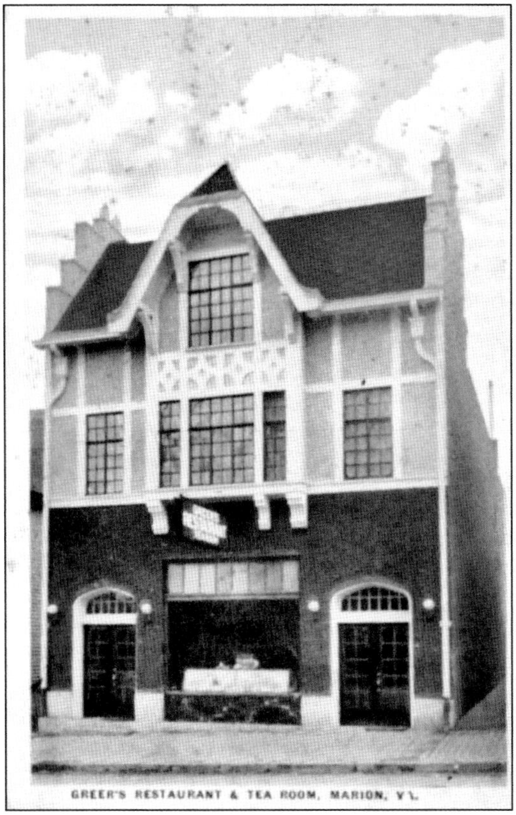

GREER'S RESTAURANT AND TEA ROOM. The Marion Hotel and Improvement Company built this elegant building in 1923. F. M. Greer leased the building to establish Greer's Restaurant and Tea Room. Wyatt's Café began operating here in 1936, making good use of the restaurant and ballroom. In 1942, the City Café was located here. A hardware store operated here and later a shoe store. (Courtesy Atwood J. Huff.)

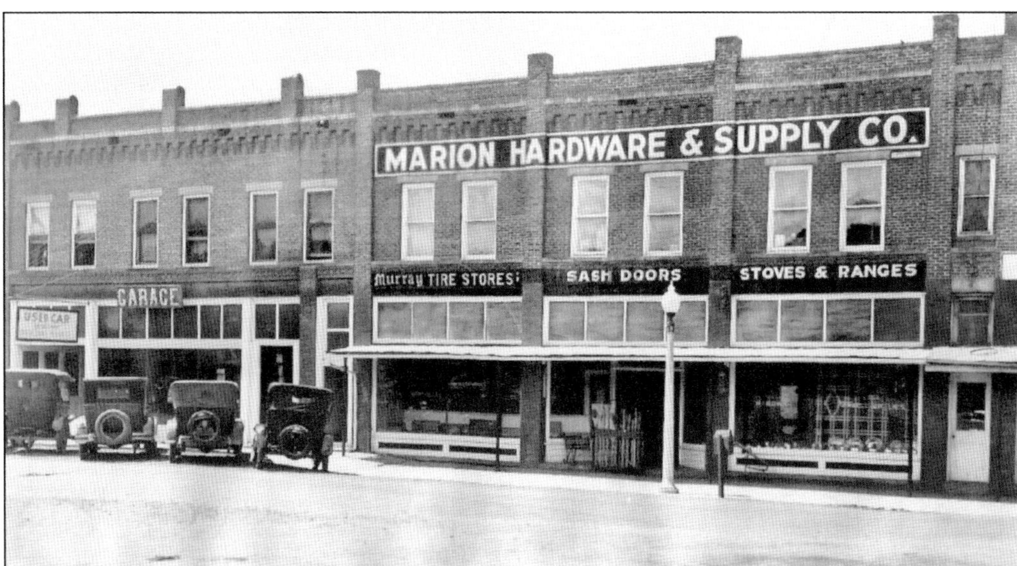

MARION HARDWARE AND SUPPLY COMPANY. Built on land purchased from W. W. Pruner in 1908, the Marion Hardware and Supply Company opened here in 1909. In 1913, the matching, two-story brick garage was added. At the time of this photograph, the used car department of Smyth County Motors was operated in this building. Murray Tires were sold here as well as appliances. (Courtesy family of A. P. Snider.)

Five

Hospitals and Medical Services

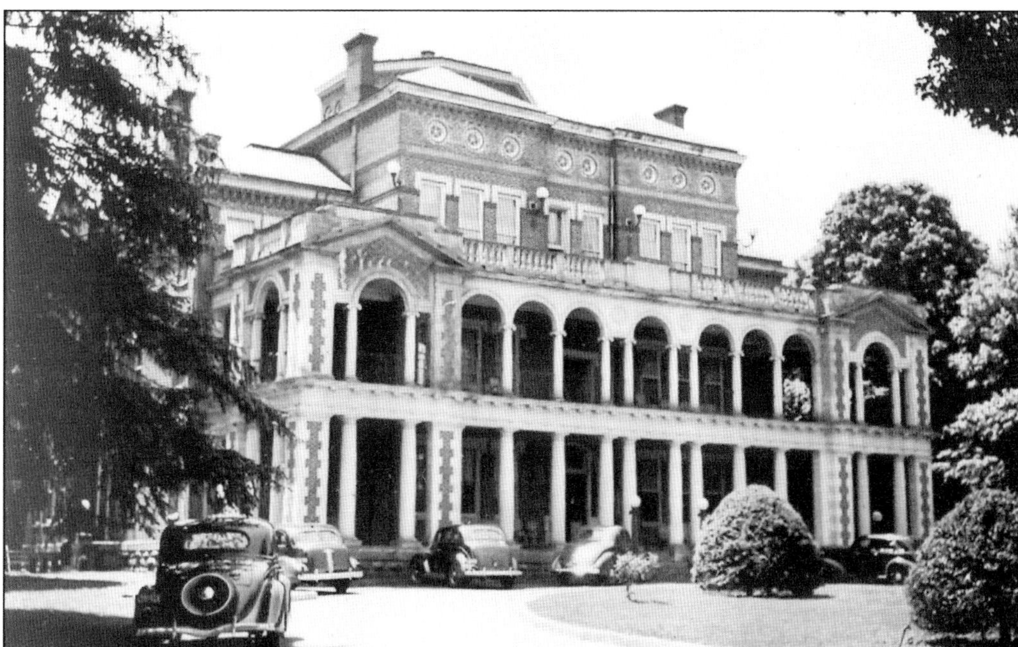

Henderson Building. Completed February 12, 1887, and standing 118 feet high, the administration building contained four floors, a plated, glass dome ceiling, and clock/bell tower. The front room opened into an octagonal rotunda with lofty floors that led to offices. This building also contained a laundry, kitchen, bakery, one dining room for men and one for woman, a sewing room, elevator, rooms for attendants, and enough room to house 280 patients. (Courtesy Edna Hutton.)

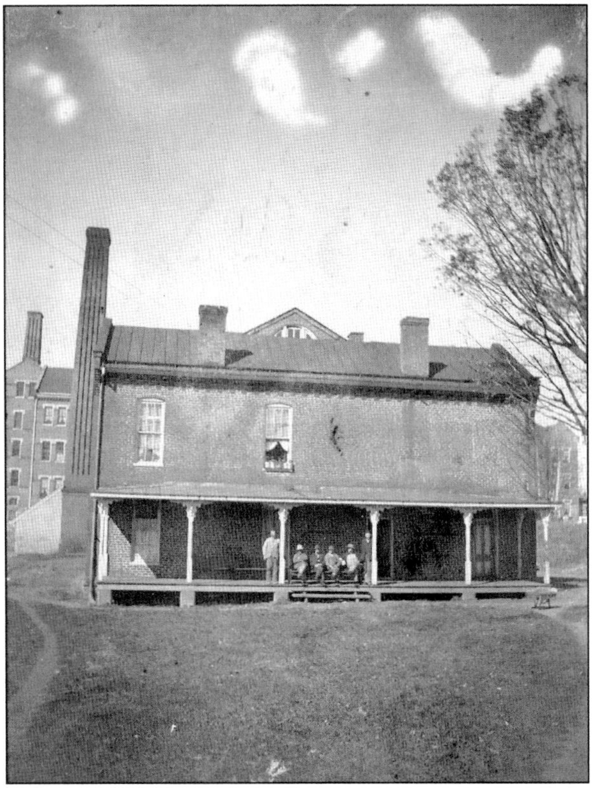

KITCHEN OF THE STATE HOSPITAL. From the beginning, the hospital was self-supporting with the farm and the foods raised here. Once located inside the Henderson Building, this kitchen also included a dining room for patients and one for employees. Food storage was greatly improved with this addition thanks to cold storage and deep-freeze units. Here employees are shown taking a break behind the kitchen. (Courtesy Dr. Paul Brown.)

HOUSING FOR EMPLOYEES. During the early years of the Southwest Lunatic Asylum, many employees worked 84 hours per week. They and their families lived on the grounds of the institute. The hospital was fully self-sufficient and included a dairy, many animals, gardens, orchards, four accessible springs, and a power plant that supplied heat and electricity. Here employees and their families gathered to have their picture taken. (Courtesy Southwest Virginia Mental Health Institute.)

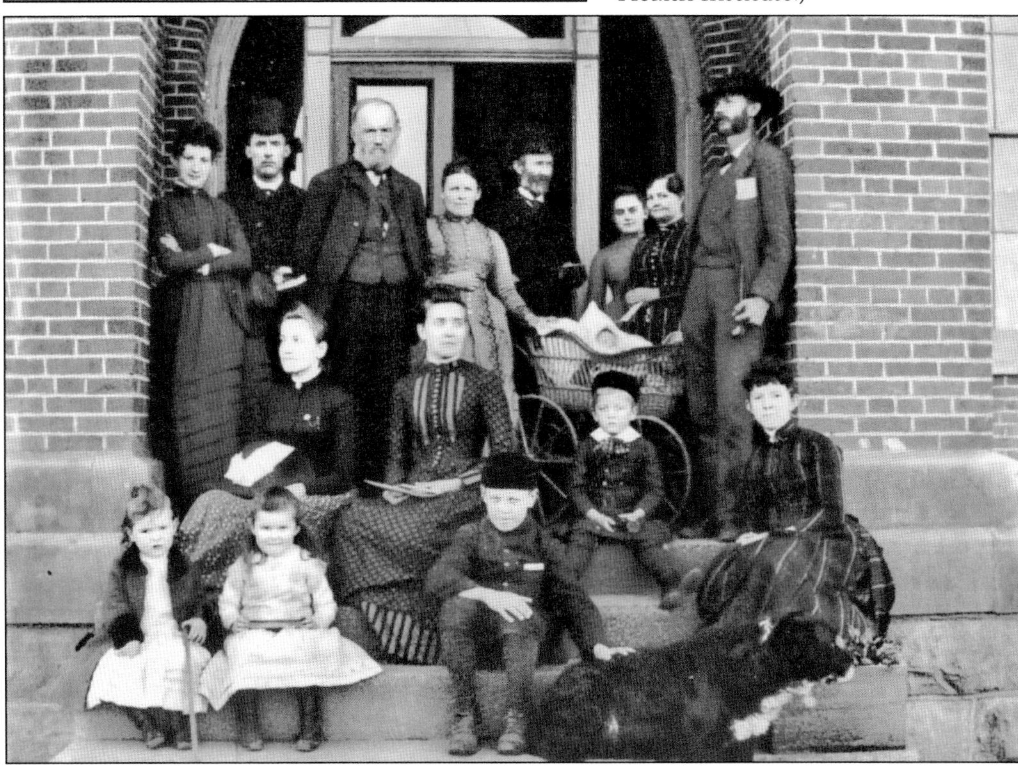

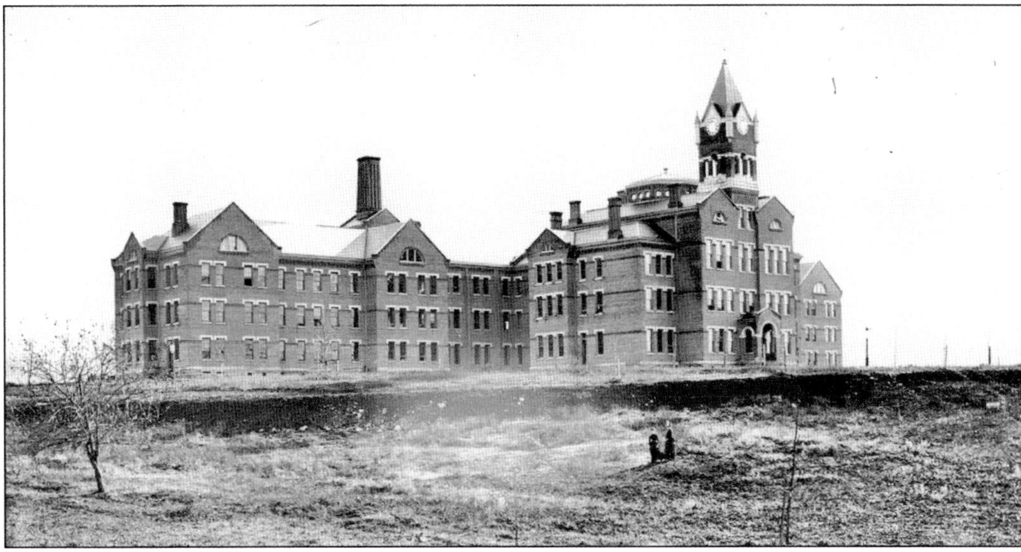

STATE HOSPITAL, SOUTHWESTERN LUNATIC ASYLUM. The Atkins farm of 199 acres was selected for this enormous structure, Southwestern Lunatic Asylum, in 1884. The Henderson Building, pictured here standing 118 feet high, was completed in 1887. Dr. Harvey Black was the first superintendent, and Dr. Robert Preston was the first physician. (Courtesy Southwest Virginia Mental Health Institute.)

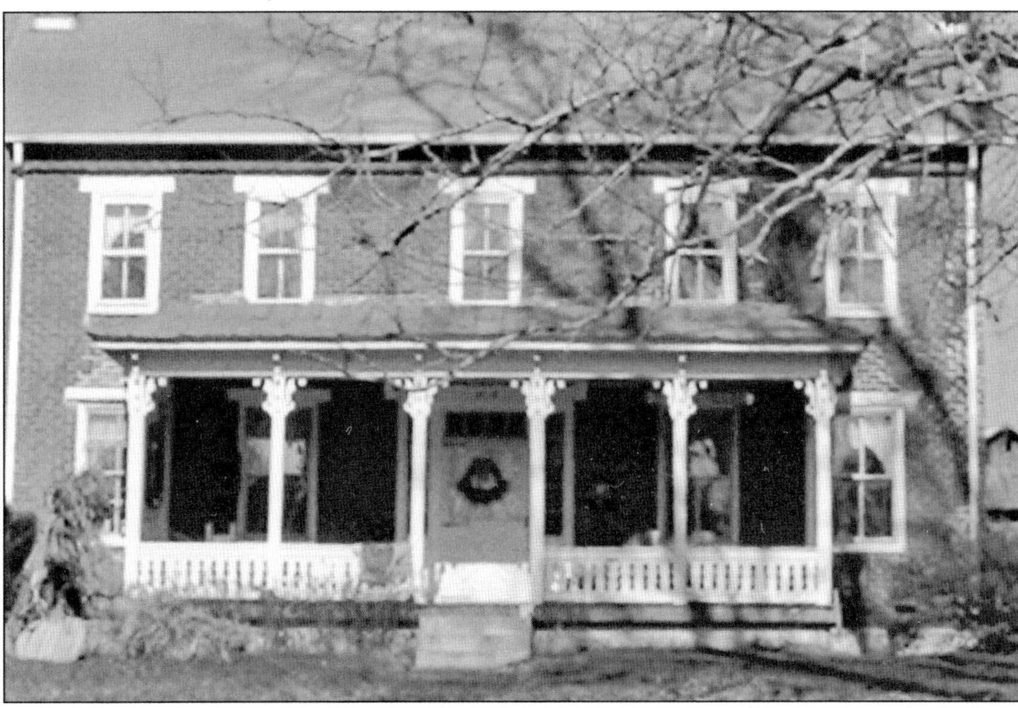

CIVIL WAR HOSPITAL. This beautiful brick, three-story home with 17-inch-thick walls was once used as a hospital during the Civil War. This pre-1830s home contains an oak and a walnut staircase. Many items of interest were found by the newest owner, Tim Crawford, including spots on the upstairs floor, which are said to be bloodstains from soldiers treated here. (Courtesy Debra Williams.)

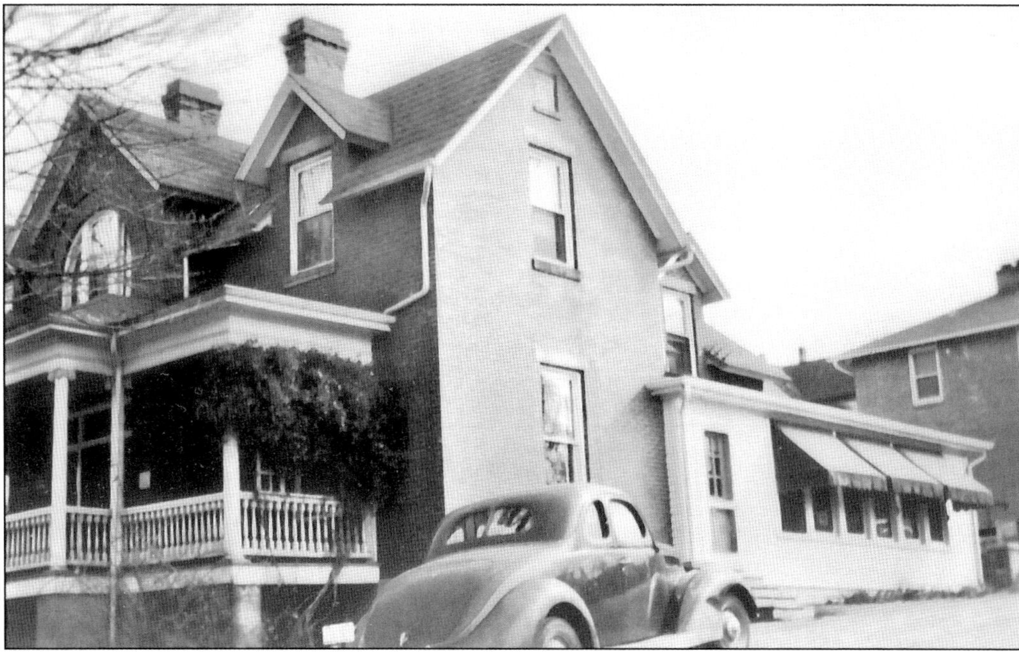

HOMELAND HOSPITAL. On August 5, 1936, Dr. J. Stuart Staley opened Marion's first hospital. Located on the corner of Main and Poston Streets, the hospital contained two offices, a lab, an X-ray room, and an operating room. Eight doctors used the facility. With room for 15 adults, 3 children, and 5 infants, overcrowding soon became an issue, and within two years, another hospital was built in Marion. (Courtesy J. S. Staley Jr.)

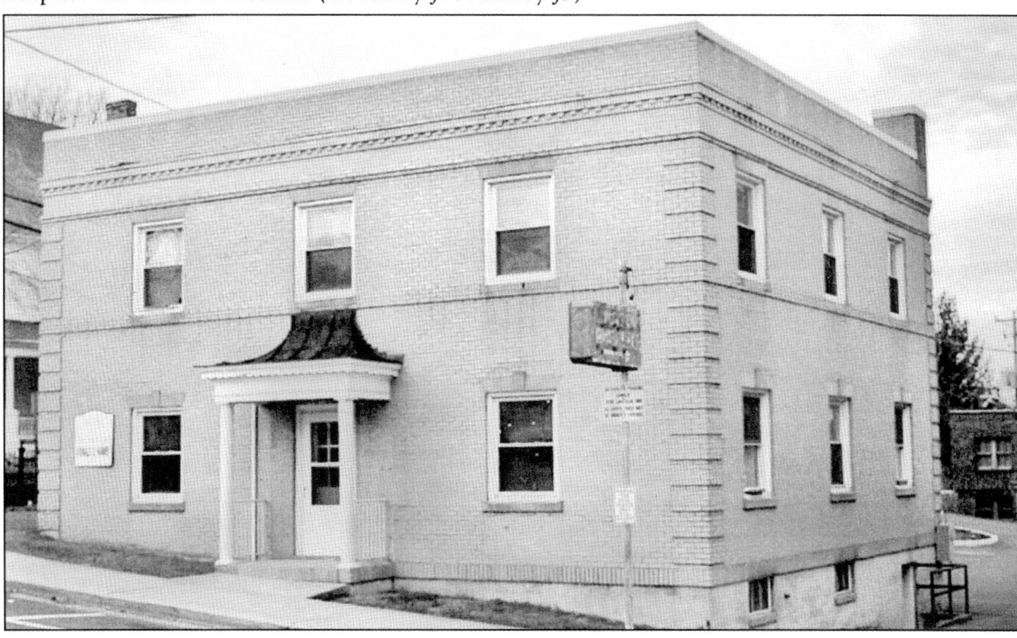

MARION'S SECOND HOSPITAL. Dr. A. B. Graybeal built this limestone structure on Church Street behind the First National Exchange Bank in 1938. The basement served as the operating room, offices were on the first floor, and patients were housed on the second floor. This building is now occupied by law offices. (Courtesy Debra Williams.)

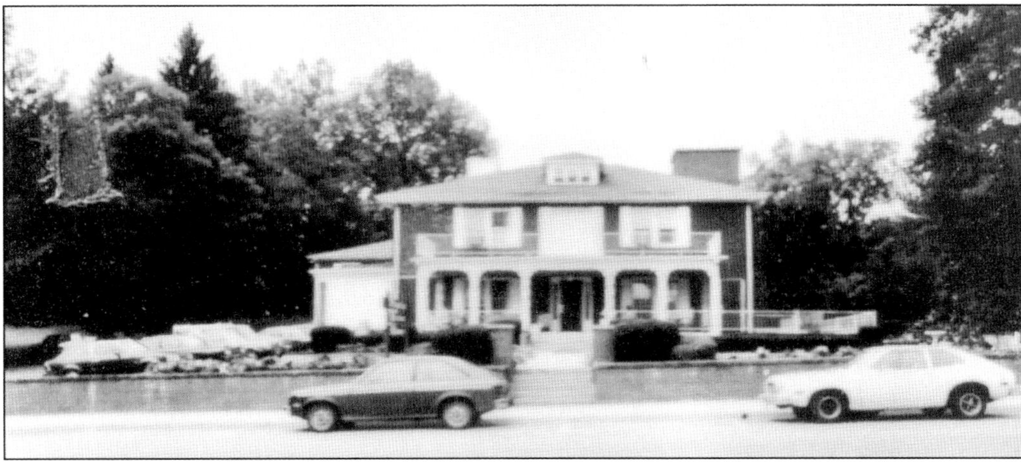

MARION GENERAL HOSPITAL. In 1952, this former apartment building, located at 221 West Main Street, was obtained by a group headed by Drs. O. O. Smith Jr. and E. V. Richardson Sr. After extensive remolding, this became Marion's fourth hospital. It was mainly used for surgical procedures. Later it became Frances Marion Manor Nursing Home. It is now the Rejuvenation Center and is privately owned. (Courtesy Bill Huber.)

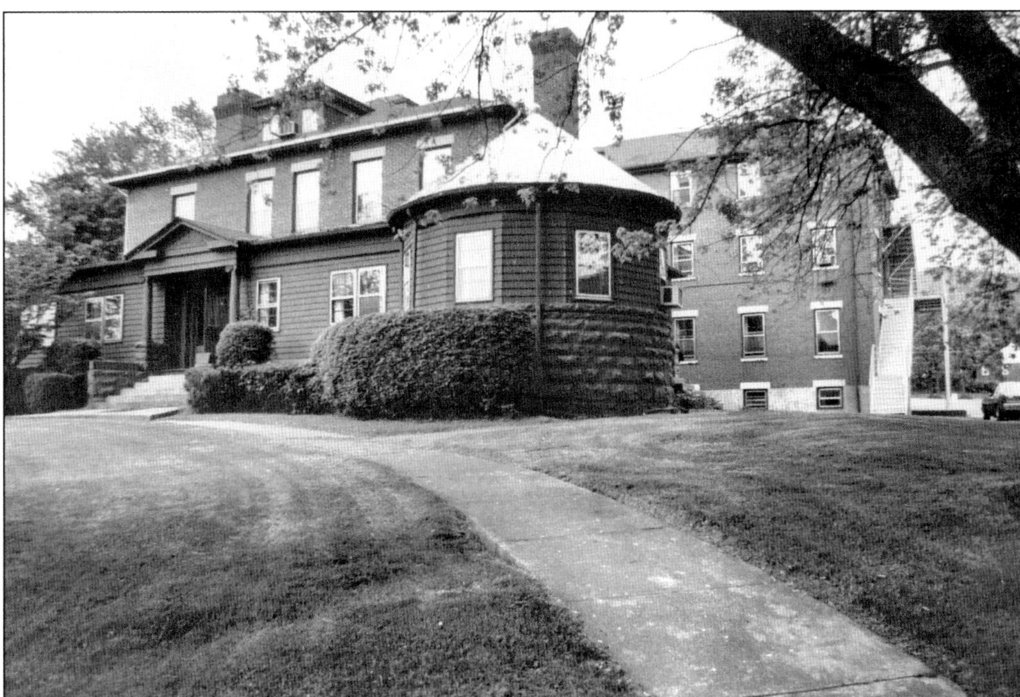

LEE MEMORIAL HOSPITAL. This beautiful mansion was constructed in 1913 as a home for the Wythe Hull family. In 1939, Drs. A. B. Graybeal and George Wright, along with about 20 shareholders, purchased the property to use as Marion's third hospital. By 1946, additions increased the capacity to a 50-bed unit. The Smyth County Community Hospital Corporation purchased the hospital in the early 1960s. (Courtesy Mack Sturgill Collection.)

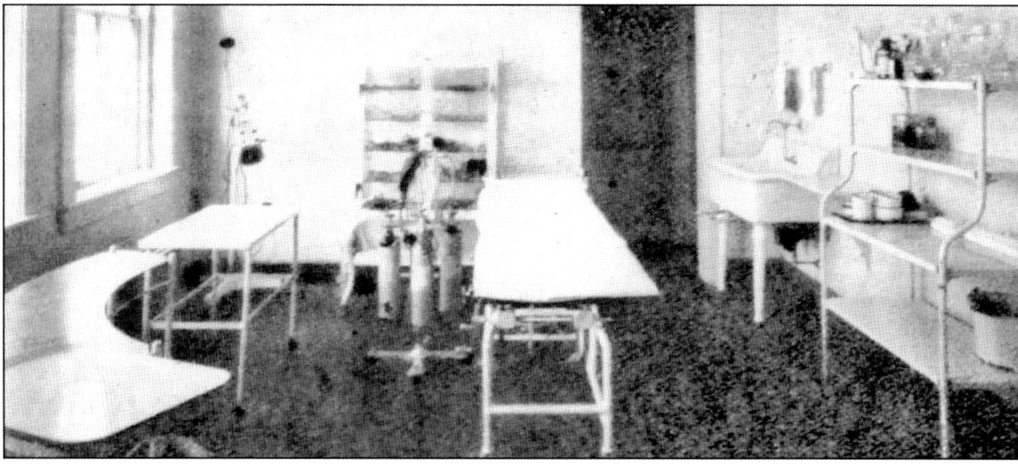

MATHIESON HOSPITAL OPERATING ROOM. The first hospital in Saltville was the "accident house," which was established in 1895 and located halfway between British Row and the Mathieson Alkali Works. It was designed as an emergency hospital for injured employees but could be used by others in the community. In 1925, Mathieson Alkali Works installed a hospital above the Mathieson Pharmacy. (Courtesy Mack Sturgill Collection.)

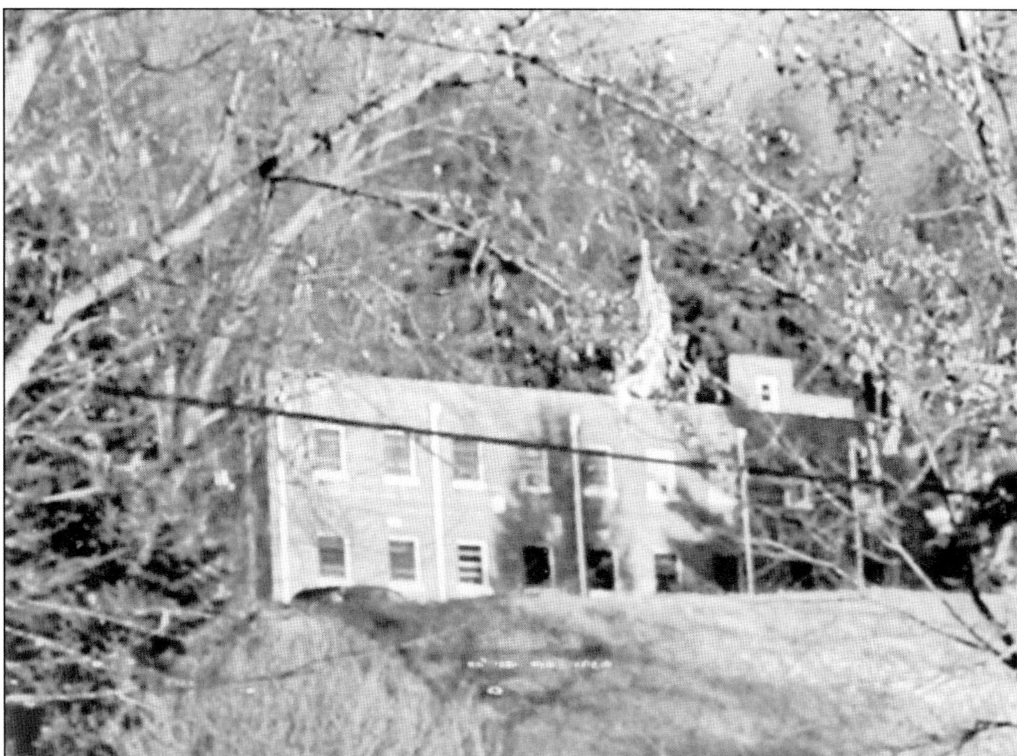

T. K. MCKEE HOSPITAL. On November 24, 1950, the hospital was relocated from the Mathieson Alkali Works General Store building to the newly constructed T. K. McKee Hospital building. The final costs of the hospital including equipment was $200,000. It was named after Dr. Thomas K. McKee, who was born at St. Clair's Bottom and began practicing medicine there in 1897. He moved to Saltville in 1912. (Courtesy Debra Williams.)

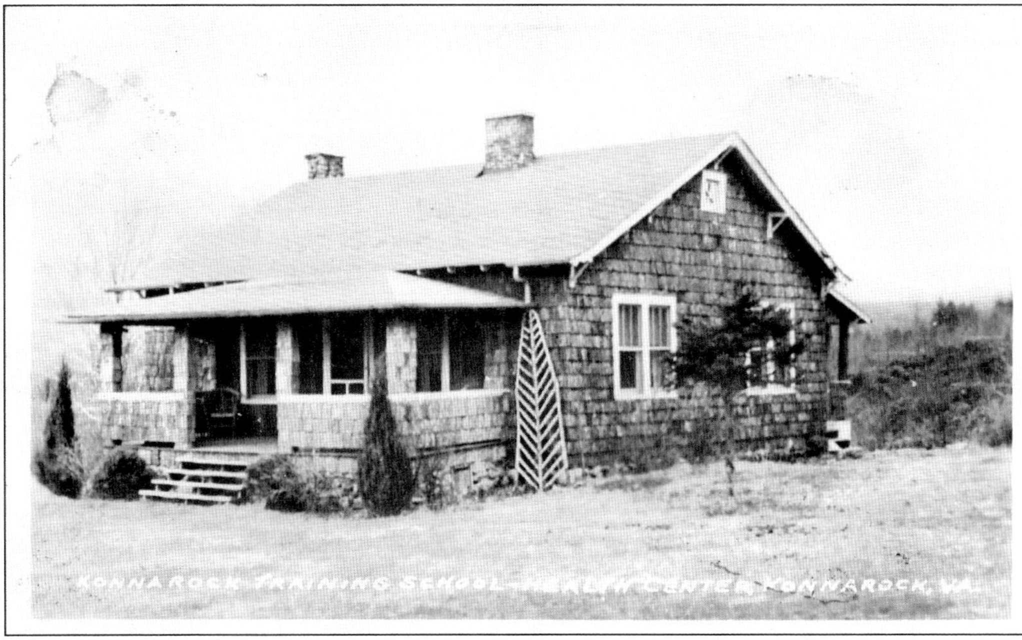

KONNNAROCK TRAINING SCHOOL HEALTH CENTER. Pictured here is the second infirmary of the Konnarock Training School (KTS), completed in 1936 on property donated by L. C. Hassinger for the school complex. The medical needs of the children served through the KTS were taken care of here as well as those of the community. This facility was supported by the Lutheran Church Synod. (Courtesy Dr. Paul Brown.)

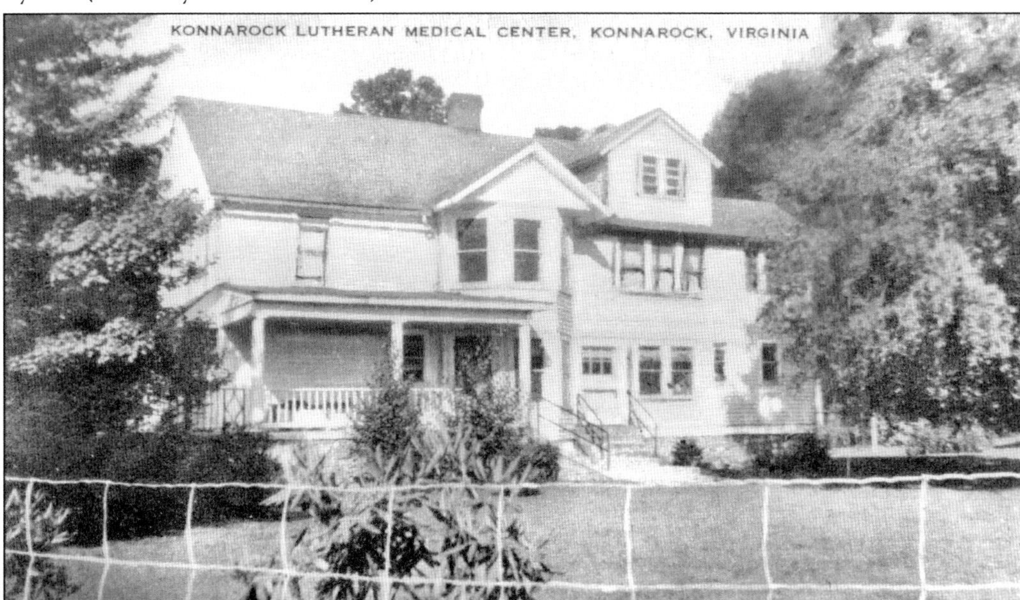

KONNAROCK LUTHERAN MEDICAL CENTER. A vacant home of the Hassinger Lumber Company was renovated, and an addition was built to form the Konnarock Lutheran Medical Center in 1939. Medical missionaries Dr. and Mrs. Heinz C. Meyer lived here as refugees from Nazi persecution. Dr. Meyer developed a program in nutrition and health. The word "Konnarock" comes from the Native American word "Konnaugh," which means high rock. (Courtesy Clegg Williams.)

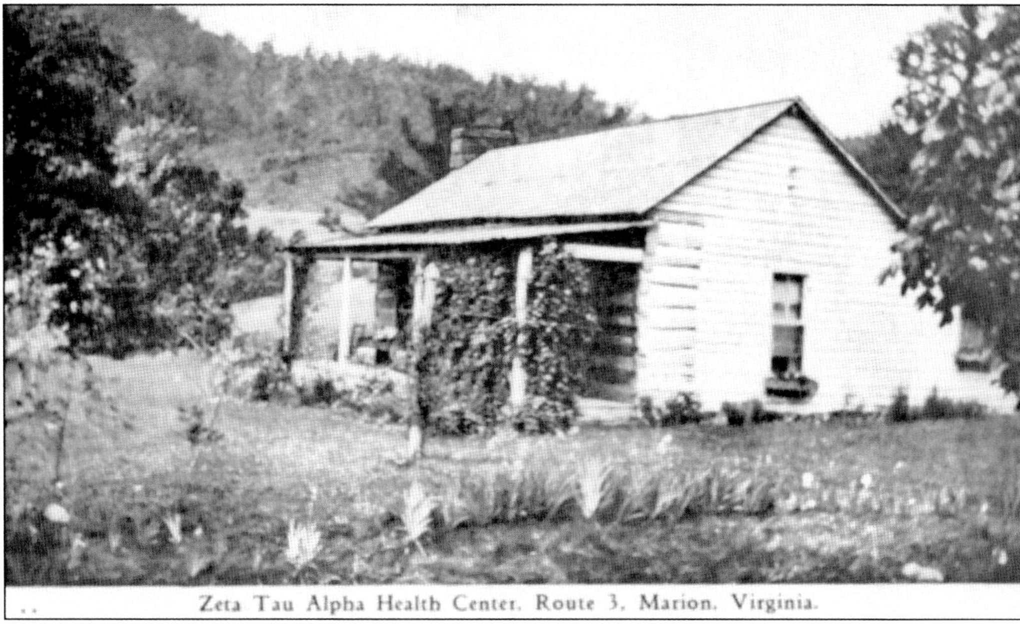

ZETA TAU ALPHA HEALTH CENTER. In the 1920s, the Zeta Tau Alpha sorority and Pastor Kenneth Killinger started a health care center for the underprivileged mountain folks. The center was located on the Killinger farm in the Mill Stone area, just north of Attaway, and stayed open for over 20 years. Miss M. L. Crosby was the first nurse and lived in the center. (Courtesy Dr. Paul Brown.)

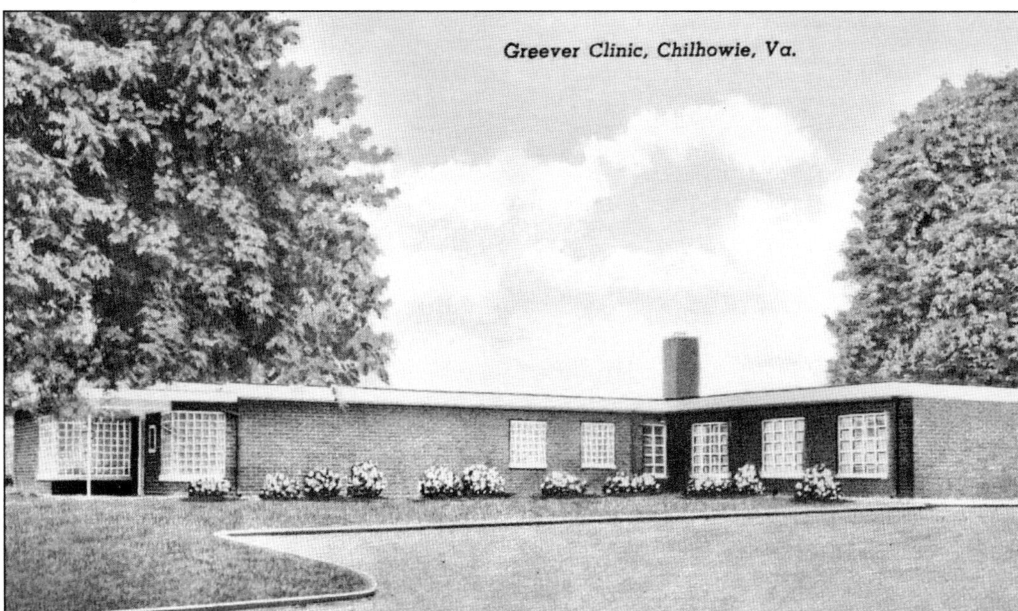

GREEVER CLINIC. The Greever brothers—Don (internal medicine) and Bill (family practice)—built this office in the late 1940s to replace the rented one on Main Street. This Chilhowie office also served as a maternity ward until the early 1960s, and many local babies were born here. The two doctors retired in the early 1990s, but the clinic still lives on through other medical associates. (Courtesy Clegg Williams.)

Six

COMMUNITY SERVICES

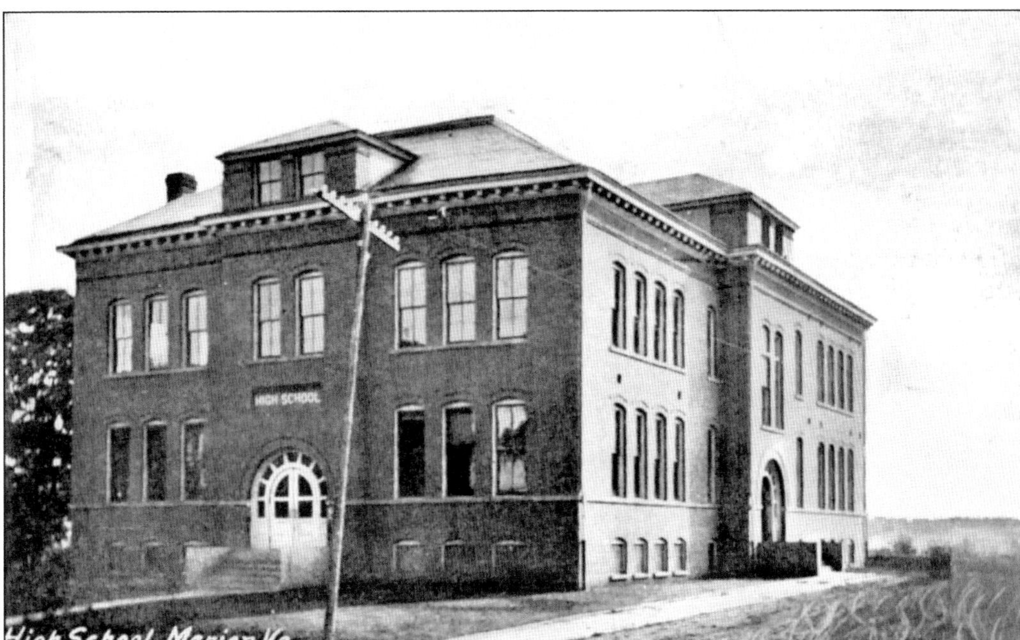

FORMER SITE OF ROYAL OAK. The second building of Royal Oak Presbyterian Church once stood on this location at the corner of Church and Strother Streets. The land was conveyed to the trustees in 1853. A cemetery was also located next to the church. Before building the Marion Grammar School on this land, the remains of the cemetery were moved to the Round Hill Cemetery. (Courtesy Mack Sturgill Collection.)

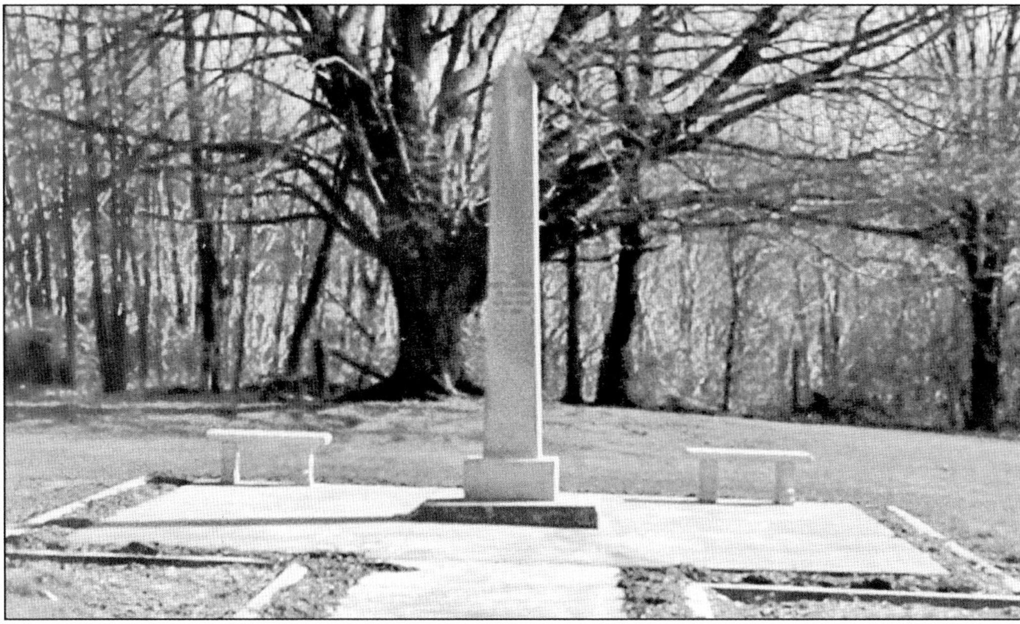

THE LOST CEMETERY. Here one can oversee the town of Marion, but to the town, the Southwest Virginia Mental Health Institute Cemetery is invisible as well as unknown. The deceased patients of the state hospital, including two Confederate soldiers who had no family to claim them, were buried in these grid-marked graves. This memorial reads "The Forget Me Nots of Heaven Known Only to God." (Courtesy Debra Williams.)

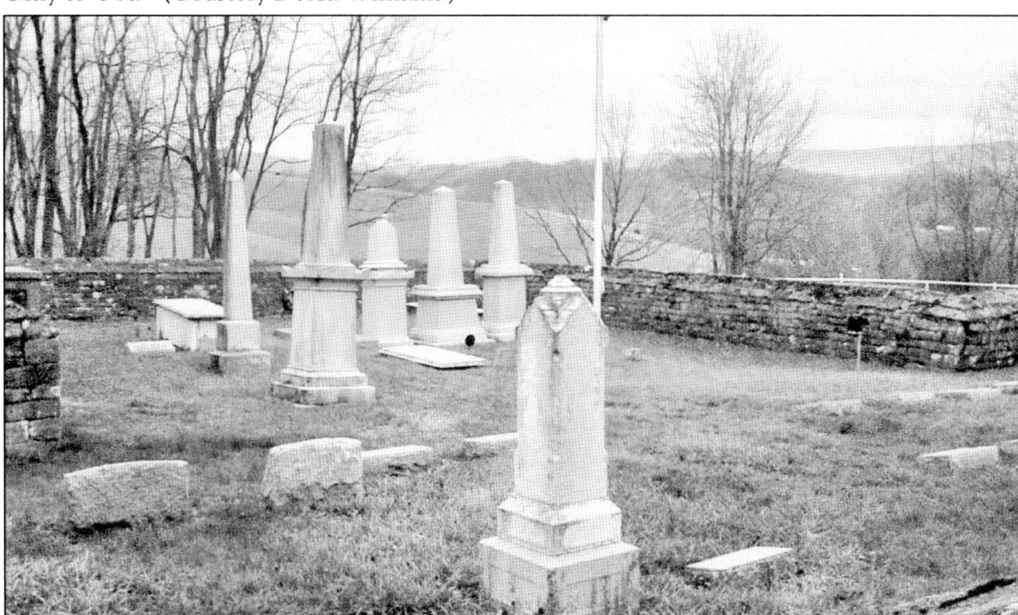

HISTORICAL ASPENVALE CEMETERY. Veterans of six wars rest at historically rich Aspenvale Cemetery. Col. John Buchanan gave this land to his sister, Mrs. Charles (Margaret) Campbell, who in 1777 was the first entombed. A wall containing no mortar was erected by slaves to enclose the Campbell-Preston section. Three other cemeteries surround it: a community cemetery, Rector family cemetery, and a cemetery for slaves and freed blacks. (Courtesy Debra Williams.)

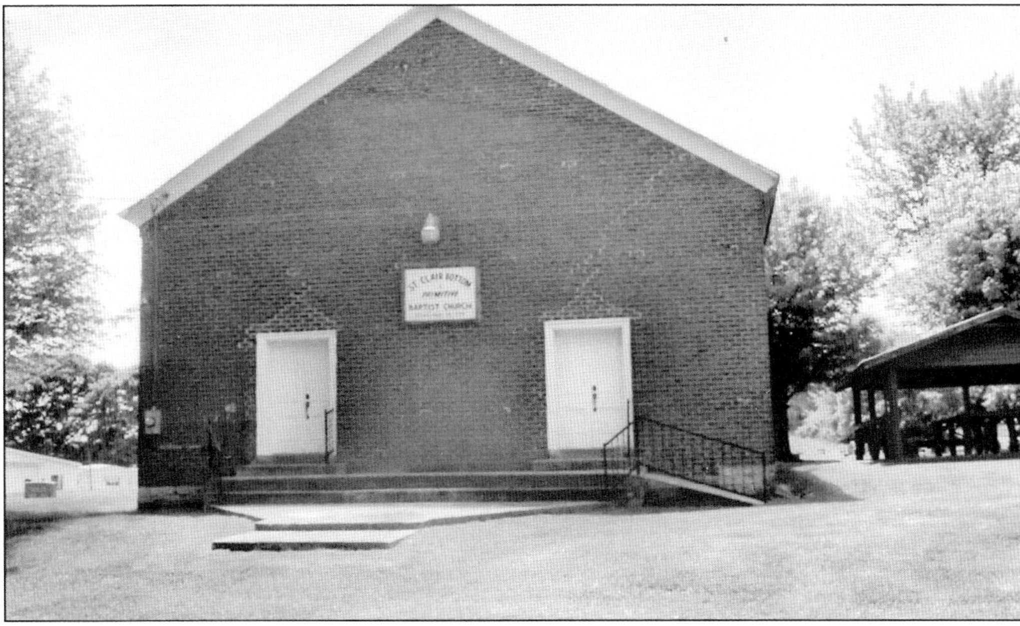

SINCLAIR'S BOTTOM PRIMITIVE BAPTIST CHURCH. Property for the original log church was obtained for 20 shillings and deeded June 20, 1792, to James Wheeler, John Thomas, and Jonathan Bishop, acting trustees for the congregation. The brick church, seen here, replaced the log structure in 1851, which once stood on the same site on the South Fork of the Holston River and is still in operation. (Courtesy Debra Williams.)

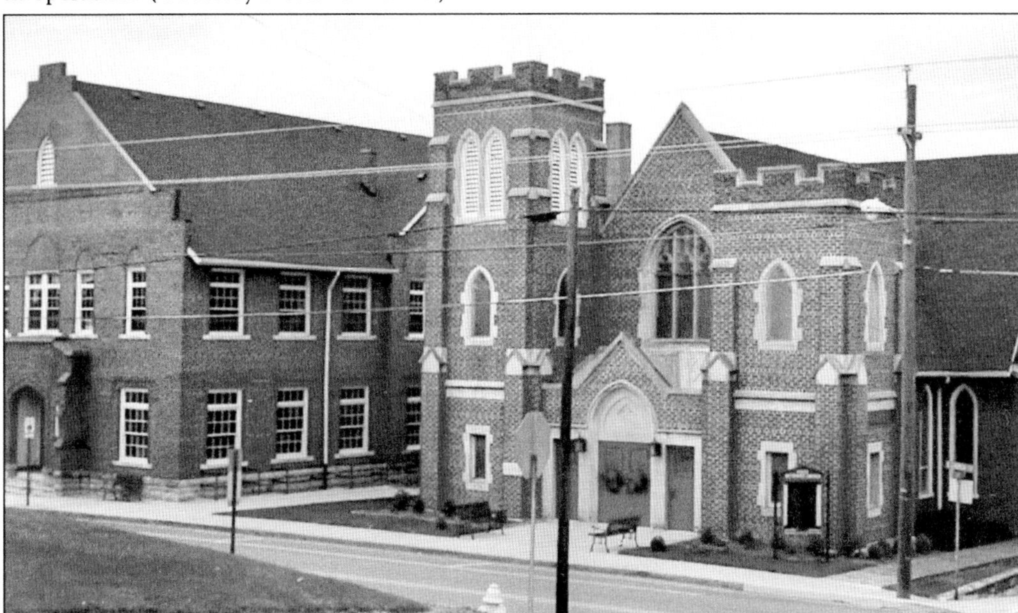

FIRST METHODIST CHURCH. In 1840, the first organized group of Methodists met at the old red courthouse and continued to meet there until the first church was constructed in 1847. This structure stood on the corner of Church and Strother Streets. Forty years later, the congregation obtained land and built this church at the present location of Church and Cherry Streets. Additions were later made to make room for the congregation. (Courtesy Debra Williams.)

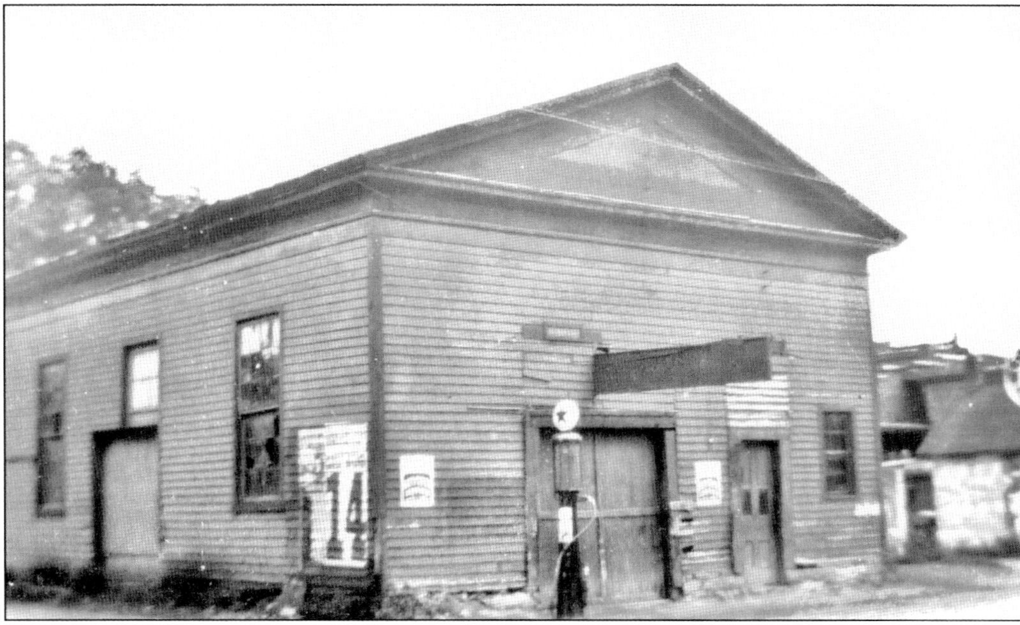

Oldest Baptist Church. In 1845, the Marion Baptist Church started with 17 members that met in the old red courthouse. This building was constructed in 1859 on Broadway, now Broad Street, and remained there until 1891, when another church was built on the corner of Church and Alley Streets. This building became the Virginia Motor Company in 1922, owned by Quincy Calhoun and F. A. Roland. (Courtesy Mack Sturgill Collection.)

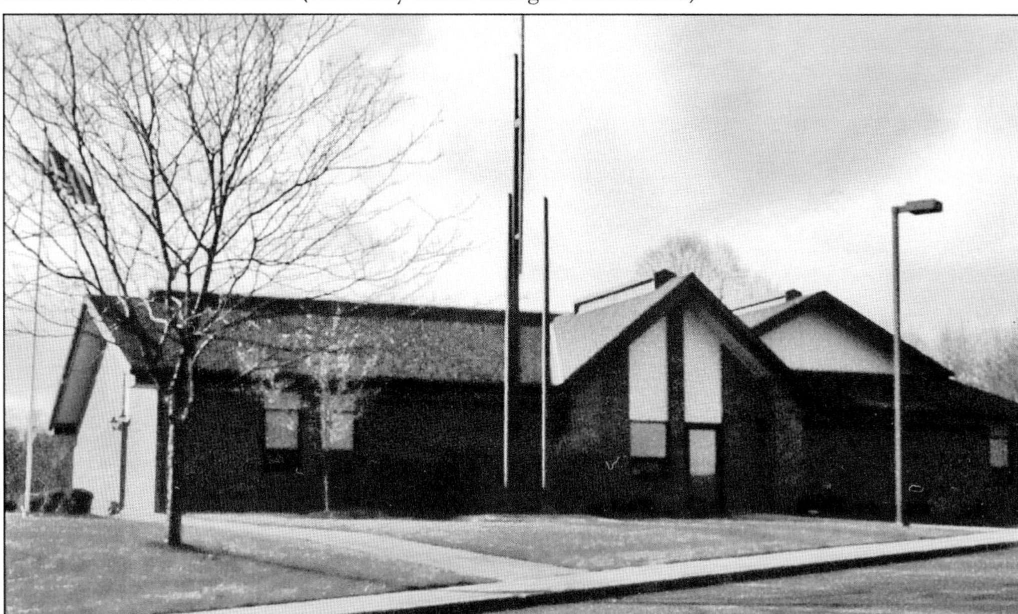

Mormon Church. The Church of Jesus Christ of Latter-day Saints has been operating in Smyth County since the mid-1800s. Until this building was erected in 1984, meetings were held in members' homes and community buildings. This church, with a non-paid ministry, is patterned after the same church Jesus Christ established during His existence on Earth. This building is located on Althea Street in Marion. (Courtesy Debra Williams.)

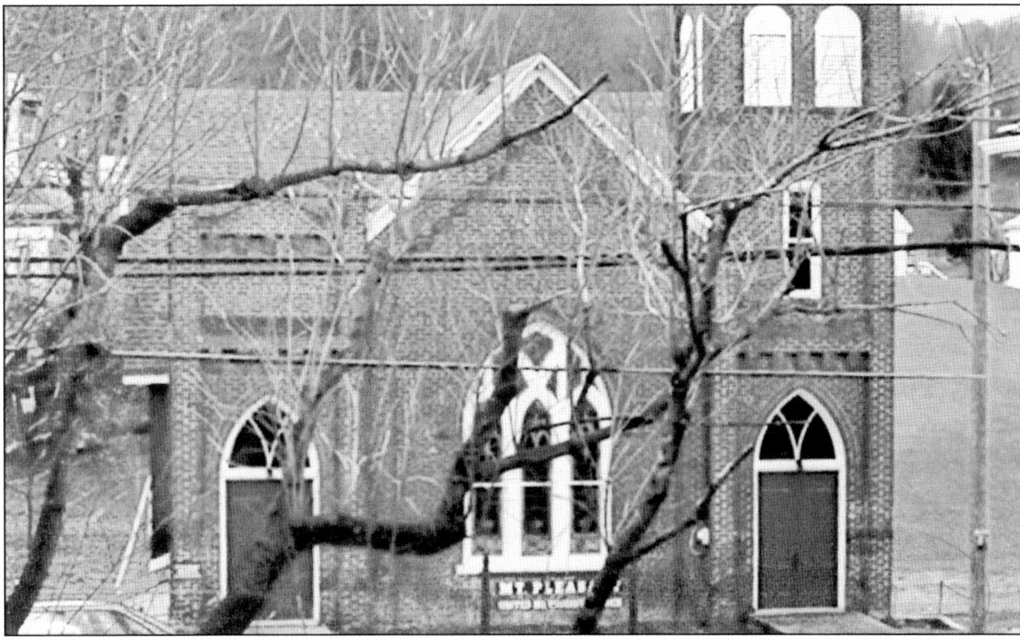

MOUNT PLEASANT UNITED METHODIST CHURCH. In 1871, freed slaves and African Americans desiring to have a place of worship organized their own church. Located on South Main Street, the original building was added onto in 1914 to form this beautiful structure that stands today. The building is under renovation, with windows being replaced with stained glass, only enhancing its character and charm. (Courtesy Debra Williams.)

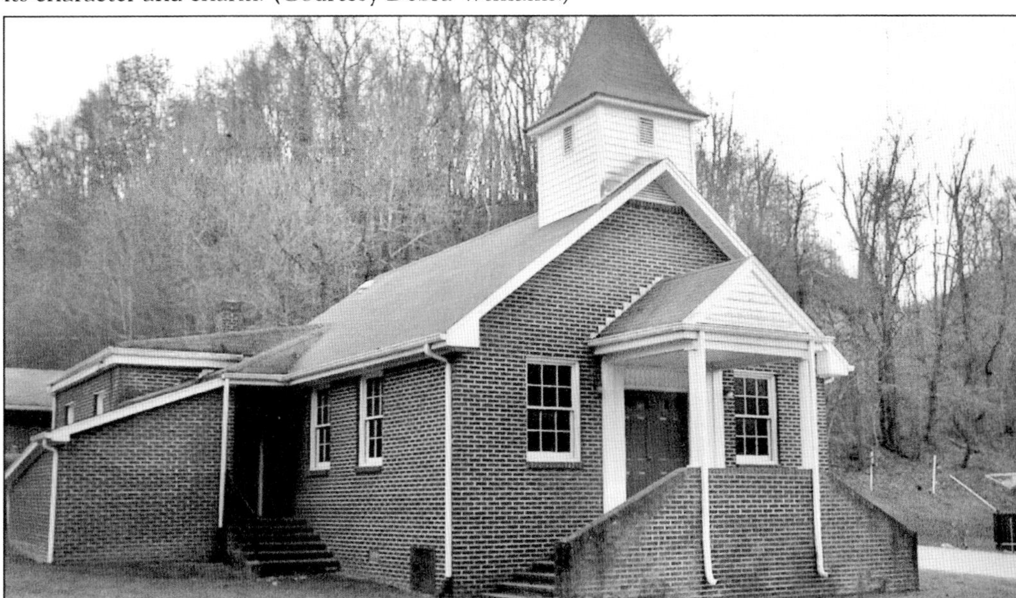

FURNACE HILL LUTHERAN CHURCH. In 1919, Rev. Kenneth Killinger invited the community of Furnace Hill to join him in a prayer meeting under a maple tree along Staley's Creek. This was the beginning of the church that has met in this neighborhood ever since. Two railroad cars and a 16-foot-square building served as temporary meetinghouses. The present building across Highway 16 was erected in 1963. (Courtesy Debra Williams.)

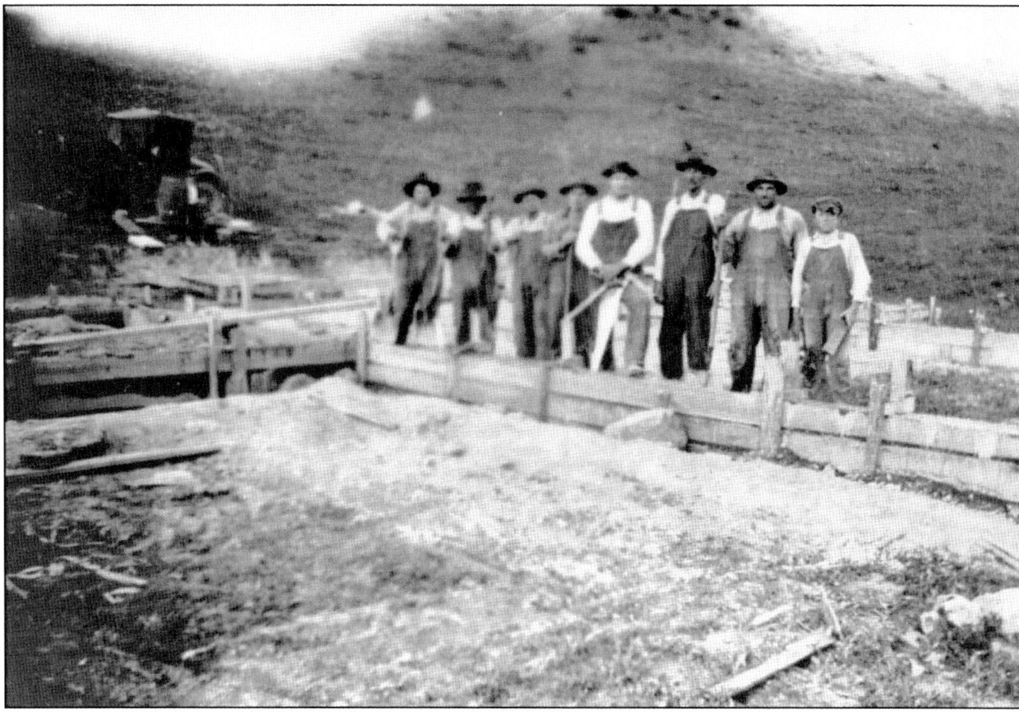

Walker's Creek Chapel. The Walker's Creek community came together to build the Walker's Creek Chapel, which was dedicated in May 1925. It took two days to pour the foundation for what is known as "the Presbyterian Church on Walker's Creek." God's Acre cemetery is close by. In 1953, when the church was remodeled, there were 51 graves there. (Courtesy Edna Hutton.)

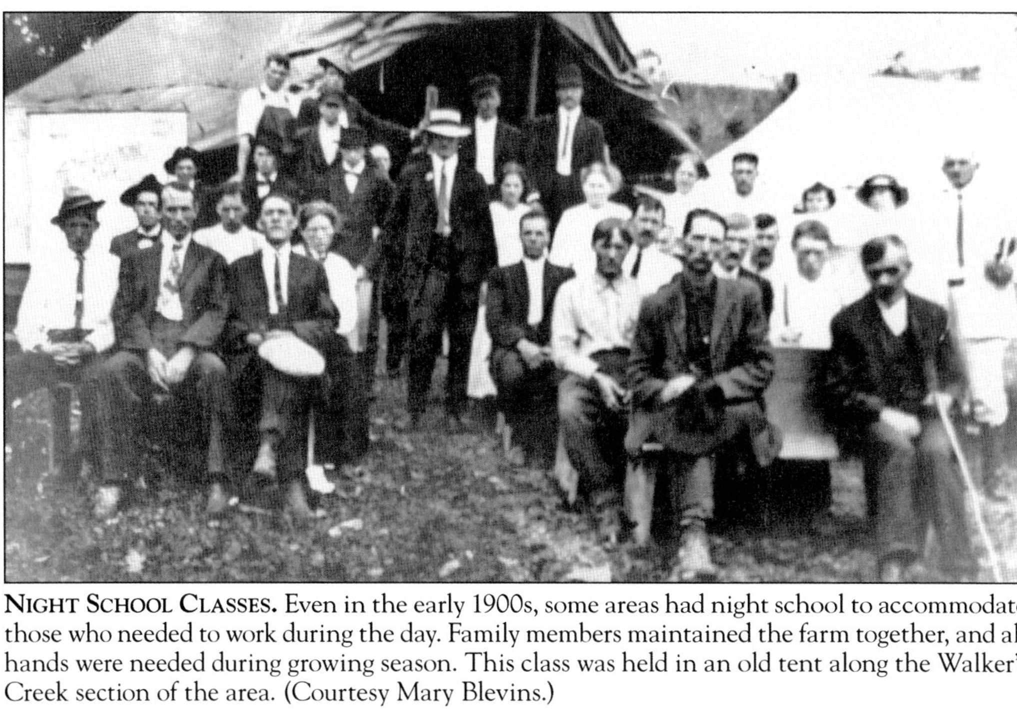

Night School Classes. Even in the early 1900s, some areas had night school to accommodate those who needed to work during the day. Family members maintained the farm together, and all hands were needed during growing season. This class was held in an old tent along the Walker's Creek section of the area. (Courtesy Mary Blevins.)

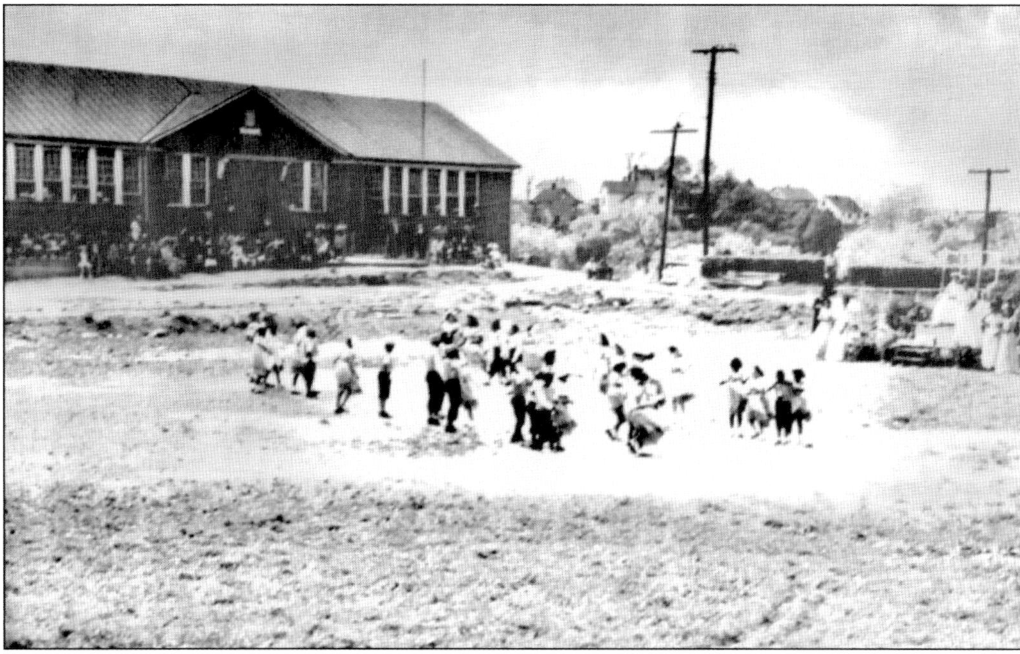

CARNEGIE HIGH SCHOOL. This photograph shows the May Day Celebration at the old Carnegie High School in the 1940s. This four-room school was constructed in the 1930s as an educational facility for local black children from funds gathered by Rev. Amos Carnegie from African American citizens and from a Julius Rosenwald Grant. (Courtesy Mack Sturgill Collection.)

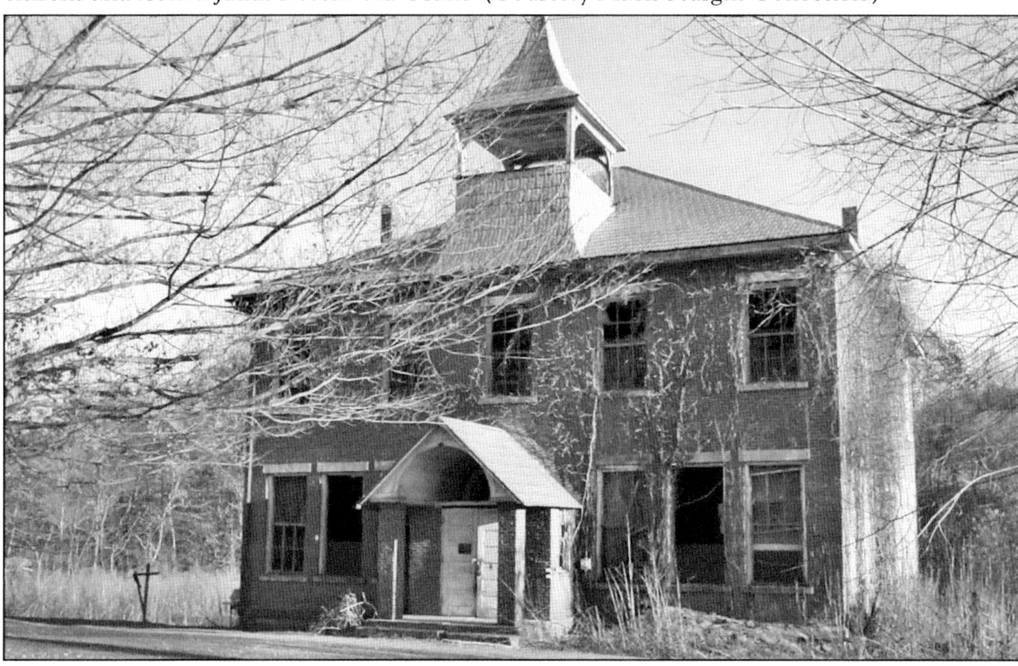

BARRICK SCHOOL. This abandoned building once rang with the laughter of the many neighborhood children who attended school here. Located in the Love's Mill area, this school was made possible by the instructions and generous donations of land and money included in the will of Solomon G. Barrick during the later part of the 1800s. (Courtesy Debra Williams.)

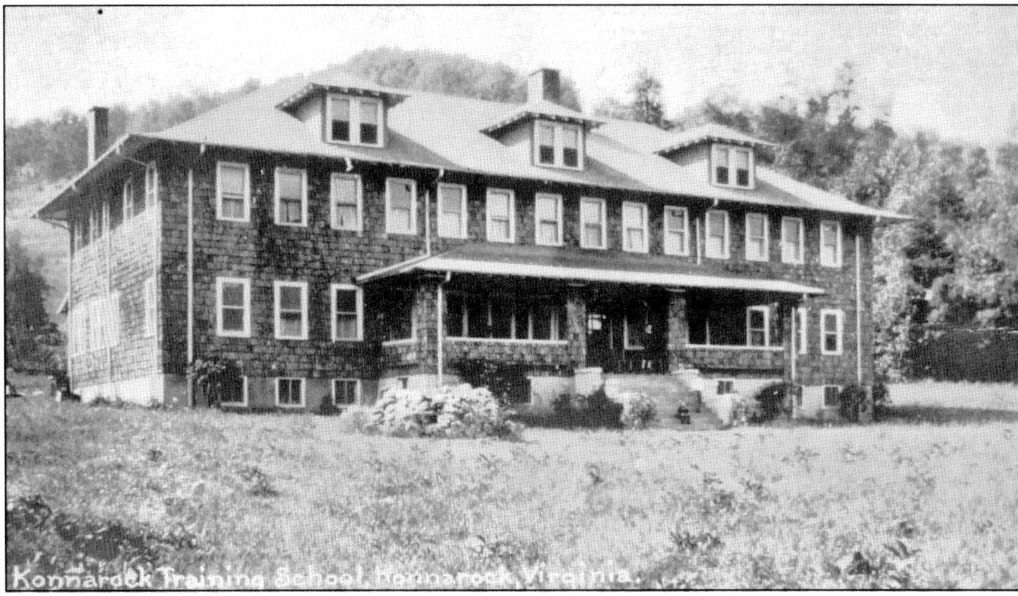

KONNAROCK LUTHERAN GIRL'S SCHOOL. Constructed in 1925 under the leadership of Rev. Kenneth Killenger, the Konnarock Lutheran Girl's School was a mission effort to reach underprivileged girls. This large building contained classrooms, a dining hall, and a kitchen, as well as a chapel that was attached to the rear of the structure. The goal was to train girls in practical life skills while providing a Christian influence. (Courtesy Clegg Williams.)

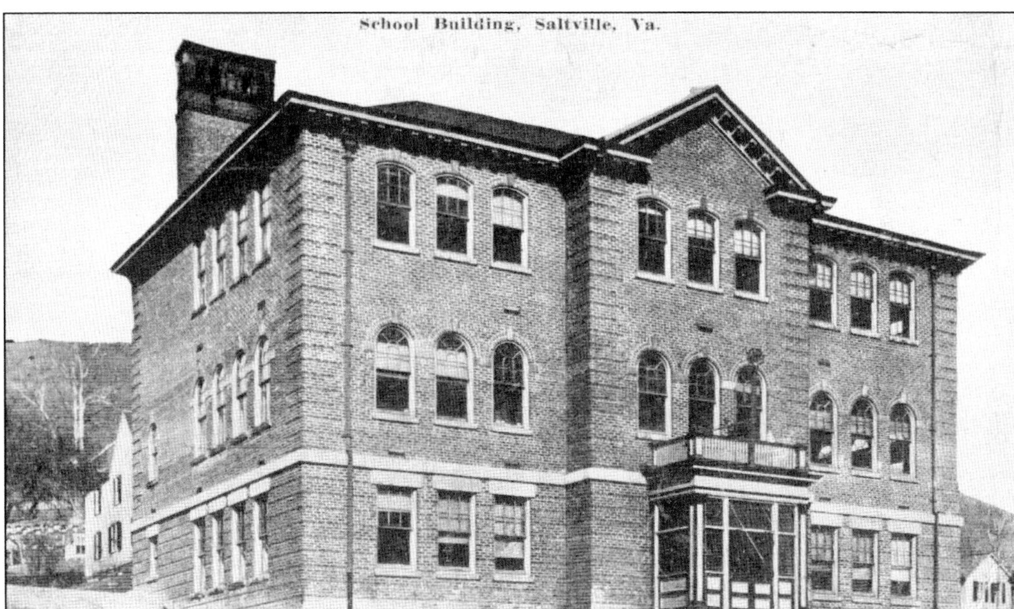

SALTVILLE HIGH SCHOOL. Built in 1905, the Saltville High School cost $30,000 and housed seven classrooms and an auditorium. Sliding doors allowed the auditorium to be divided into two rooms if need be. In the 1906–1907 school year, there were 45 pupils enrolled. This number had increased to 207 for the 1924–1925 school year. A new high school was built in 1925. (Courtesy Mack Sturgill Collection.)

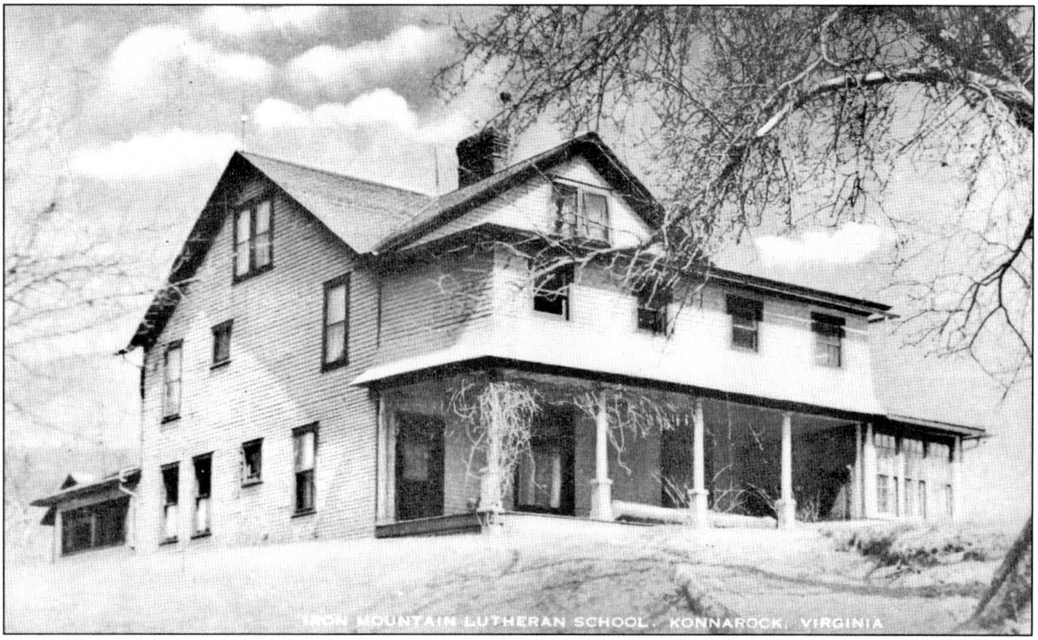

IRON MOUNTAIN LUTHERAN SCHOOL. Located in nearby Washington County, the Iron Mountain Lutheran School for Boys began as a 200-acre farm. C. L. Hassinger and the Hassinger Lumber Company had constructed a 7-room house, a chapel, and a 33-room hotel. The entire property was bought in the 1930s for $20,320, and the hotel, which could house up to 70 boys, was used as the dormitory. (Courtesy Dr. Paul Brown.)

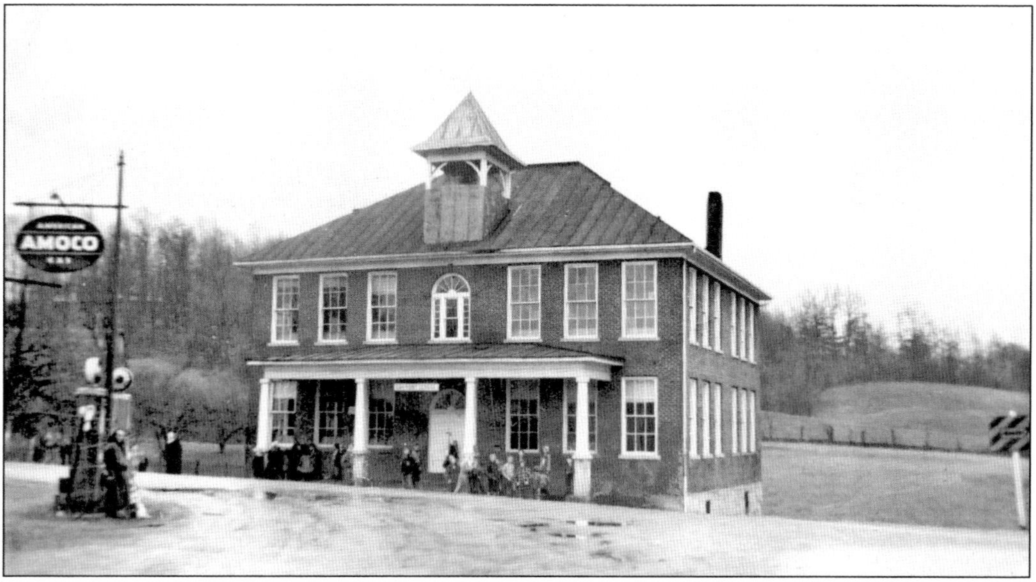

OAK POINT SCHOOL. Built in 1905 to replace the dilapidated Oak Point Academy, this school served the Adwolfe area until the 1970s. Afterward, the upstairs was used for concerts of local musicians, giving them a chance to show off their talents and entertainment for people of the area. The 4-H Club used the building before it was torn down to make room for the Adwolfe Fire Department and Community Center. (Courtesy Mack Sturgill Collection.)

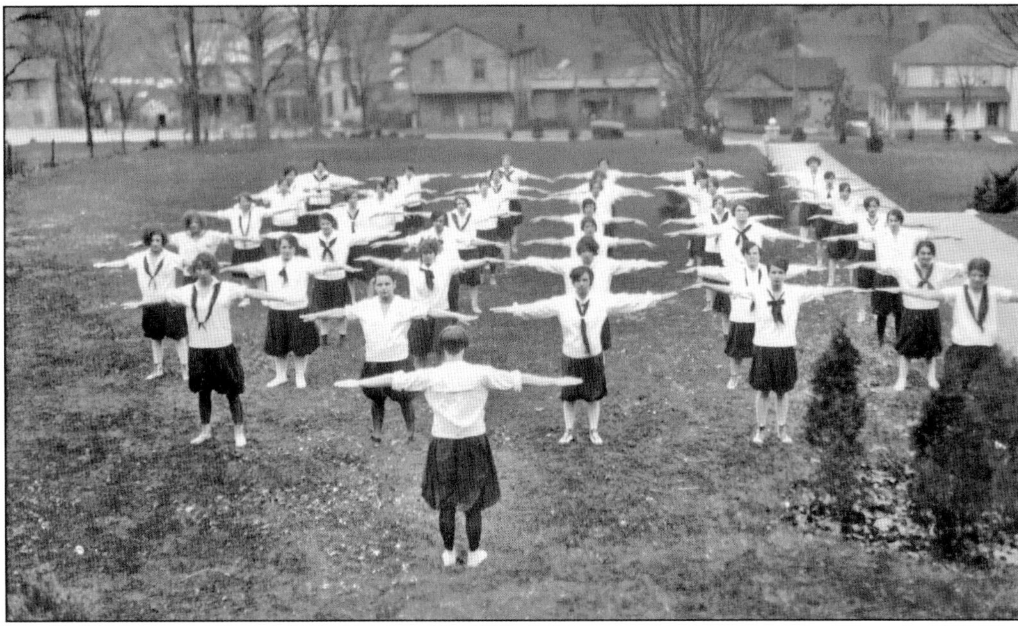

SITE OF THE YANKEE CAMP. For several years after the War Between the States, 300 Union soldiers were stationed in makeshift barracks along Main Street to ensure the Southern town was complying with the new laws of the land. The barracks sat where the houses are in the background. These young ladies of Marion College are exercising in the front yard of the college. (Courtesy Mack Sturgill Collection.)

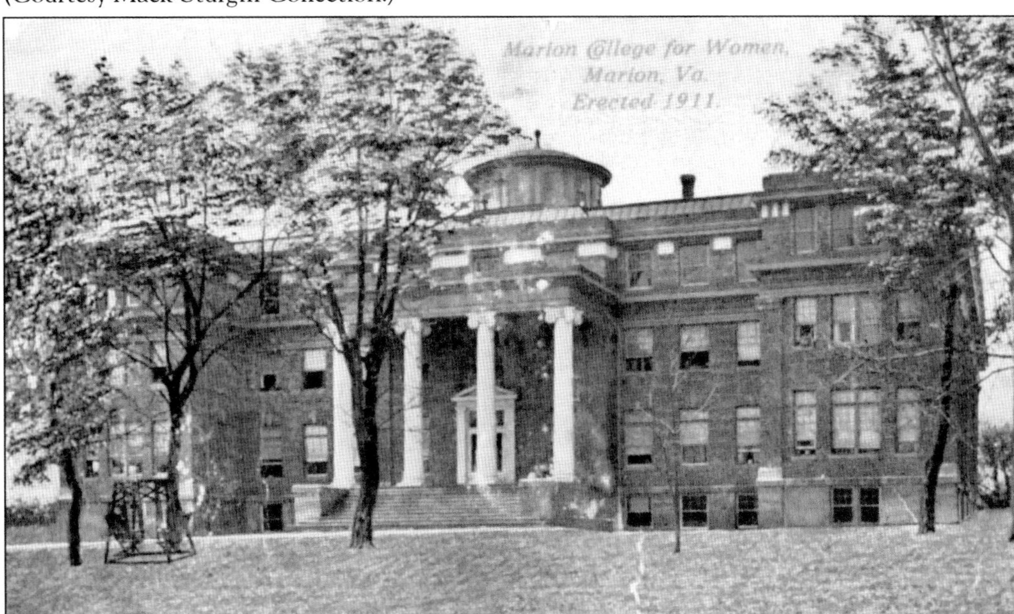

MARION COLLEGE. The Evangelical Lutheran Synod of Southwestern Virginia founded Marion Female College in 1873. After several name changes, it eventually became known as Marion College in 1934. What was once a college for women began to enroll local male students in 1933. The present building was constructed in 1911–1912 and became the home of the Blue Ridge Job Corps in 1967. (Courtesy Dr. Paul Brown.)

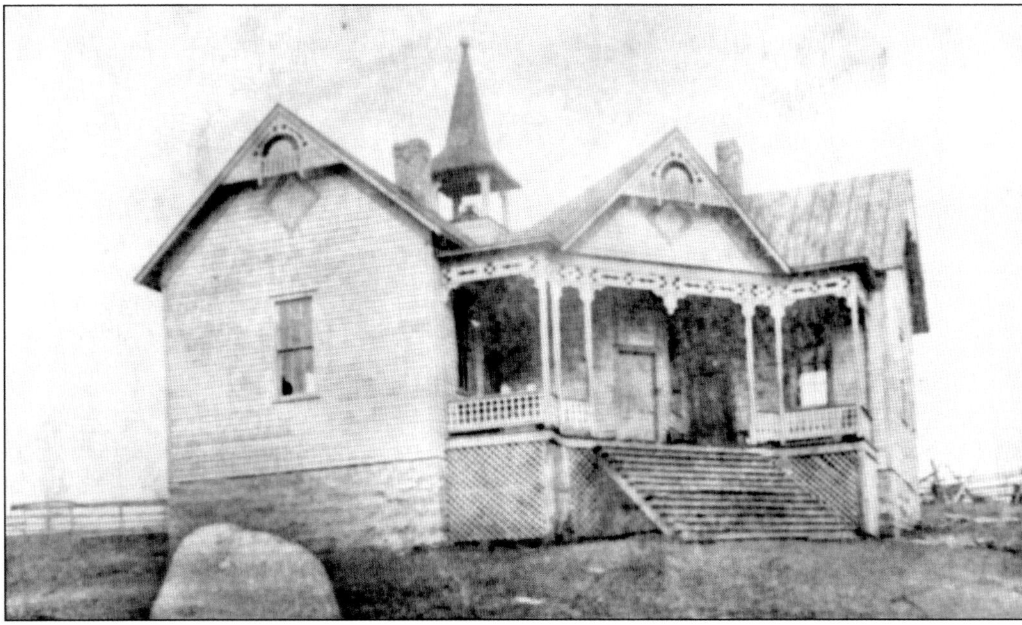

OLD ZION SCHOOL. This "V"-shaped school was located in the Nebo area of the county and was quite ornate for a school building; note the spindles and decorative trim. The children carried their lunches in pails and sacks and warmed themselves around pot-bellied stoves in the two-room school. Children from grades 1 through 11 attended here. (Courtesy Kenny Sturgill.)

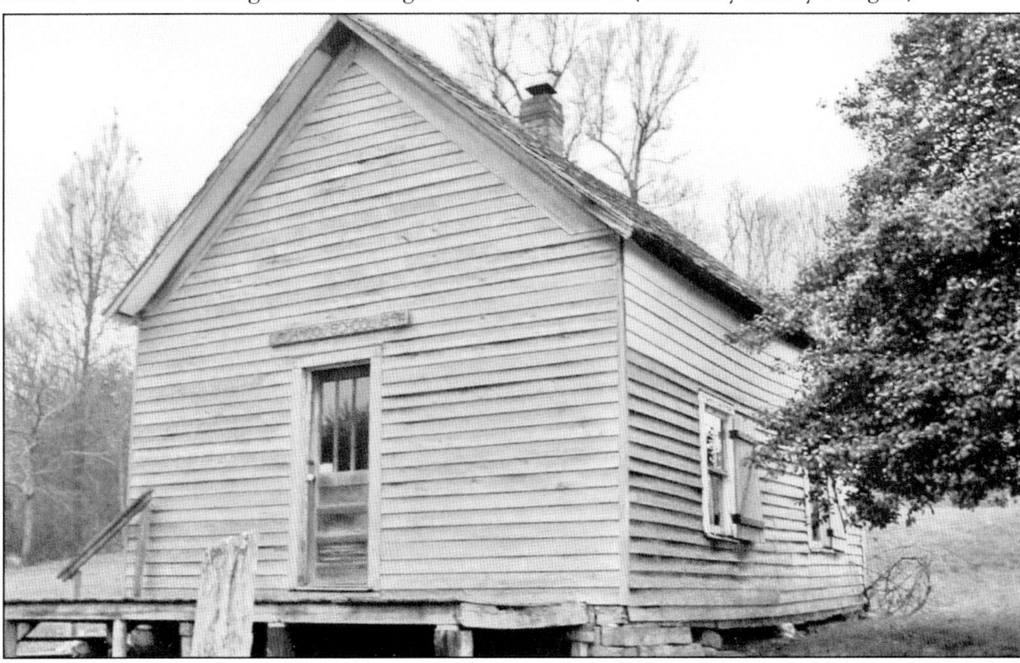

LINDAMOOD SCHOOL. Established in 1894, this one-room schoolhouse is located at the Settler's Museum in Atkins and mirrors the education of more than 100 years ago. Children huddled around the pot-bellied stove for warmth on those cold winter days. Restrooms were out back as was the springhouse, from which water was carried in, and one dipper was used for everyone to drink from. (Courtesy Debra Williams.)

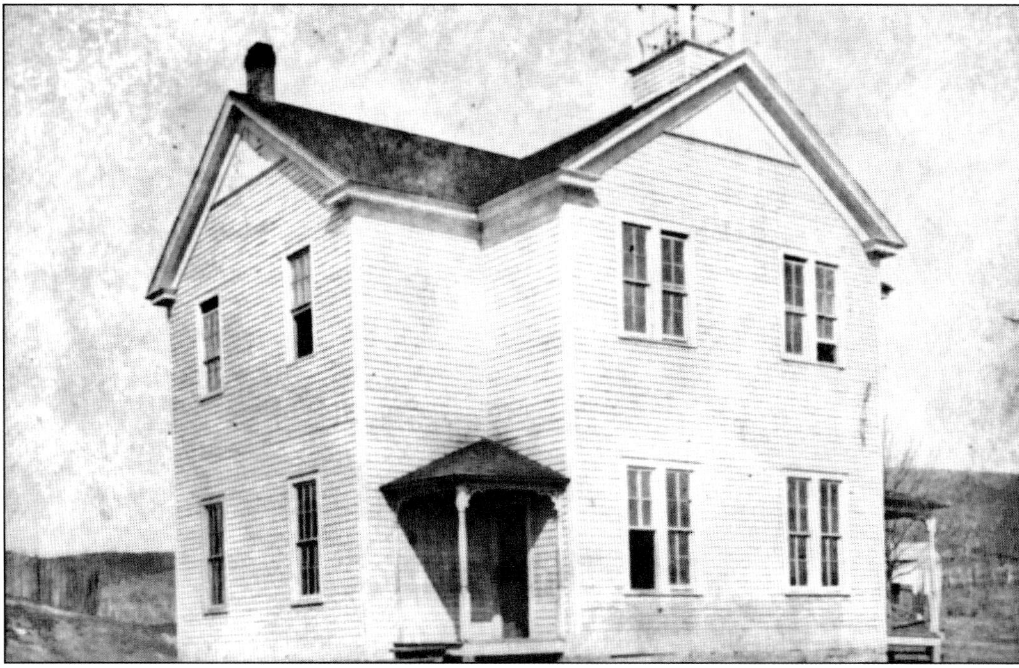

CHILHOWIE HIGH SCHOOL. In 1900, Liberty Academy merged into Chilhowie Graded School, and a separate high school was formed five years later in 1905. This elementary school building, which was located on the old Macadam Road in Chilhowie, was used to teach three years of high school. Three of the four classrooms were used for elementary school. There were 21 high school students enrolled for the 1906–1907 school year. (Courtesy Mack Sturgill Collection.)

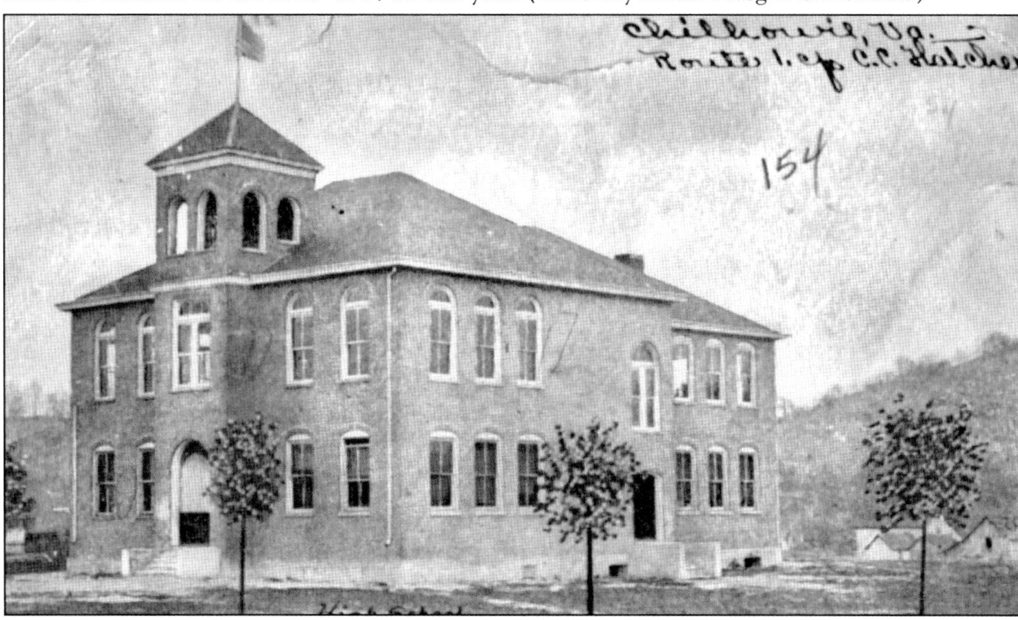

CHILHOWIE GRAMMAR AND HIGH SCHOOL. Built *c.* 1910, this brick school building was constructed at a cost of $15,000. Two of the nine classrooms were used for high school students. It served all grades until a new brick high school was built across the road on what is now Chilhowie Street. This building then became the grade school building. (Courtesy Clegg Williams.)

Seven

PEOPLE, PLACES, AND THINGS

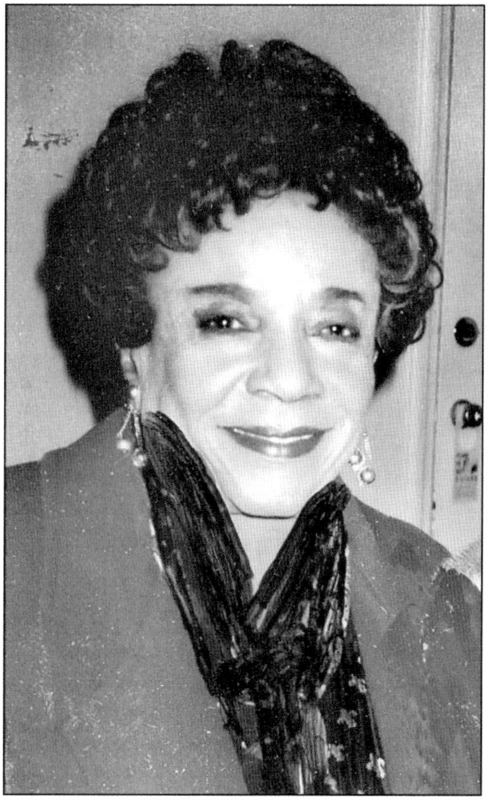

EVELYN LAWRENCE DAY. July 22, 2006, was set aside in Marion as Evelyn Lawrence Day by the town council to honor its own historian and educator of more than 40 years. Evelyn Thompson Lawrence, a Marion native, has been an inspiration to blacks and whites alike. Since her retirement, she volunteers at Valley Nursing Home, contributes to local history, and serves on various social and educational boards. (Courtesy Evelyn Lawrence.)

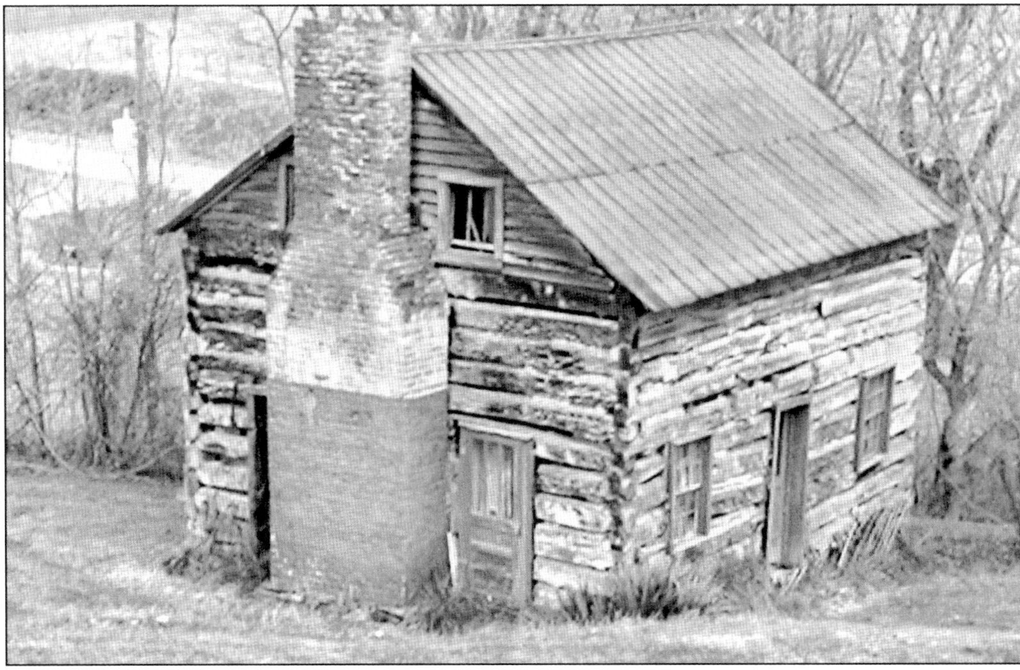

OLD BUCHANAN CABIN. This pre-1850s cabin, located on private property just off of Spring Branch Road, was once part of the Buchanan estate. The upstairs was never finished though the cabin was later added onto to accommodate the two Colley children who lived here with their parents. One of those children, Roy, later tore off the additions, leaving the original, hand-hewn log house. (Courtesy Debra Williams.)

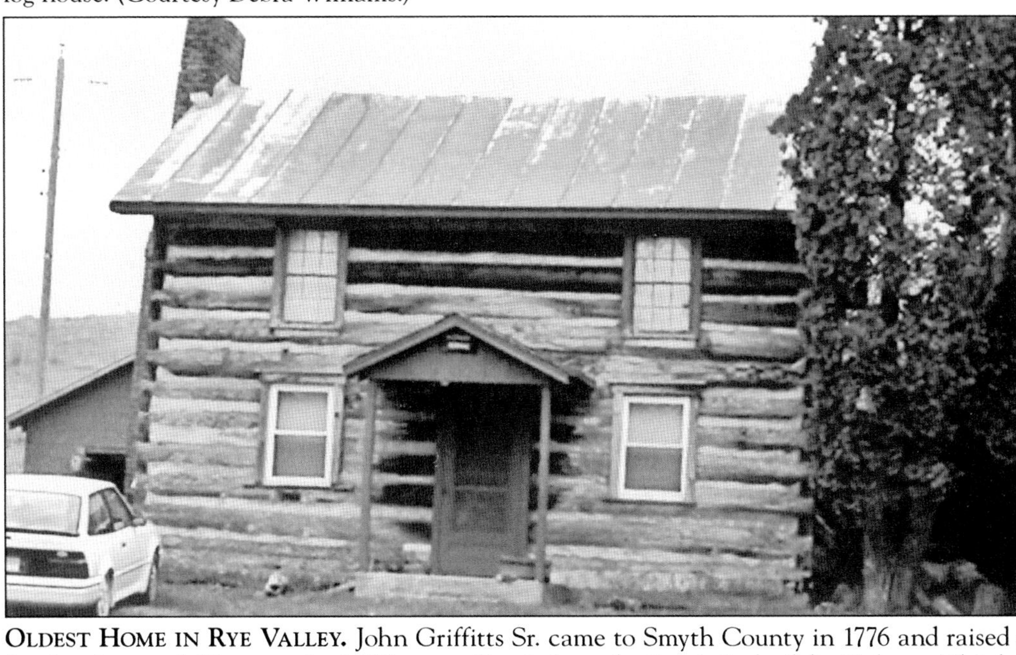

OLDEST HOME IN RYE VALLEY. John Griffitts Sr. came to Smyth County in 1776 and raised a family of seven children on the 1,650 acres of land along the South Fork of the Holston. This log cabin was built in 1852 by Griffitts on the site of his first home in the Teas section of the county. (Contributed by Debra Williams.)

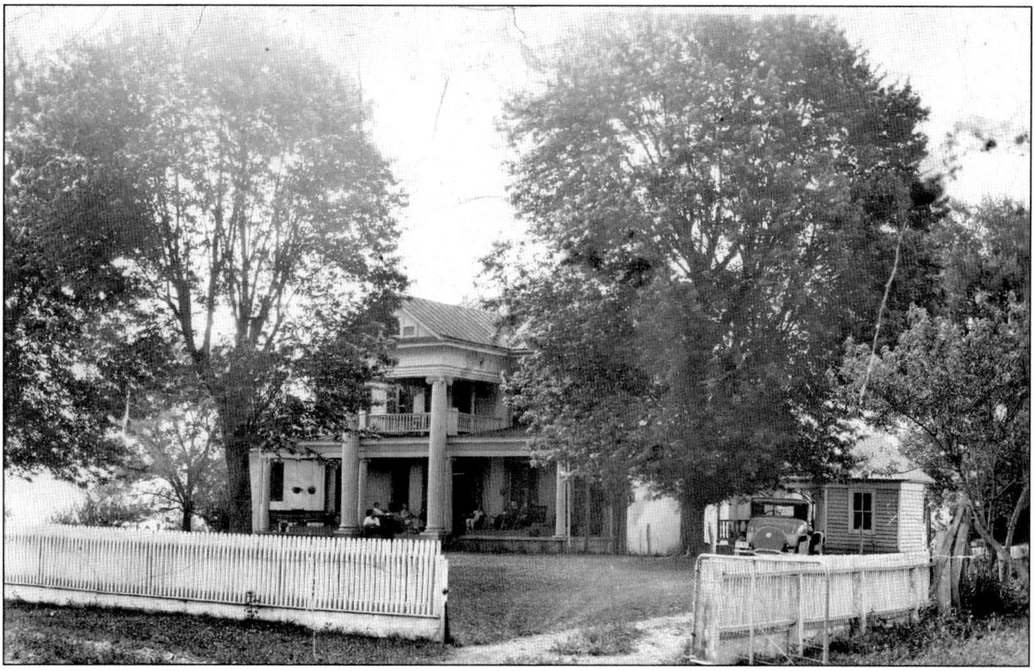

FORT KILMACHROMAN. Built in 1776 on the edge of Smyth and Washington Counties, this was a popular neighborhood fort. The survey of 2,600 acres, dated in 1746, was one of the earliest recorded and belonged to James Patton. The Huff family renovated this fort into their beautiful home place that still stands today. (Courtesy Atwood J. Huff.)

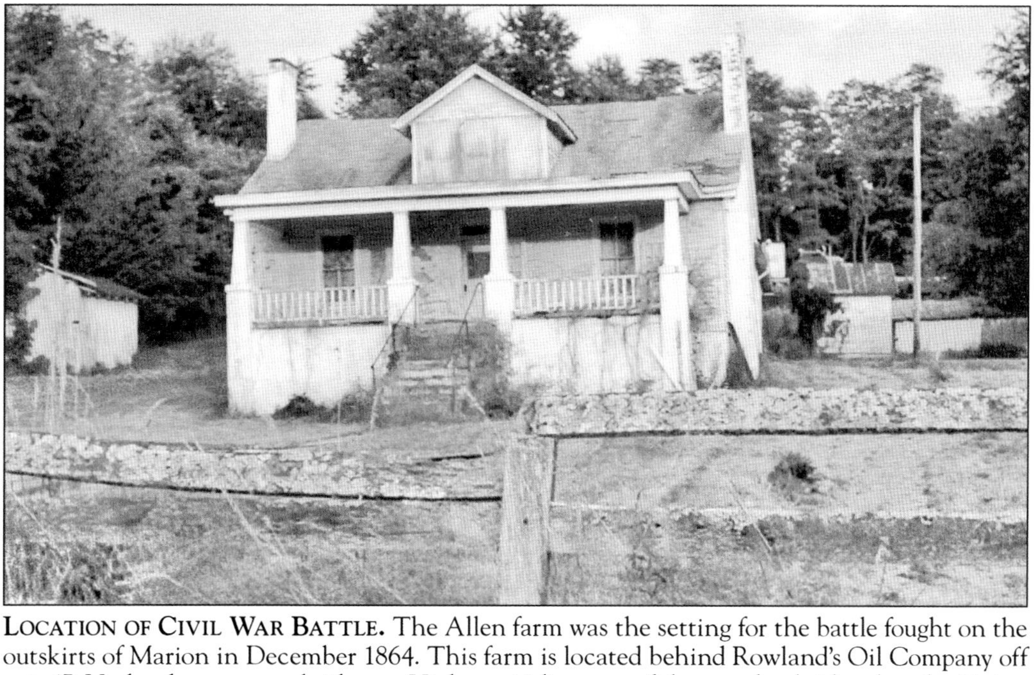

LOCATION OF CIVIL WAR BATTLE. The Allen farm was the setting for the battle fought on the outskirts of Marion in December 1864. This farm is located behind Rowland's Oil Company off exit 47. Under the concrete bridge on Highway 11 lie parts of the wooden bridge that the Union soldiers tried several times to burn. The fire was extinguished by nine-year-old Susan Allen. (Courtesy Debra Williams.)

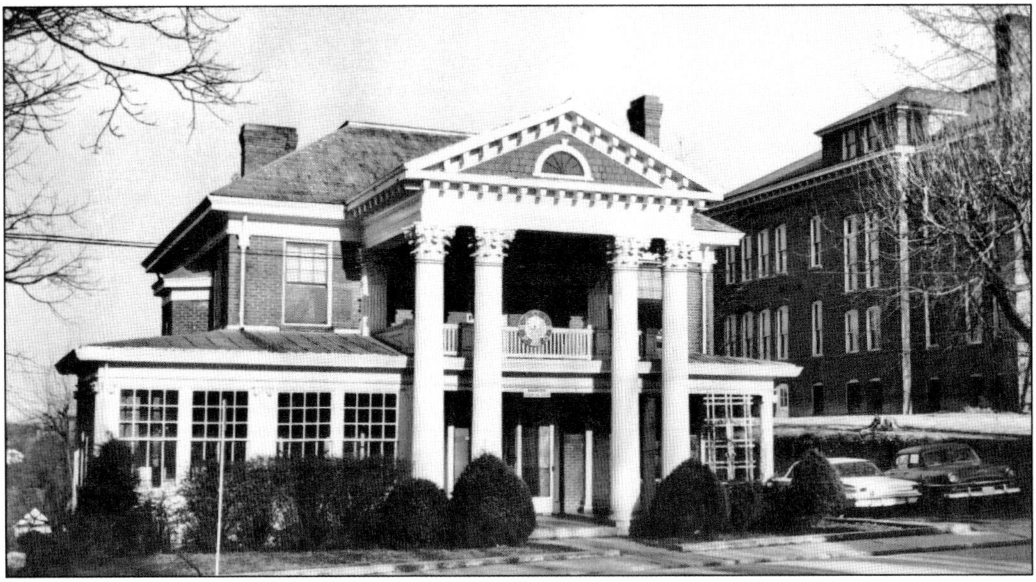

HOME OF A. T. LINCOLN. Politician A. T. Lincoln served in the House of Delegates, state senate, and at the 1901–1902 Constitutional Convention. Lincoln was known for having the first automobile in the county and was the president of the Smyth County Telephone Company. This elaborate dwelling was erected *c.* 1912 and was once owned by Lincoln. This is now the home of Gary and Bonita Frazier. (Courtesy Debra Williams.)

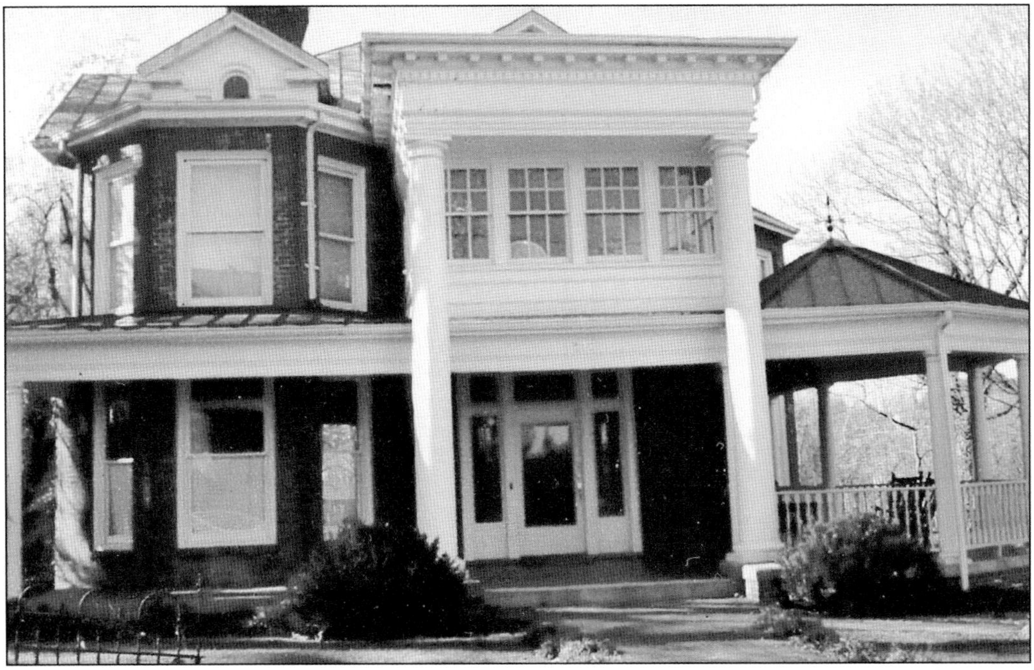

C. C. LINCOLN SR. HOME. Because Charles Lincoln Sr. was part owner of the Look and Lincoln Firm, and because of the location of his house on Church Street, this was the first home in Marion to be wired for electricity. Look and Lincoln ventured into many trades, but their best known was the Virginia-Lincoln Furniture Company, which was the second largest of its kind in the world. (Courtesy Debra Williams.)

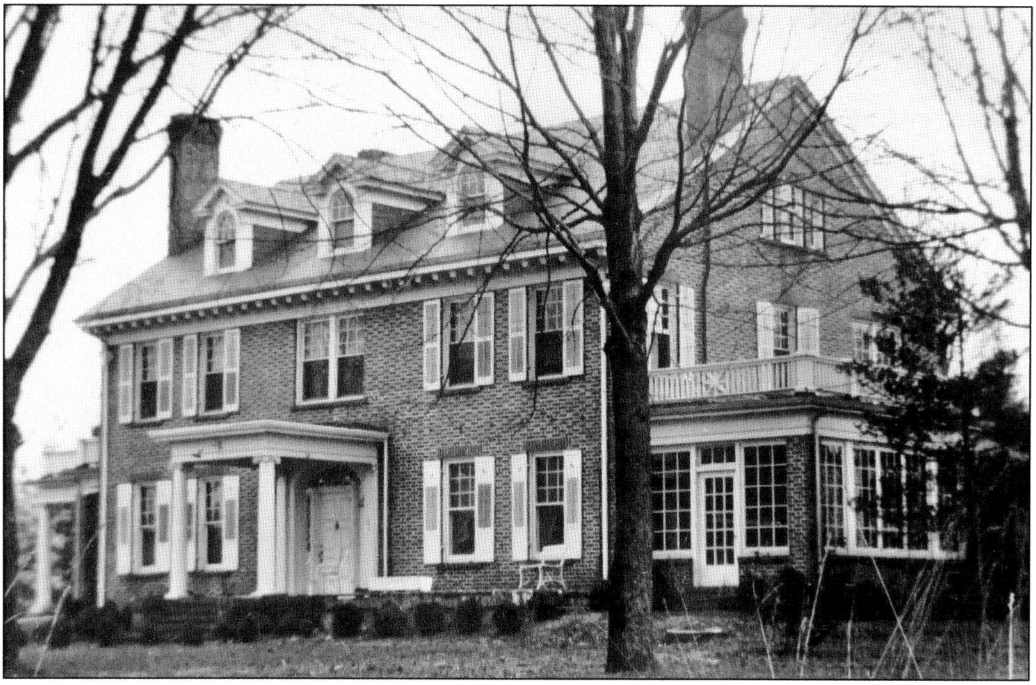

BIRBON HALL. This magnificent, three-story structure with hardwood floors, glass doorknobs, and library off to the side was built in 1917 by W. V. Birchfield Sr. The third story was used as a ballroom for entertaining. The home was purchased by Deward Miller in 1954 and later became a bed-and-breakfast. It is now a private residence. (Courtesy Mack Sturgill Collection.)

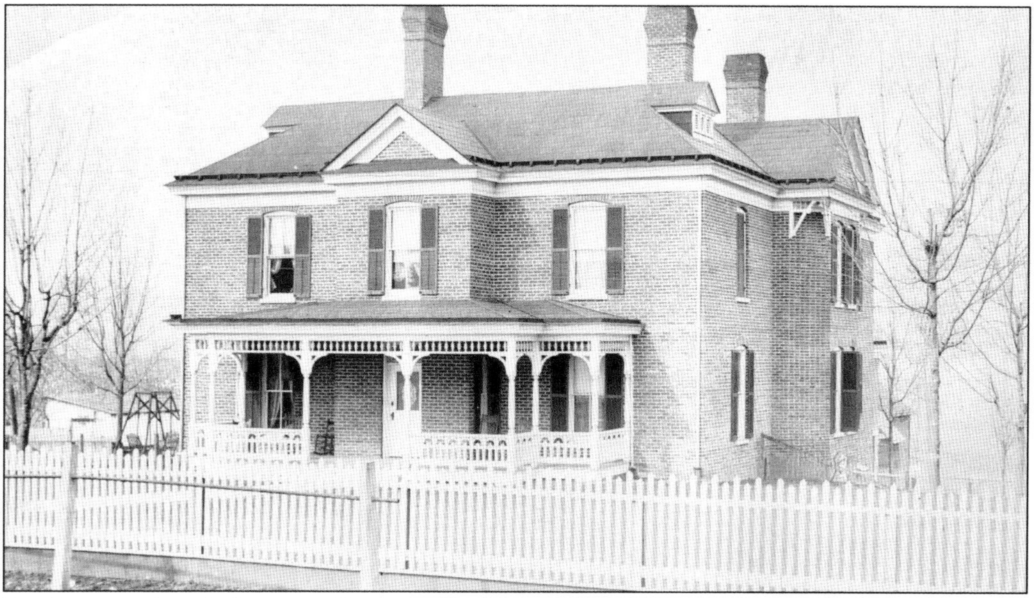

DR. ROBERT COLE'S SUMMER HOUSE. This beautiful brick home is located on Needmore Road in Chilhowie. Dr. Cole's practice was located in New York, and for a change of pace during the early 1900s, the Cole family vacationed at this lovely home in the country. The acreage around the home was later sold, and other houses sprang up around the quiet neighborhood. Notice the hitching post in front of the house. (Courtesy Dr. Paul Brown.)

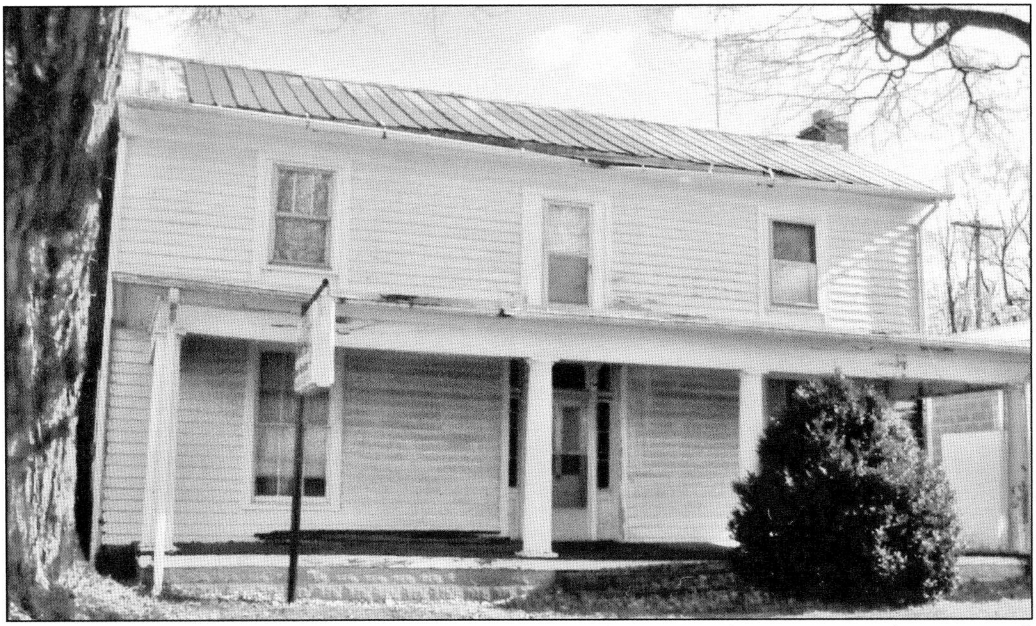

A. G. PENDLETON HOUSE. During the Civil War, Pendleton served as a major in the Stonewall Brigade, also known as "Smyth Blues." In 1879, Pendleton married Missouri Thomas, the daughter of businessman Obijah Thomas. They had two children and made their home here on Pendleton Street. Missouri's mother, Priscilla Scott Thomas, widow of Obijah, died while living with her in 1885. Later this house served as Catron's Funeral Home. (Courtesy Debra Williams.)

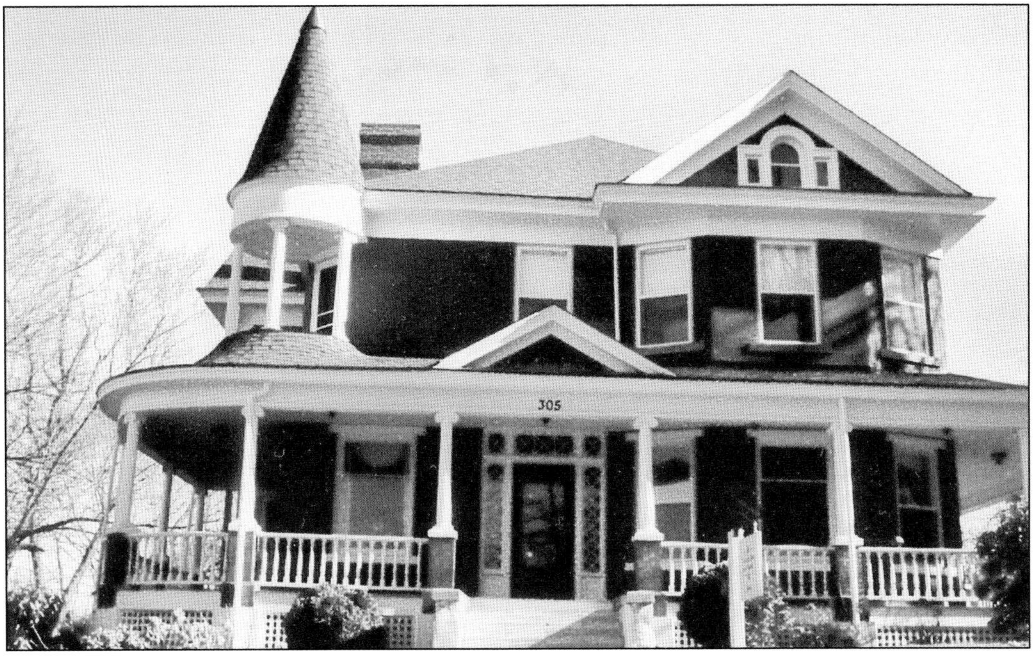

LINCOLN HOUSE BED-AND-BREAKFAST. Willard L. Lincoln had this brick, Queen Anne–style house erected in 1904. It remained in the family until 1945. The descendants of Lincoln reacquired the house in 2001. Author Betsy Lemmon Sayers has since converted her ancestor's home place into a lovely bed-and-breakfast, which would make Mr. Lincoln proud. (Courtesy Debra Williams.)

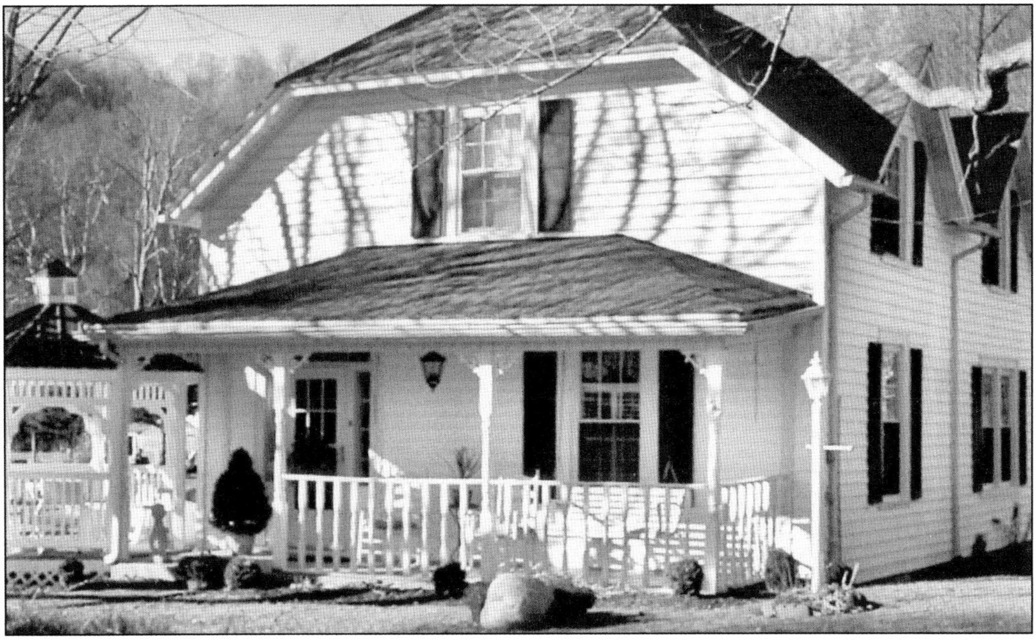

SUGAR GROVE DOCTOR'S HOME AND OFFICE. During the early 1900s, this white bungalow on Water Street was the home of Dr. Ross, whose office was just to the left side of the house. Since Sugar Grove had such a small population, Dr. Ross substituted his income by plumbing on the side. (Courtesy of Debra Williams.)

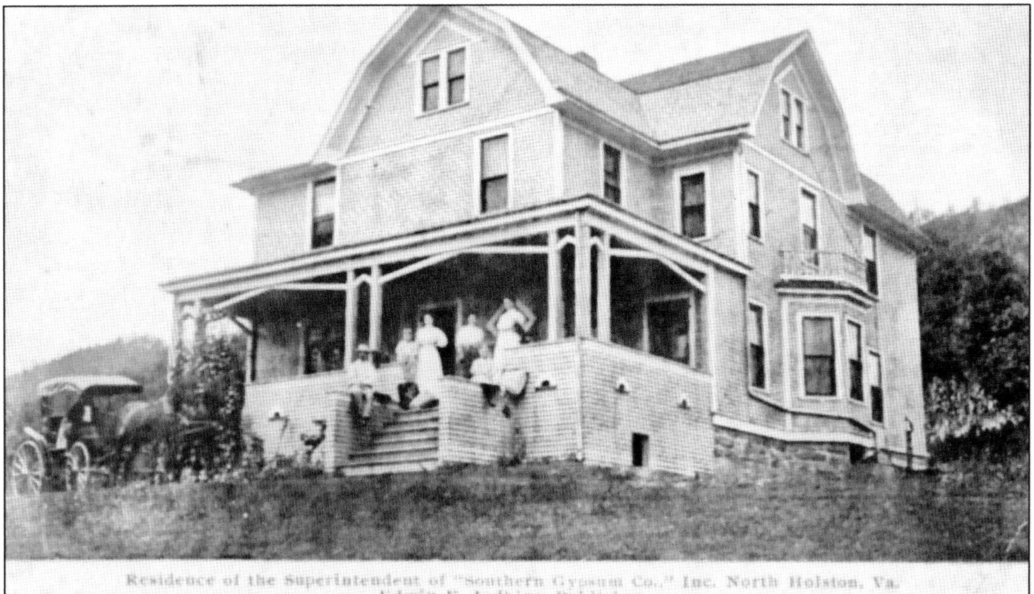

SOUTHERN GYPSUM COMPANY. Shown in this photograph is the residence of the superintendent of Southern Gypsum Company in North Holston. With Dr. F. A. Wilder in charge, Southern Gypsum bought the Pearson Plaster Banks, located three miles above Saltville. A 1907 prospecting experiment revealed the presence of a million and a half tons of gypsum. Afterward, a plant was constructed to turn the gypsum into a high-grade wall plaster and also Portland cement. (Courtesy Clegg Williams.)

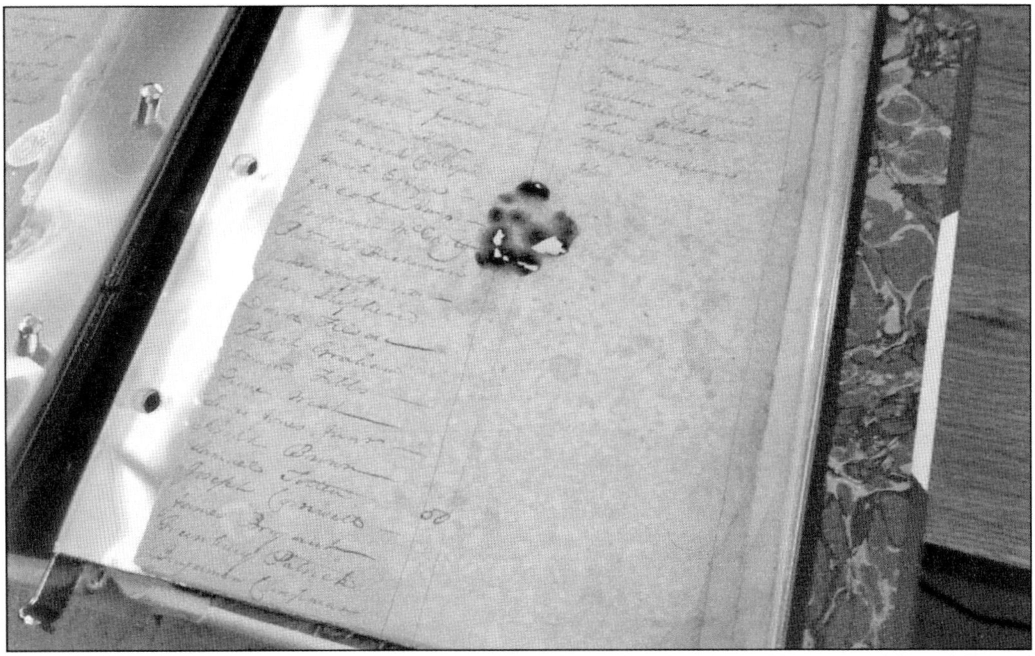

COURT RECORDS SAVED. In December 1864, Maj. James B. Harrison and his 300 soldiers followed William Sexton, county clerk, who was trying to save the court records from being destroyed by the Union. The troops caught up with Sexton on Staley's Creek Road, just south of present-day WOLD Radio, and set fire to the wagon carrying these records. Preteen Catherine Killinger carried the scorched books to safety and saved the county records. (Courtesy Debra Williams.)

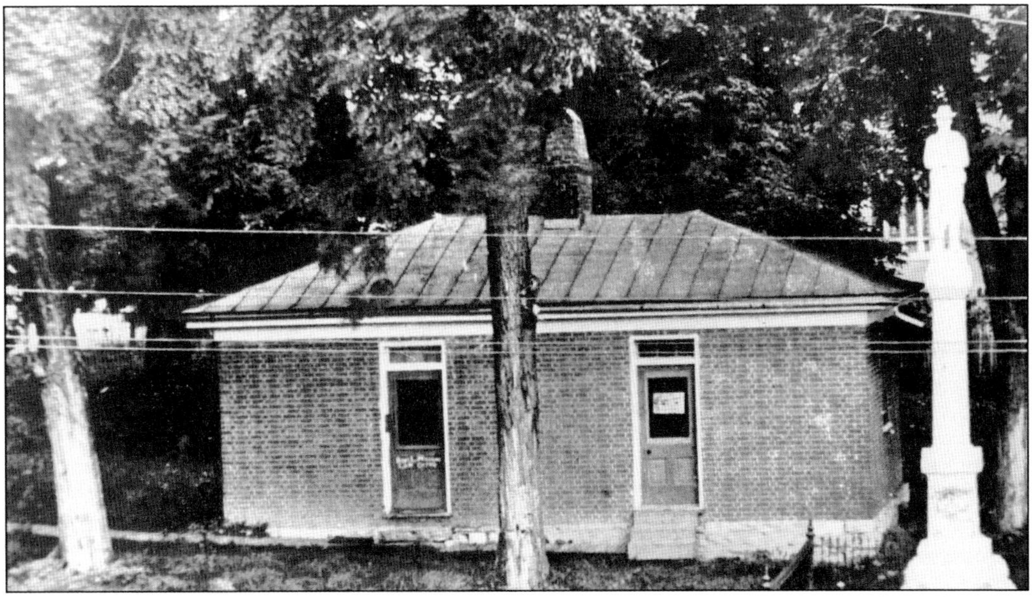

D. C. MILLER LAW OFFICE. This two-room brick office was used by Judge D. C. Miller, who came to Smyth County during the Civil War. He developed the education system for the county and was instrumental in bringing the Southwest Lunatic Asylum to Marion, for which he did all the legal work. He became the county's first superintendent of schools before becoming a county judge. (Courtesy Mack Sturgill Collection.)

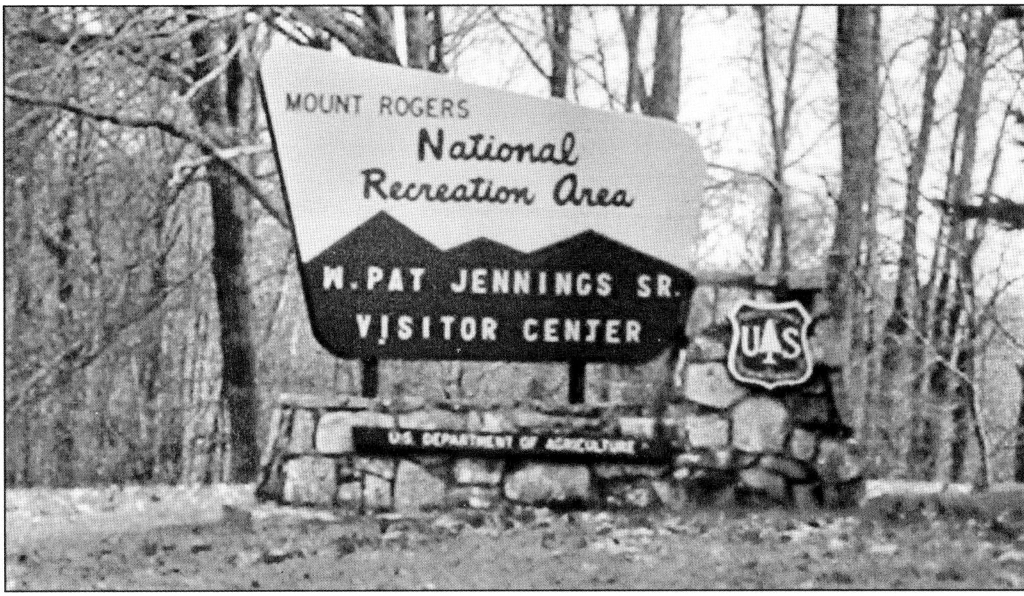

PAT JENNINGS VISITOR CENTER. Located along the pathway of the Appalachian Trail, this visitor center was named after Sen. Pat Jennings of Marion. Charles Wassum Jr. bought up 4,000 acres along Mount Rogers and met with Pat Jennings, hoping to obtain his aid in using this land to increase the economy. In 1966, Congress established Mount Rogers as a National Recreation Area that now consists of 120,000 acres. (Courtesy Debra Williams.)

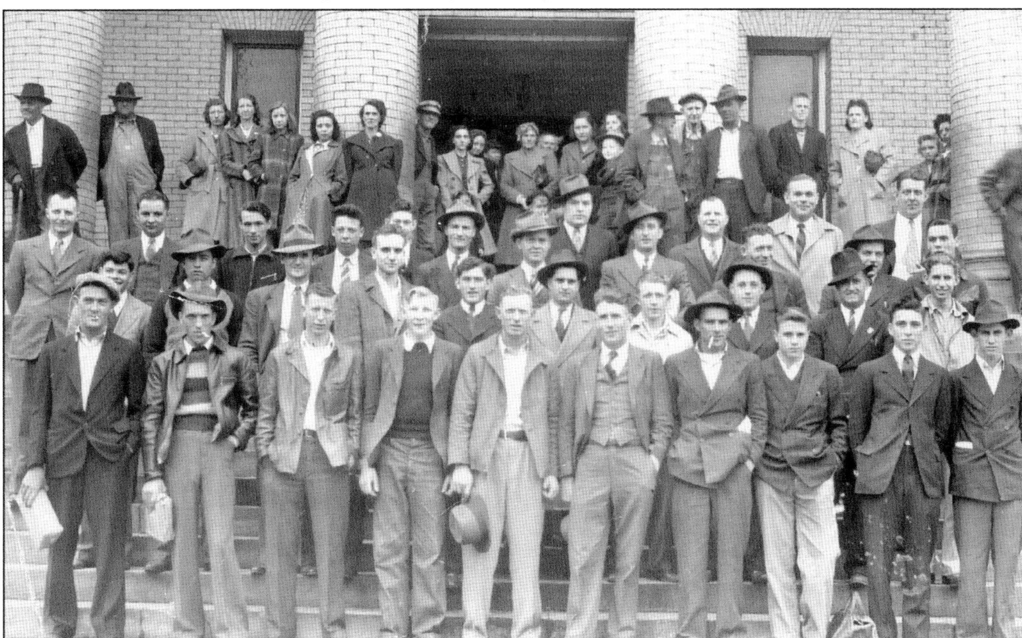

WORLD WAR II DRAFTEES. These men are posing for the picture that was taken for all draftees before going off to war. They are standing in front of the courthouse because the draft board was located inside. Here the family members have come with them for support and to see the soldiers off. Draftees from Smyth County caught the train or a bus to their destination. (Courtesy Judy Millsaps.)

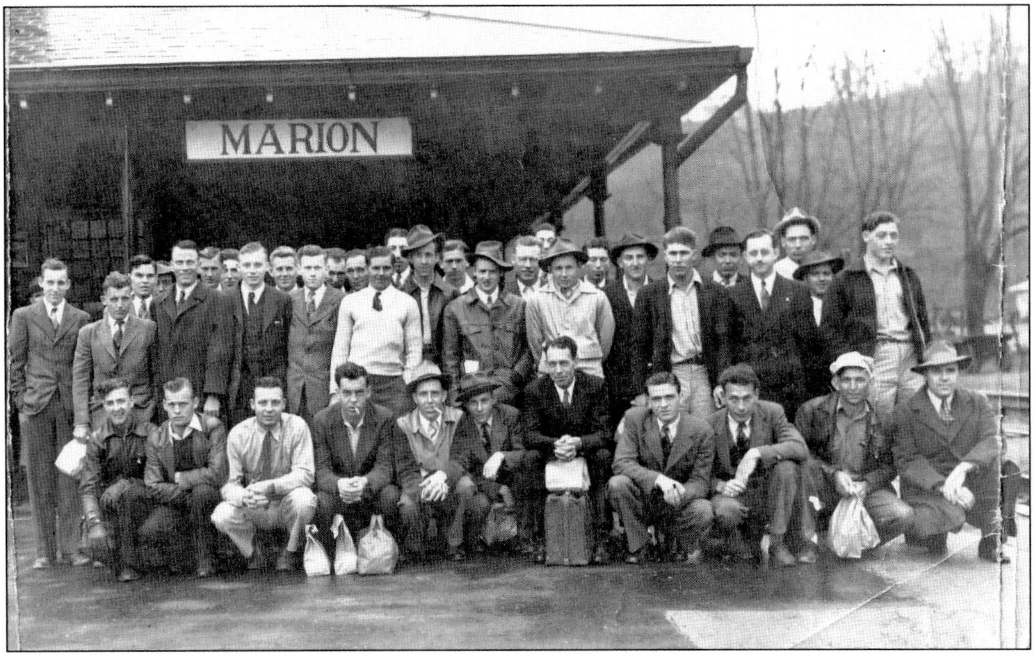

WAITING FOR THE TRAIN. These men are posing in front of the Marion Train Depot awaiting their ride to battle training. Notice the brown-bag lunches these men have for their long trip. Men leaving and bidding family members farewell was a common occurrence at train stations all over the world during wartime. The N&W Railroad moved the most freight in its history during World War II. (Courtesy of Judy Millsaps.)

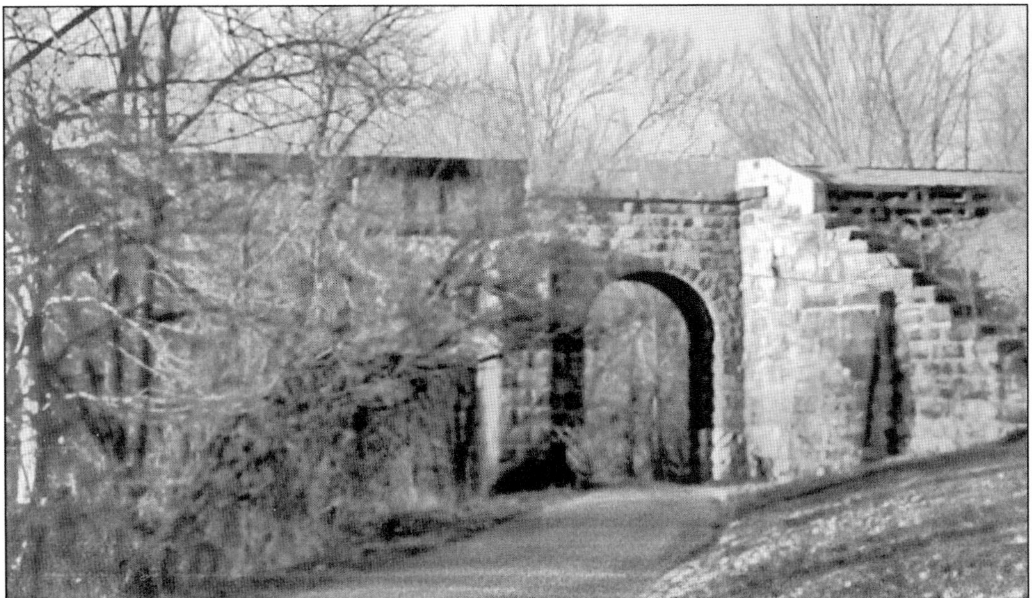

TRESTLE AT SEVEN MILE FORD. This huge limestone train trestle was built more than 150 years ago when the railroad came through this area. The one-lane entrance through the trestle is a representation of change, it being constructed when only slow-moving horses and wagons needed access along the middle fork of the Holston. (Courtesy Debra Williams.)

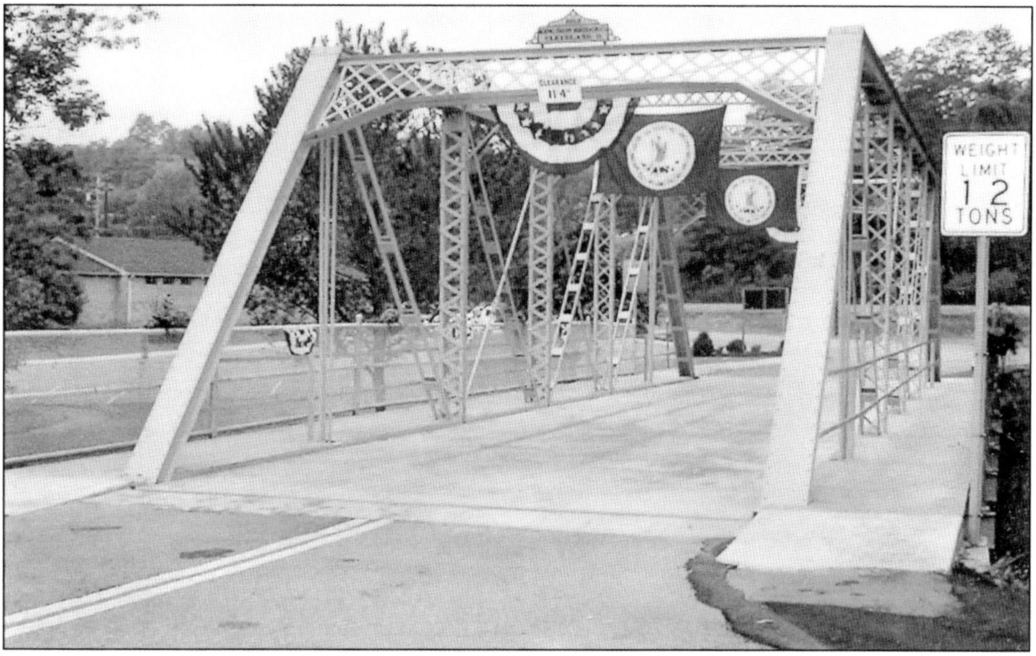

OLDEST BRIDGE IN VIRGINIA. This metal truss-type structure was built by the town of Marion in 1885 at East Chilhowie and Main Streets. At the time, the train depot was just beyond the bridge. Being the oldest two-lane bridge of its kind in Virginia, the town voted in 2003 to make repairs to the bridge instead of replacing it with a concrete structure. (Courtesy of Debra Williams.)

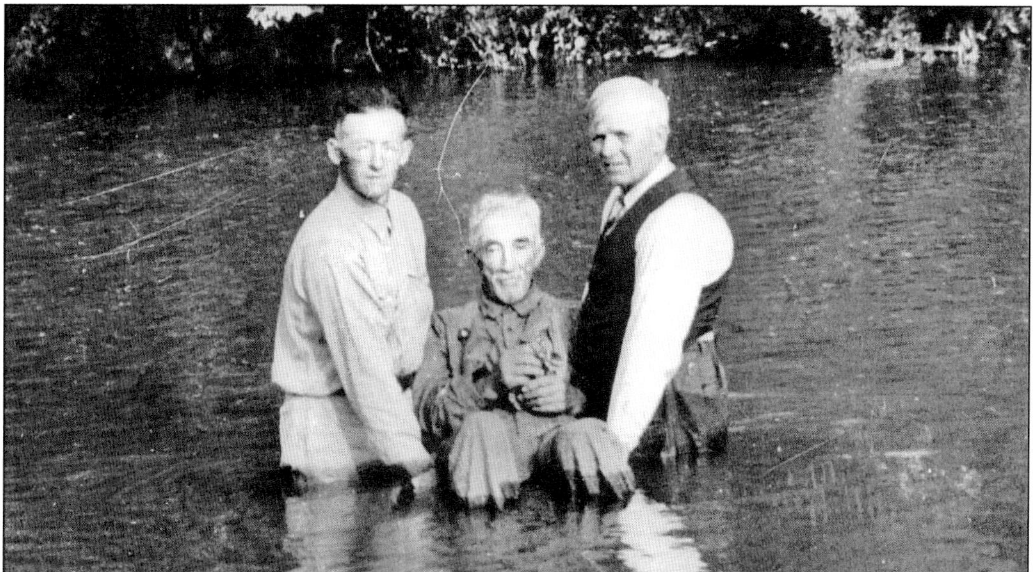

OLD-FASHIONED BAPTISM. Most churches that believe in baptism by immersion now have inside baptismal fonts, but not so long ago, creeks and rivers were the settings for baptisms. Regardless of the time of year, people gathered on the banks to witness their families and friends as they made their commitments. This elderly gentleman appears to be very enthusiastic. (Courtesy Carolyn Holman.)

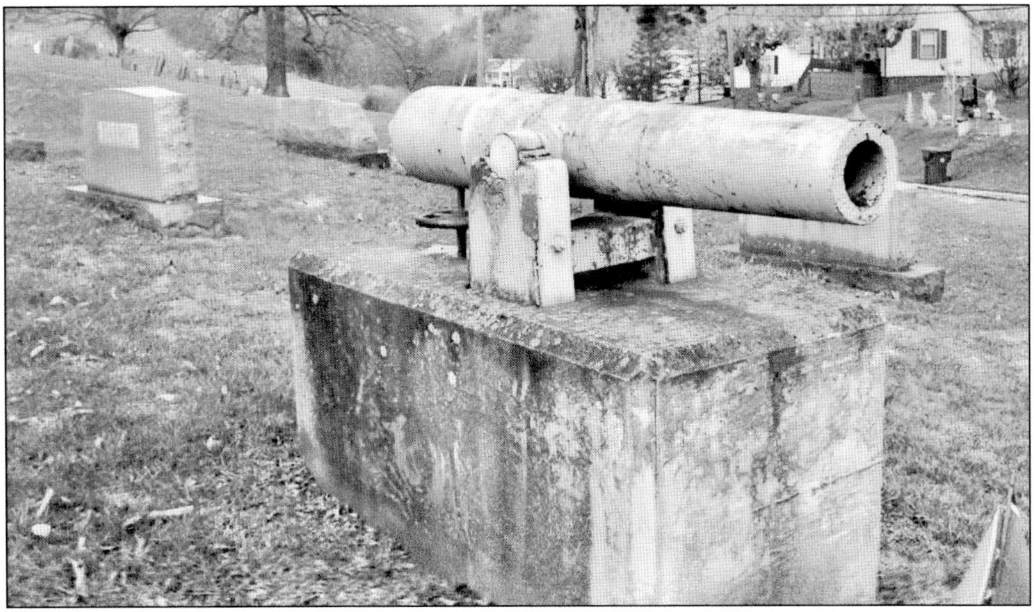

Old Cannon at Elizabeth Cemetery. After the Civil War, cannons were so plentiful around Saltville that some were used as boundary survey markers. In the 1920s, the only remaining cannon was placed at the entrance of the Elizabeth Cemetery. This cannon is a smoothbore, iron, Confederate 12-pound howitzer model 1862, weighing 850 pounds, which was manufactured at the Tredegar Foundry in Richmond by J. R. Anderson and Company. (Courtesy Debra Williams.)

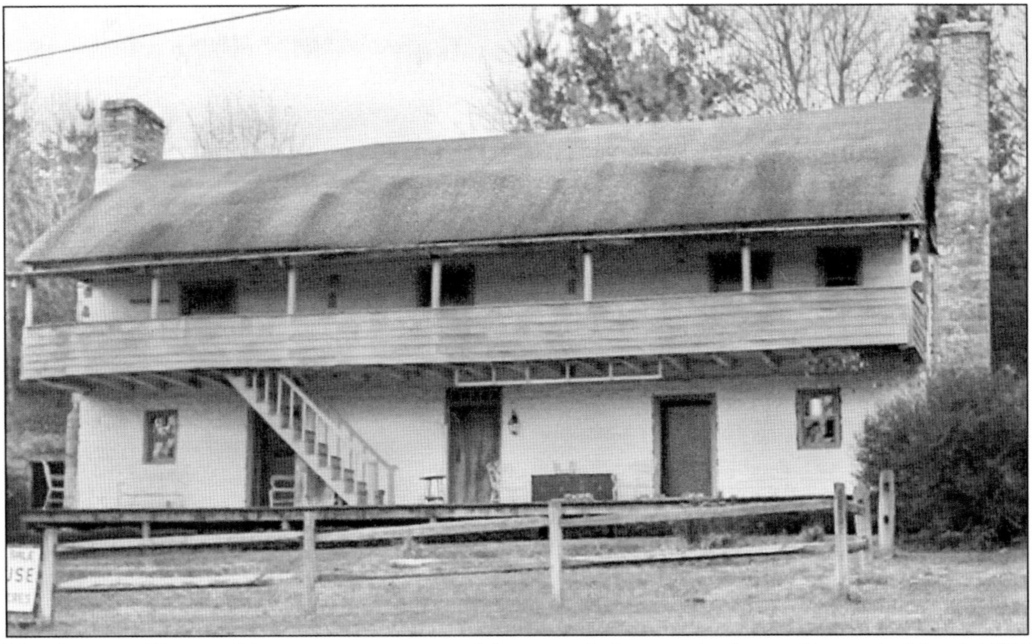

The Indian Fields. This tract was a part of the recorded survey by James Patton in March 1746 and later inherited by grandson James Thompson. The buffalo trail ran along the middle fork of the Holston and crossed over this land. This mansion of its era, now known as the Colletti House, was erected by Thompson and argued to be the oldest house in this area. (Courtesy Debra Williams.)

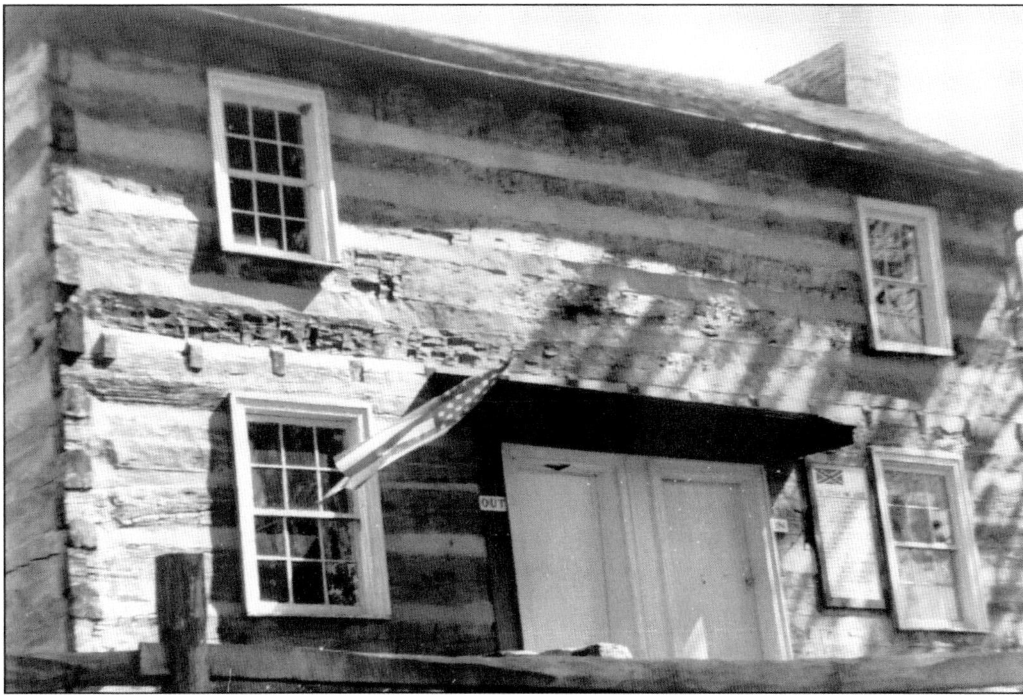

KING-STUART HOUSE. This house was built by Irish immigrant William King around 1795. He was an early owner of the saltworks. William A. Stuart, the brother of Confederate cavalry general J. E. B. Stuart, purchased a share of the saltworks and the home in 1856. J. E. B. Stuart's widow, Flora, lived here and established a grammar school on the first floor. (Courtesy Mack Sturgill Collection.)

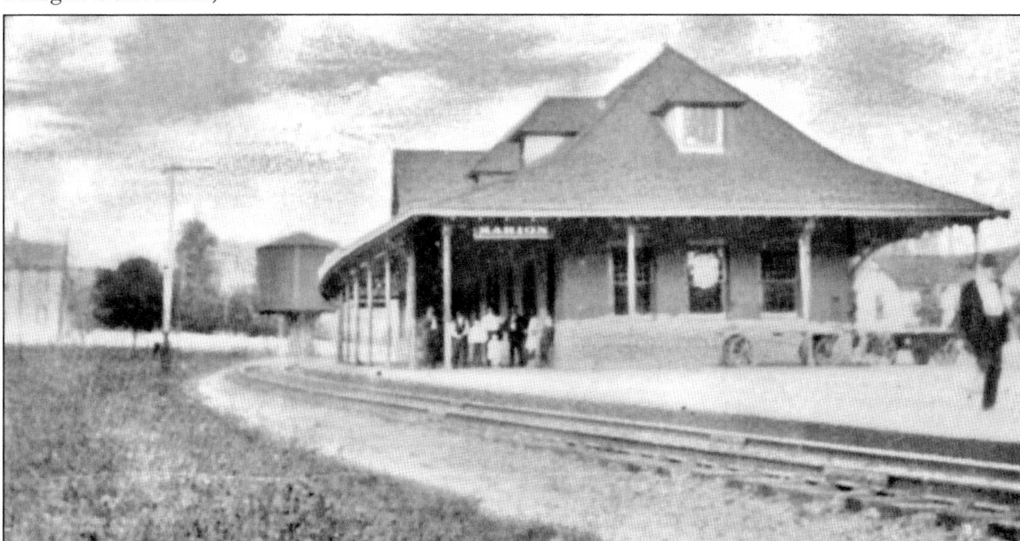

NORFOLK AND WESTERN PASSENGER STATION. In 1904, the Norfolk and Western Railway purchased a one-half acre lot from Zachariah and Alice Atkins to construct this passenger station. At the time, this station was for passengers only. Freight was shipped at an older station that was located one-half mile farther west. Notice the water tank to the left that supplied the steam engines. (Courtesy Clegg Williams.)

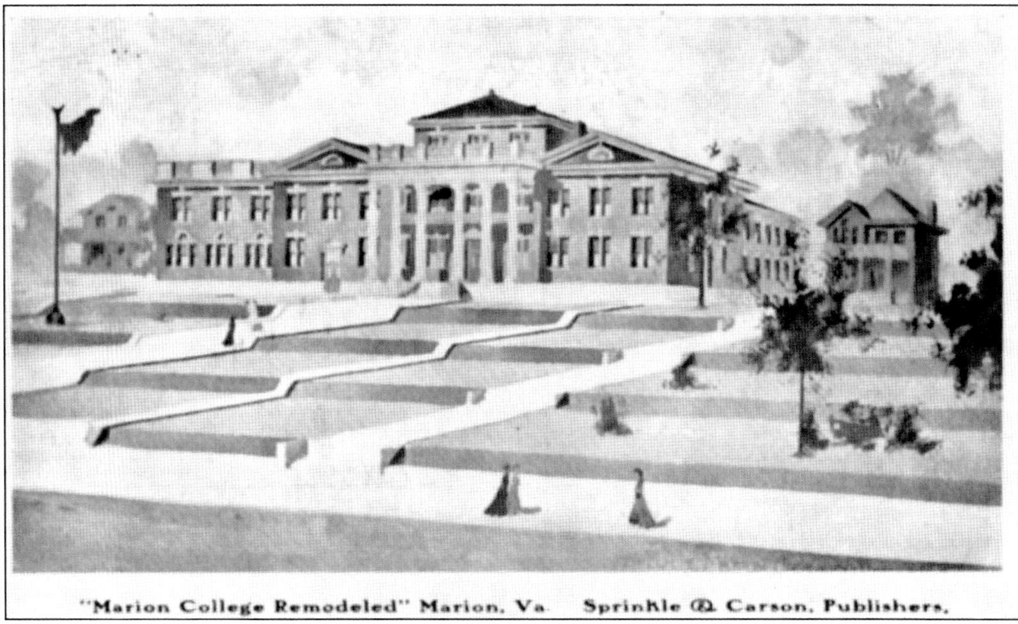

MARION COLLEGE REMODELED. This 1909 postcard shows the plans to remodel Marion College. The new building, which turned out to be quite different, was completed in 1912. It contained student dormitories, classrooms, a cafeteria, and an auditorium. In 1924, a gymnasium was added. The school's focus was to provide a Christian environment for female students while teaching domestic science, foreign language, art, culture, and music. (Courtesy Dr. Paul Brown.)

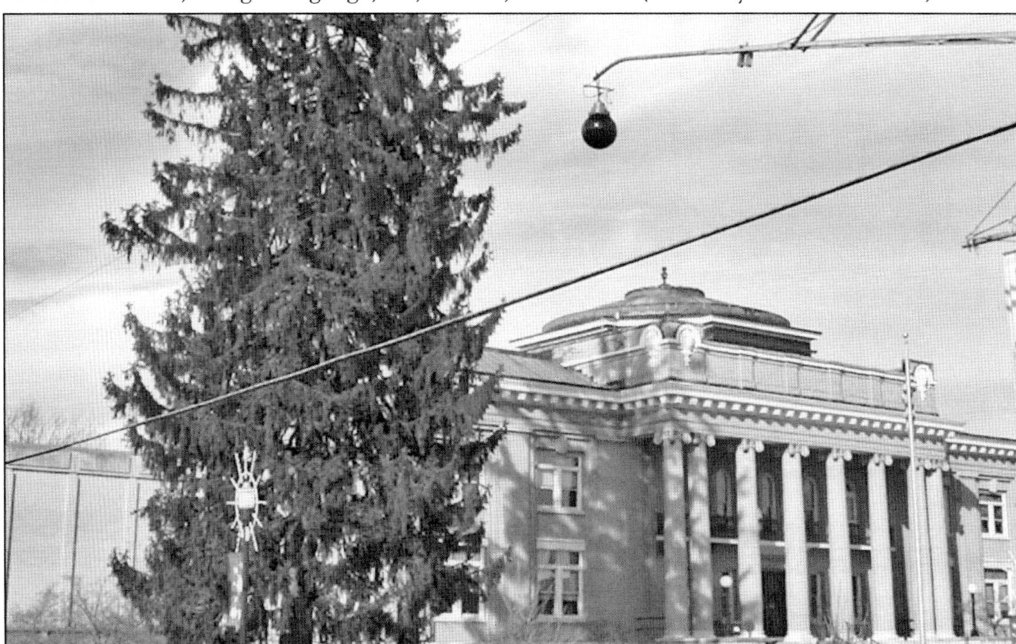

MARION'S POLICE SIGNAL. According to Walter Byrd, before there were two-way radios in police cars, Marion had a red light that could be seen down Main Street. When assistance was needed, the light signaled an officer who came to the station to get information. The light still remains today. (Courtesy Debra Williams.)

Eight

Gone, But Not Forgotten

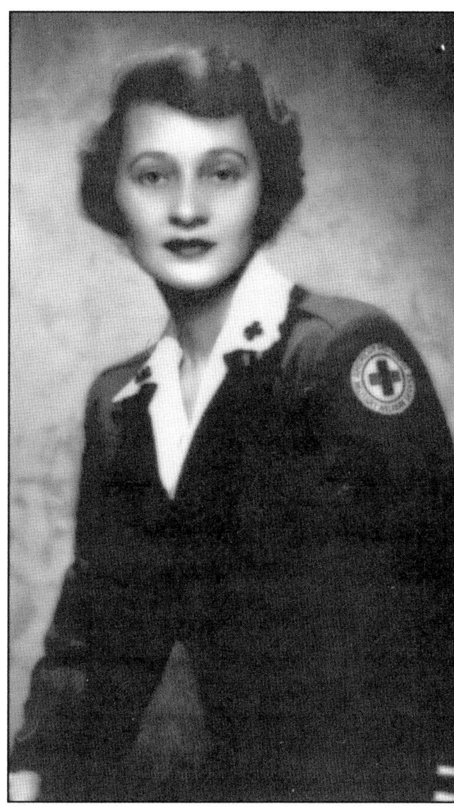

Lucy Herndon Crockett. This photograph is of Lucy Herndon Crockett in World War II Red Cross dress. She traveled with Basil O'Conner, national chairman of the Red Cross during the war, and was his speechwriter. Crockett was an author, an illustrator, and a designer. The movie *Proud and Profane*, which made its debut in 1956, was taken from her book, the *Magnificent Bastards*. (Courtesy Ron Fisher.)

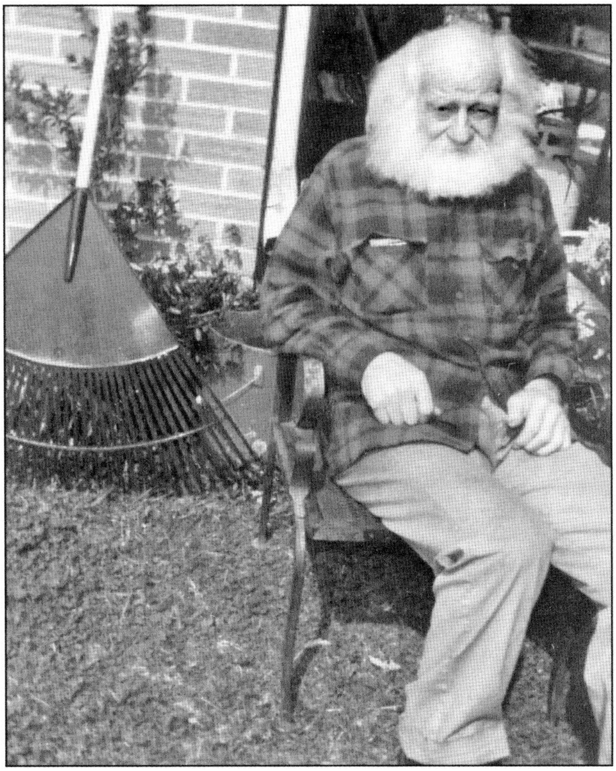

HOMER DAVENPORT. A well-known character in the Saltville area, Homer Davenport, made Clinch Mountain his home. He lived off of the land, traveling to town only to buy staples that could not be found in nature. Homer Davenport preferred living on his mountain in isolation to living in town, but he was friendly and could be seen from time to time hitching rides to town. (Courtesy Dewey Davenport.)

EARLY REFRIGERATORS. Before refrigerators, people build a stone or cinder-block shelter over a small stream. Items that should stay cold, such as milk, were placed into the water. Other items were placed around the walls or on shelves inside to keep cool. Many housed a resident black snake to keep mice away from the food. (Courtesy Debra Williams.)

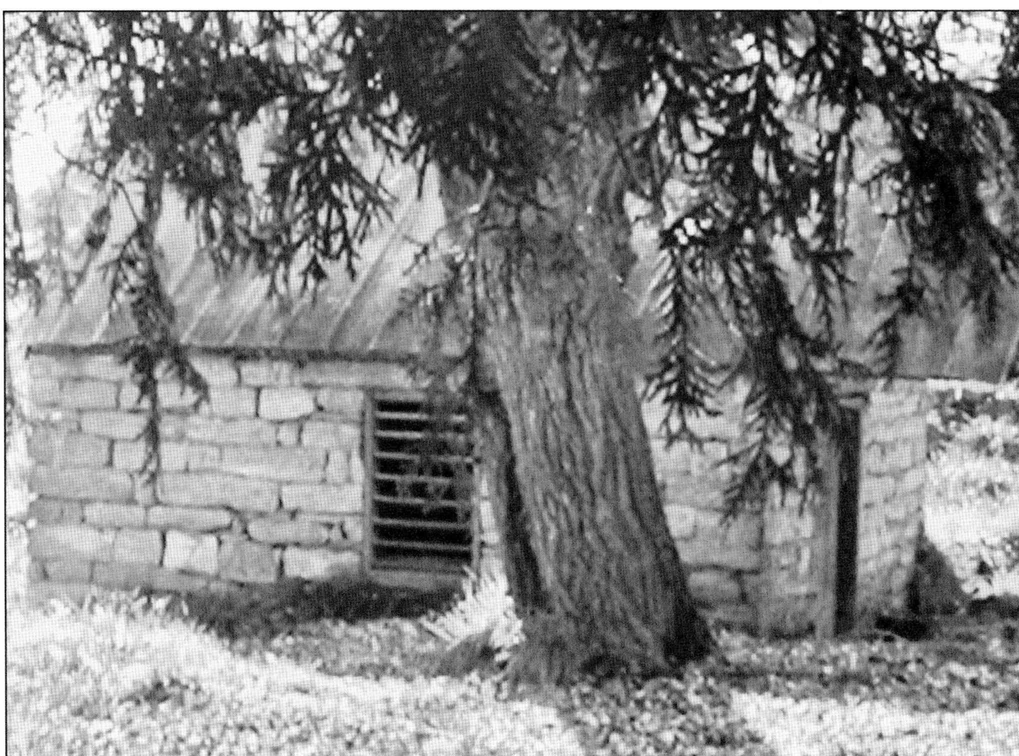

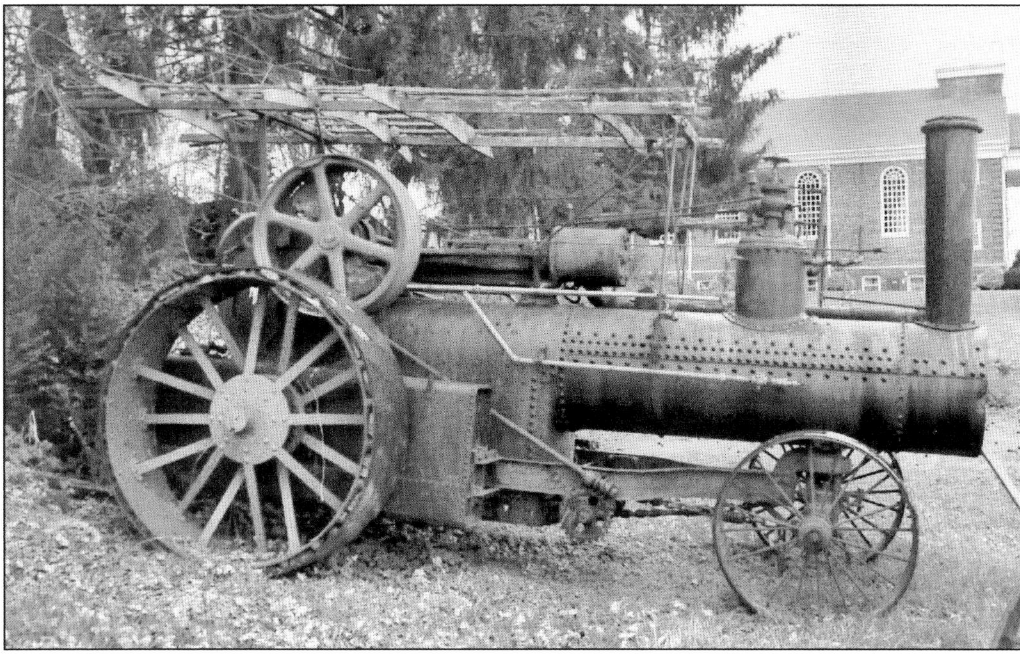

STEAM ENGINE. Invented in the late 1700s, steam engines didn't make their big debut in farming until the 1850s. Even then, they had their drawbacks. The steam engine was very heavy and would usually collapse bridges. In addition, boiler explosions were frequent and dangerous. This engine has been located along Highway 11 in Chilhowie for many years. (Courtesy Debra Williams.)

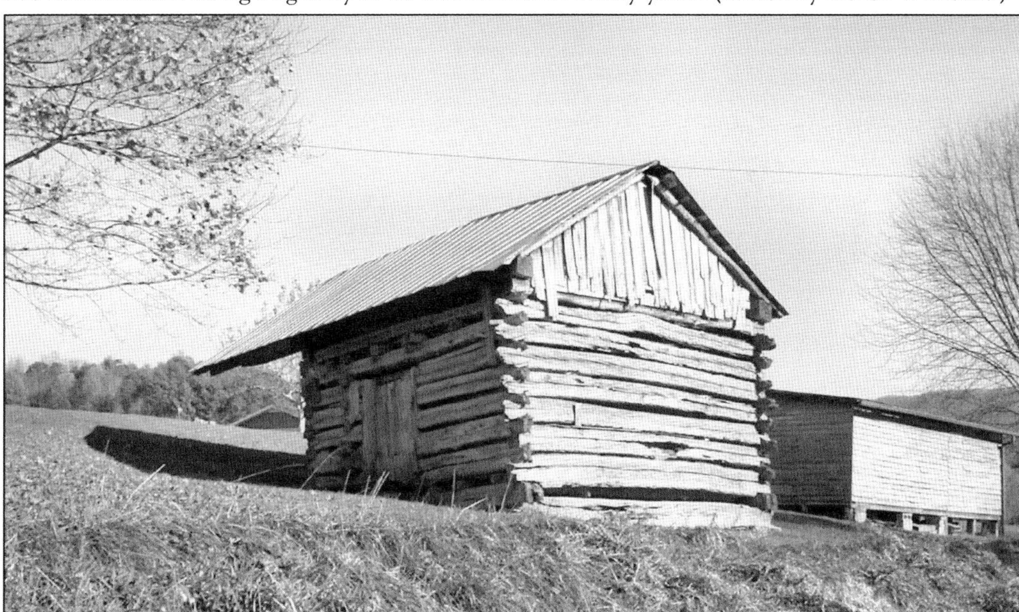

THE MCCLURE MILL. In the Mill Creek area, the McClure family built their farm, where George McClure and his siblings were raised. Later George raised his family here. Most of the farm is still intact after more than 100 years, including this family mill. Like many people in those days, the McClures raised their own grain on the farm, but few ground grain in their own mill. (Courtesy Debra Williams.)

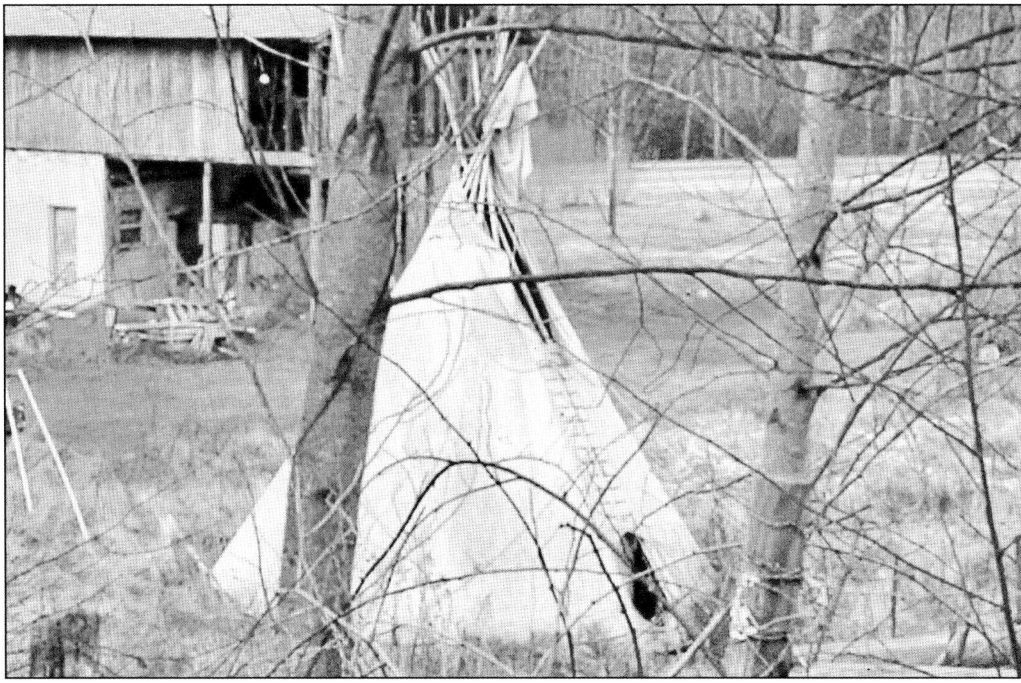

EARLY MOBILE HOUSING. The tepee was an efficient and common form of housing for those Native Americans who moved frequently to hunt for food. Tepees were quickly erected and dismantled and usually made of hide that hung midway up the stacked wood. This allowed for ventilation without drafts. This modern tepee is located just off Highway 16 South in the Sugar Grove area. Tepees were a common form of housing out West and not in Virginia. (Courtesy Debra Williams.)

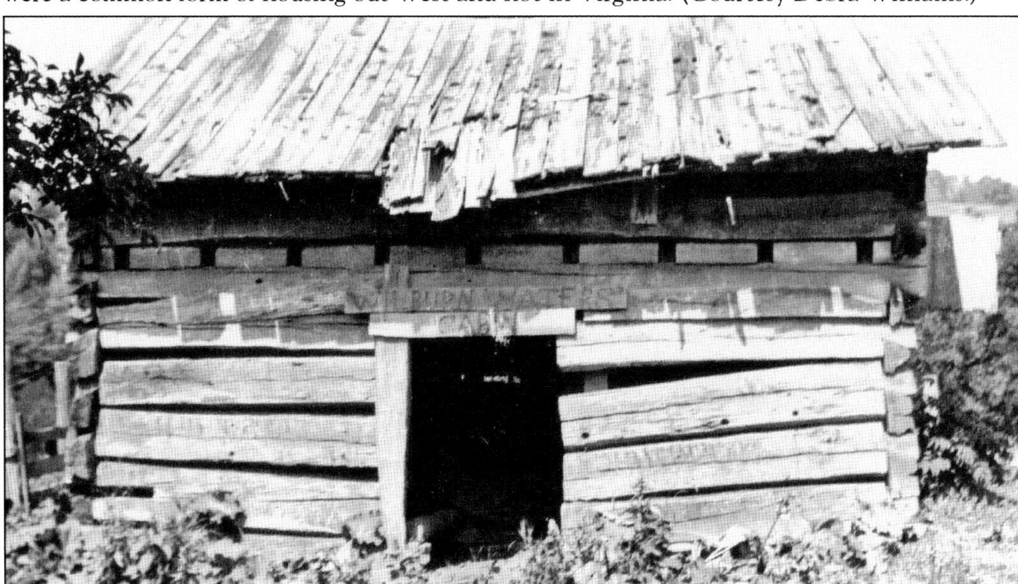

WILBURN WATERS'S CABIN. This cabin, located on Whitetop Mountain, was the home of Wilburn Waters. He was a hermit and famous in the region for hunting large game including bears. Upon living here for 20 years, he had killed 80 bears, 36 wolves, over 300 deer, and too many wild turkeys to count. (Courtesy Mack Sturgill Collection.)

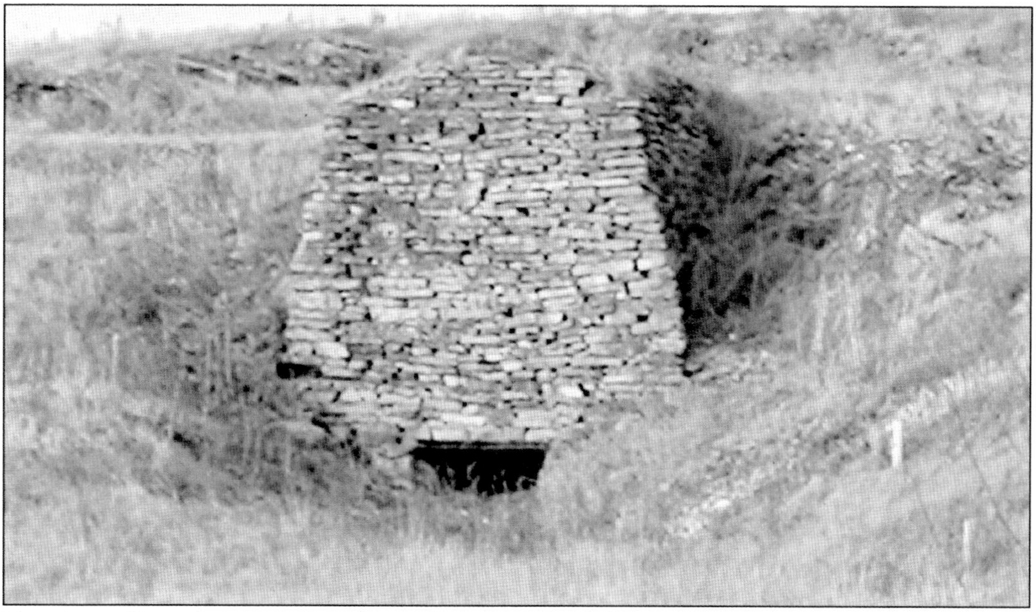

Teas Lime Kiln. Limestone was burned on top of the kiln until it formed a powder that dropped down into containers in the bottom. Lime could be used as a neutralizer for acidic soil; in making mortar, cement, and glass; in sugar refining; and in leather tanning. Medical uses include antacid and treatment of burns. This kiln is located in the Teas community and is in very good condition for its age. (Courtesy Debra Williams.)

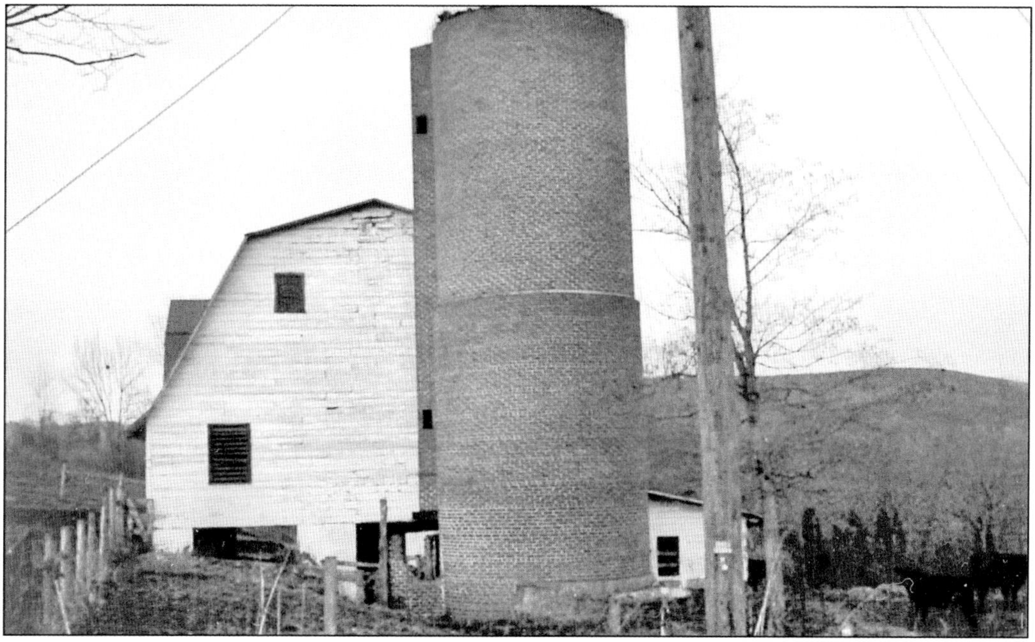

Convict Camp. During the late 1940s, in the McMullin section, Smyth County was the location of an all-black, self-sustaining convict camp. This barn is about all that is left of the camp run by Sgt. Melvin Orr. The inmates built roads for the highway department and were inexpensive labor on local farms. For entertainment, the convicts had a baseball team and played against the various local teams. (Courtesy Debra Williams.)

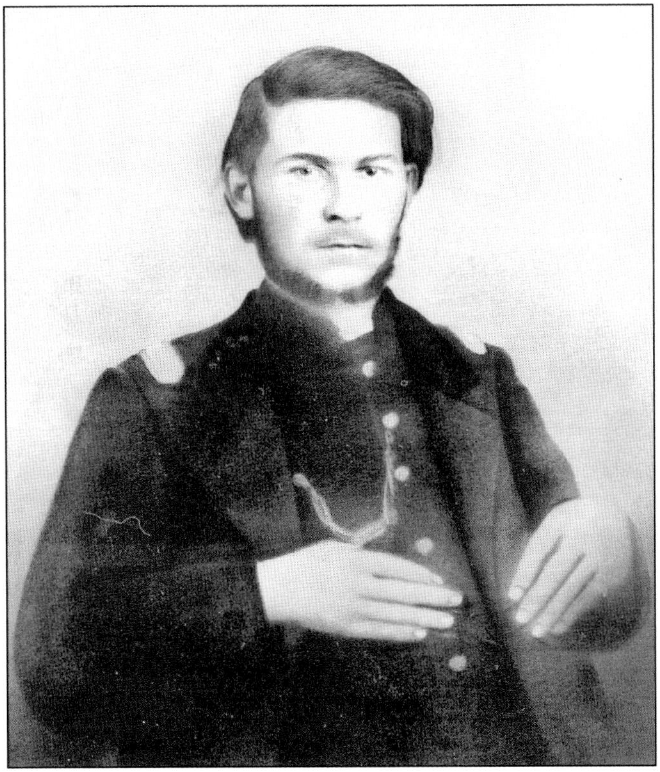

CAPT. DAVID AUXIER KILLED DURING THE BATTLE OF SALTVILLE. On October 4, 1864, this Union soldier died after being left two days earlier by his brother and uncle. Auxier's widow traveled from Kentucky to give her husband a proper burial. His body was taken from its shallow grave and placed into a private cemetery at McCrady. This was the only known marked Yankee grave from that battle. (Courtesy Museum of the Middle Appalachians.)

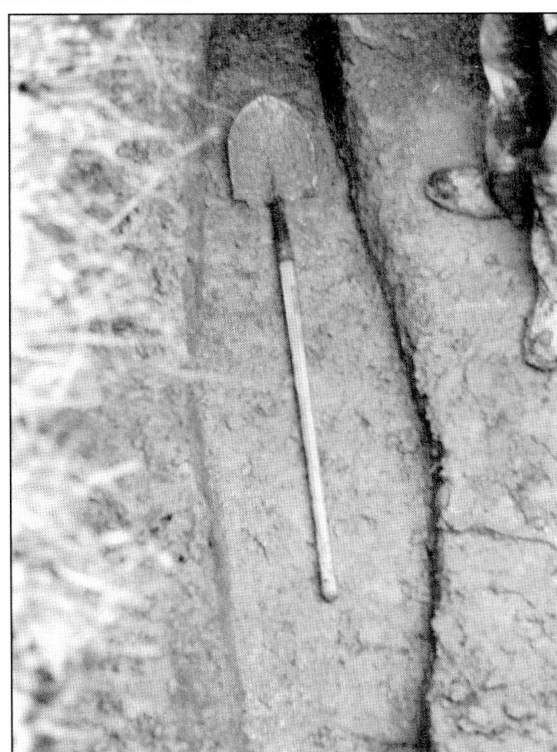

CIVIL WAR CAPTAIN GOES HOME AFTER 126 YEARS. After decades of searching, descendants of David Auxier located his grave in Saltville. In less than four feet of dirt, excavators found the bedrock was hand-hewn to fit the shape of the coffin forming this vault. The remains included teeth, bone fragments, nails, and Union infantry officer's buttons. Auxier's remains were given a military burial at his family plot in Kentucky. (Courtesy Museum of the Middle Appalachians.)

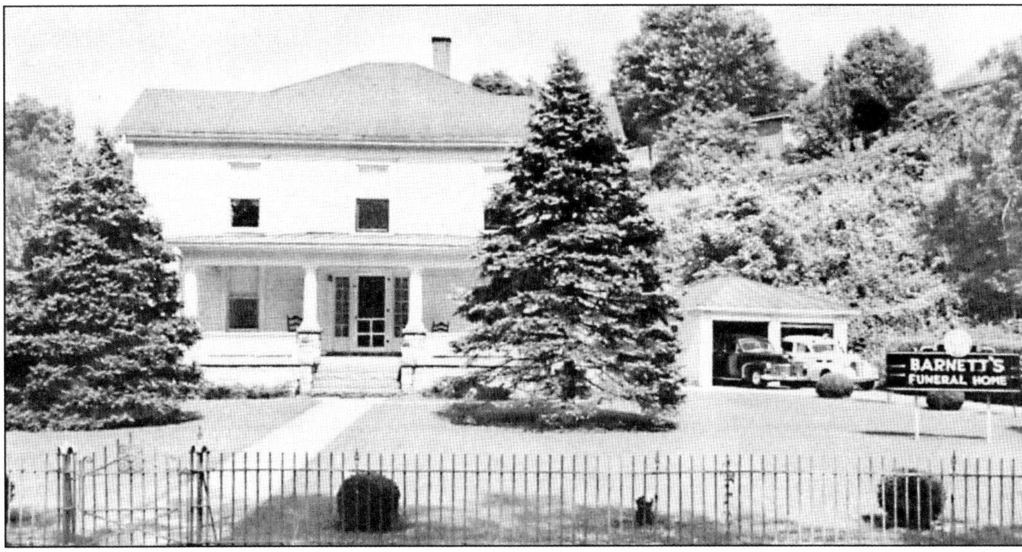

Barnett's Funeral Home. This beautiful house became Barnett's Funeral Home in 1946. As years passed, additions included more room for services and for a bigger chapel. Son and later owner Peyton Barnett was well known throughout the community and ran this business until his death in the mid-1990s. The building was razed for office space. (Courtesy Mack Sturgill Collection.)

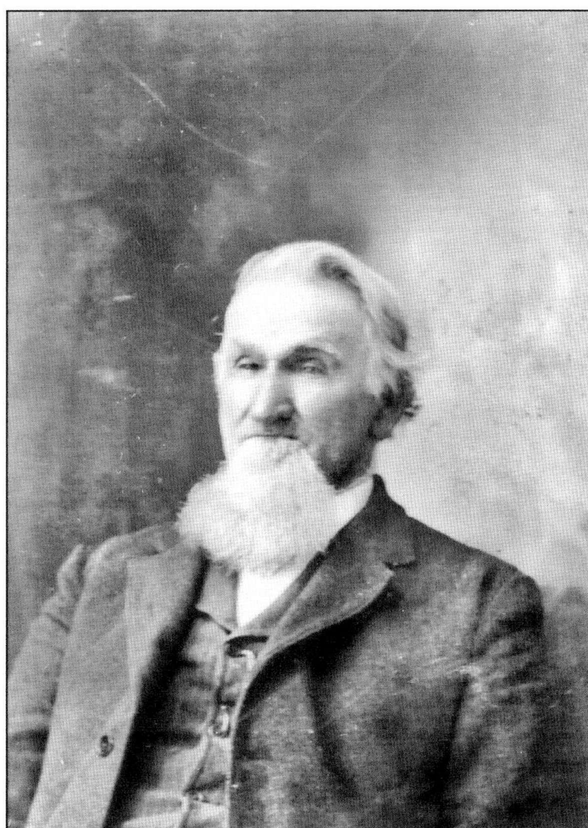

W. C. Seaver (1823–1909). In 1844, W. C. Seaver, a cabinetmaker, came to Marion and started Southwest Virginia's first furniture manufacturing company. Seaver and his two sons opened a store on the corner of Main and Commerce Streets. They later expanded into wagons and caskets. Their advertisement read "dealers in furniture, hardware, stoves, funeral directors, and embalmers." His business now lives on as Seaver Brown Funeral Service. (Courtesy Jimmy Warren.)

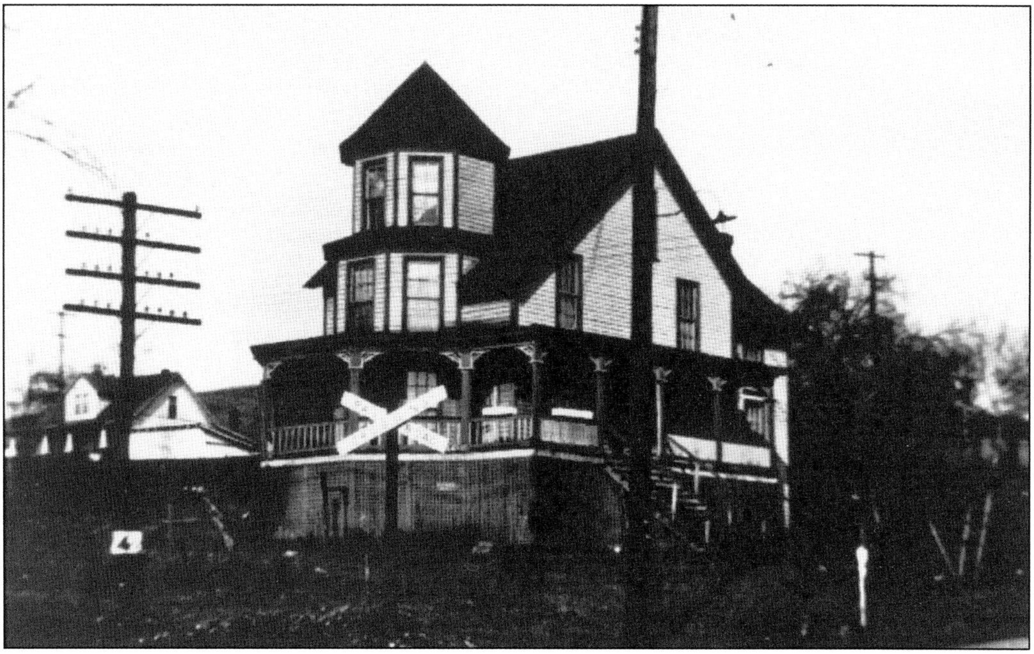

A. C. HILL HOUSE. Located on the corner of Chatham Hill Road and Chilhowie Street, this Queen Anne–style home was built in 1887 by Alphens Hill. The three-story structure was one of the first sites visitors saw when stepping off the train because it was located diagonally across the street. In the 1970s, it was torn down. Only part of the foundation still remains. (Courtesy Mack Sturgill Collection.)

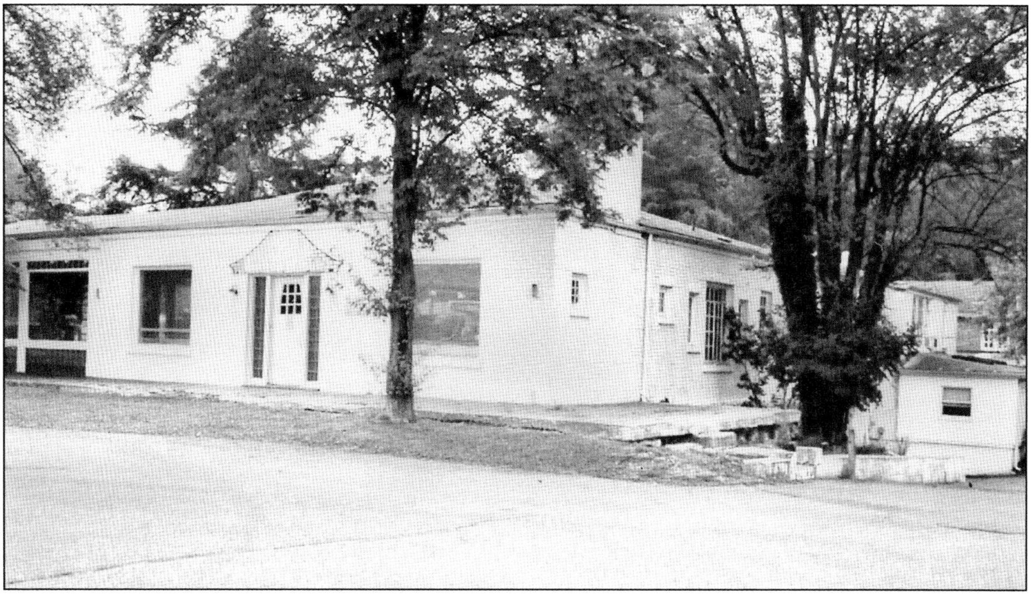

HOME OF C. C. LINCOLN JR. This modest-looking structure was built by C. C. Lincoln Jr. *c.* 1921 along North Main Street. The one story with a basement extended out back of the residence and contained an indoor swimming pool. It was converted into Southwest Virginia Business Institute and later into office space. Walgreens bought the land and razed the structure to make room for their drugstore. (Courtesy Debra Williams.)

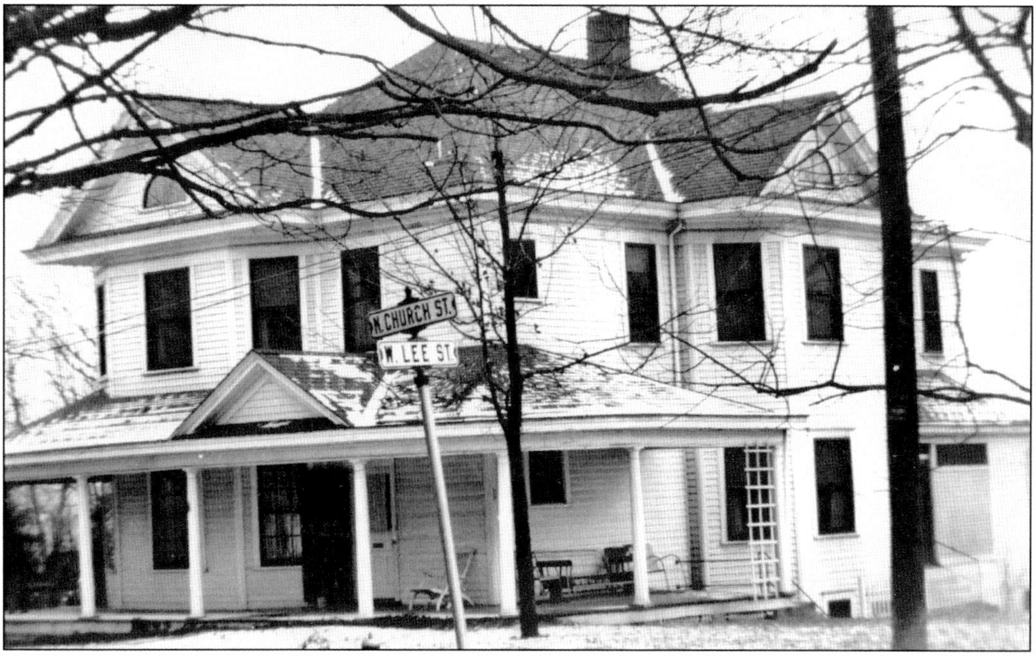

S. W. DICKINSON HOUSE. This Century Colonial Revival–style house was located on the corner of Lee and Church Streets *c.* 1883. Dickinson was a strong leader in the community, served on the first board of directors of Southwestern State Hospital, and helped organize the Medical Society of Southwest Virginia in 1884. The house was destroyed by fire in 1997. (Courtesy Mack Sturgill Collection.)

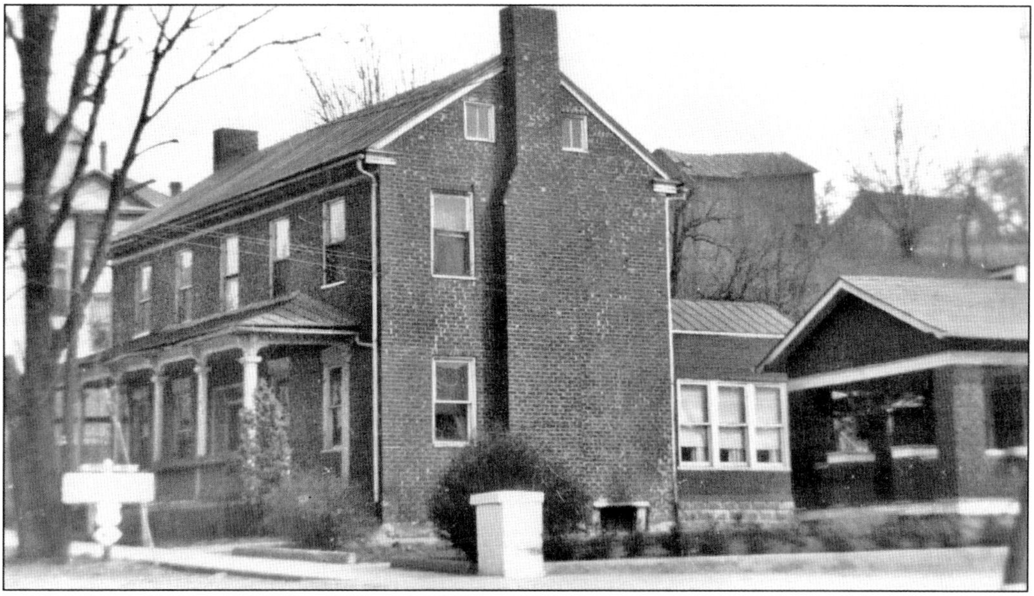

STEVENSON HOUSE. This house was built by J. M. Crockett *c.* 1853 on the corner of North and East Main Streets. Oscar Stevenson purchased the brick home in 1909. During the winter, the police blocked off the street and children pulled their sleds to the top of East Main, sliding down into the yard of this home. Stevenson operated the Marion Theatre on Church Street. The house was torn down to make room for a car lot. (Courtesy Mack Sturgill Collection.)

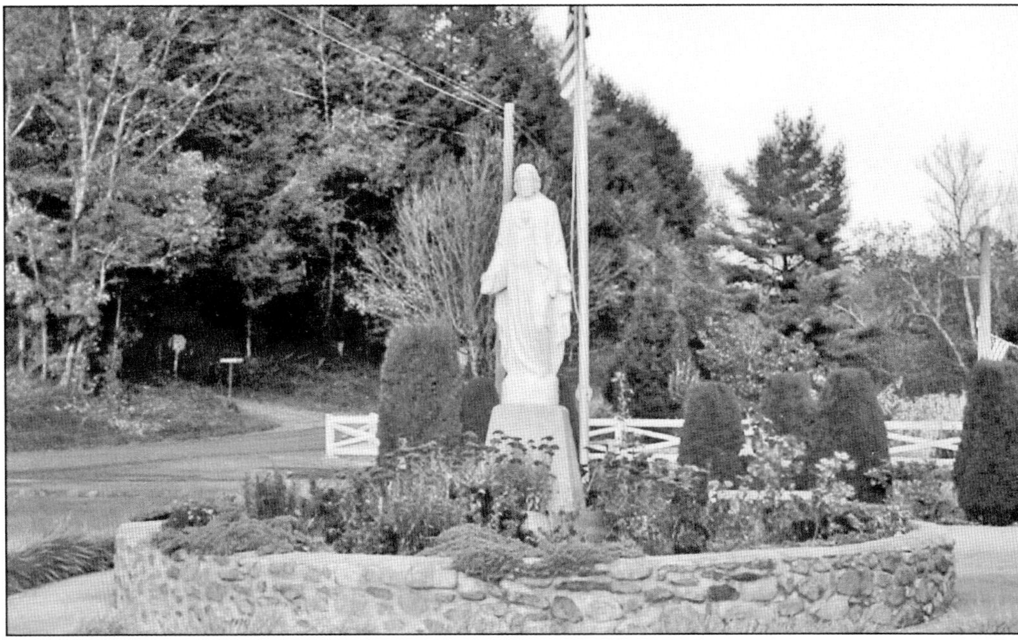

COMMUNITY VETERANS MEMORIAL. This sacred area was established as a veteran memorial by the Konnarock, Green Cove, Laurel Valley Community Association. This statue of hand-carved marble was made in Italy and donated by Lynn, Alan, and Karen Beeson. A plaque set in stone here reads, "Konnarock, Green Cove, Laurel Valley Communities Honor those Men and Women who have served our Country in the Armed Forces." (Courtesy Debra Williams.)

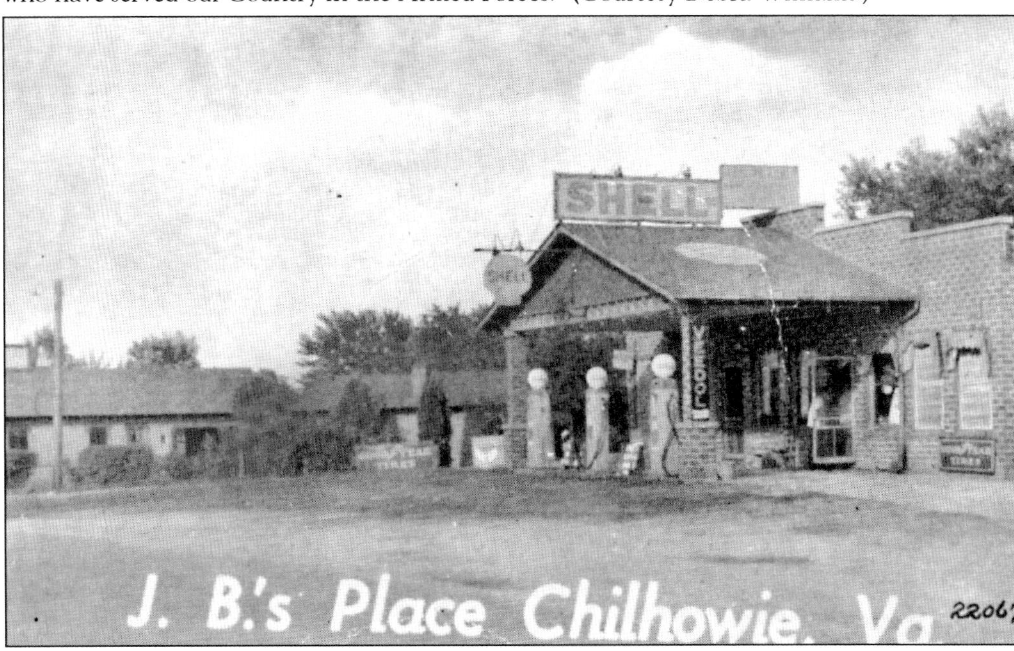

J. B.'S PLACE. This gas station, called J. B.'s Place, was owned by J. B. Poole and located on Highway 11 beside Hotel Poole. These two businesses were located at the current Valley Health Care site in Chilhowie. J. B.'s Place was a Shell gas station that offered Veedol oil and Goodyear tires. Notice the three gas pumps out front with glass globes. (Courtesy Clegg Williams.)

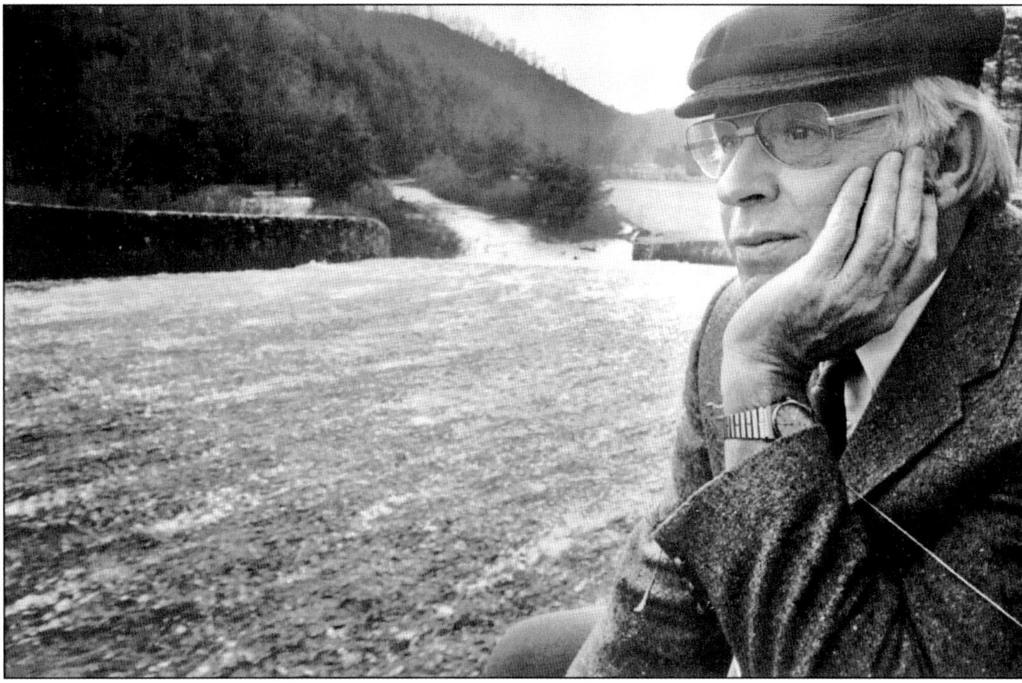

MACK H. STURGILL. A local genealogist, writer, speaker, and historian, Mack Sturgill was the historical gossip with the "golden shovel." He had a knack for digging up undiscovered historical treasures. He wrote *Abijah Thomas and His Octagonal House*, *Hungry Mother History and Legends*, and *Memories and Recollections at the Age of Ninety Five*. He coauthored the *History of the Sturgill Family, 1650–1983* and *Smyth County Virginia Cemeteries* volumes. (Courtesy Mack Sturgill Collection.)

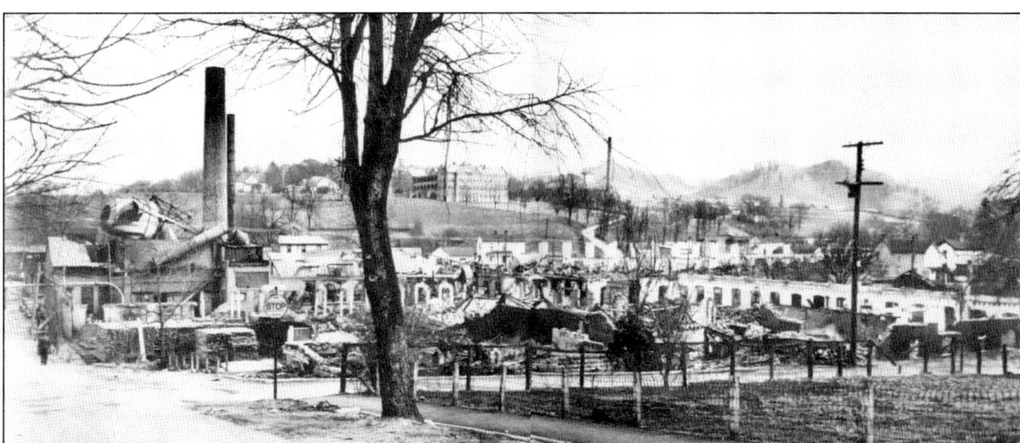

REMAINS OF VIRGINIA-LINCOLN CORPORATION. Where the Marion Post Office is located, a furniture factory was established by W. C. Seaver in 1875. He sold out in 1906 to L. P. Collins, B. F. Buchanan, and C. C. Lincoln Sr. The company, under Lincoln's direction, grew into the largest manufacturer of dining room furniture in the world. This photograph was taken on January 27, 1943, after a fire. (Courtesy Mack Sturgill Collection.)

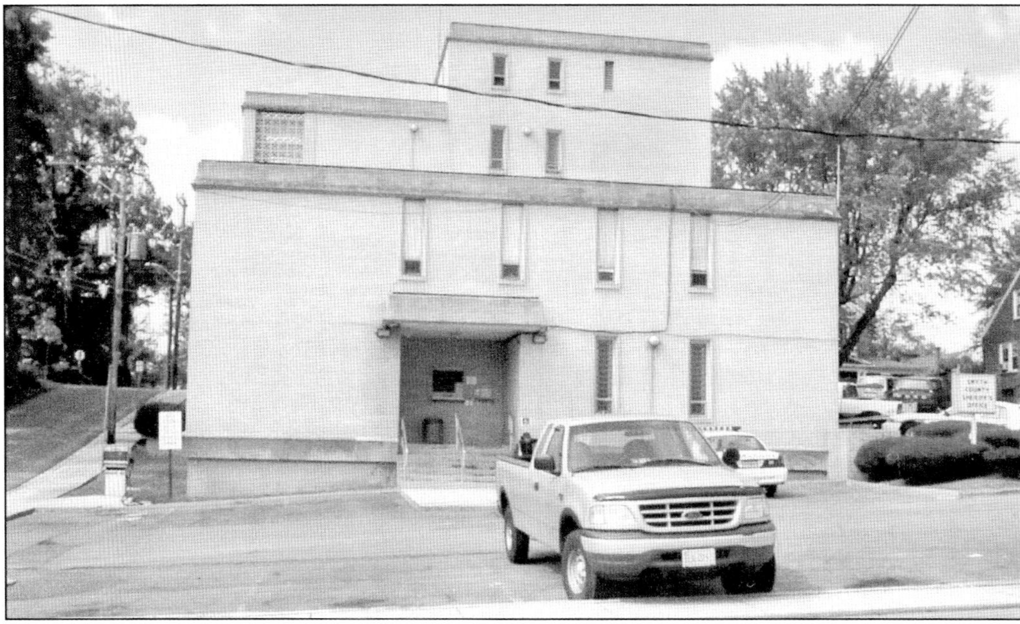

THE LAST COUNTY JAIL. This county jail was erected *c.* 1970 behind the courthouse. All four floors contained cells, but only women were housed on the fourth floor. The kitchen and many of the offices were on the second floor. Overcrowding became a problem with a capacity of only 55 inmates. The jail was closed April 8, 2005, and moved to a regional facility in Abingdon. (Courtesy Debra Williams.)

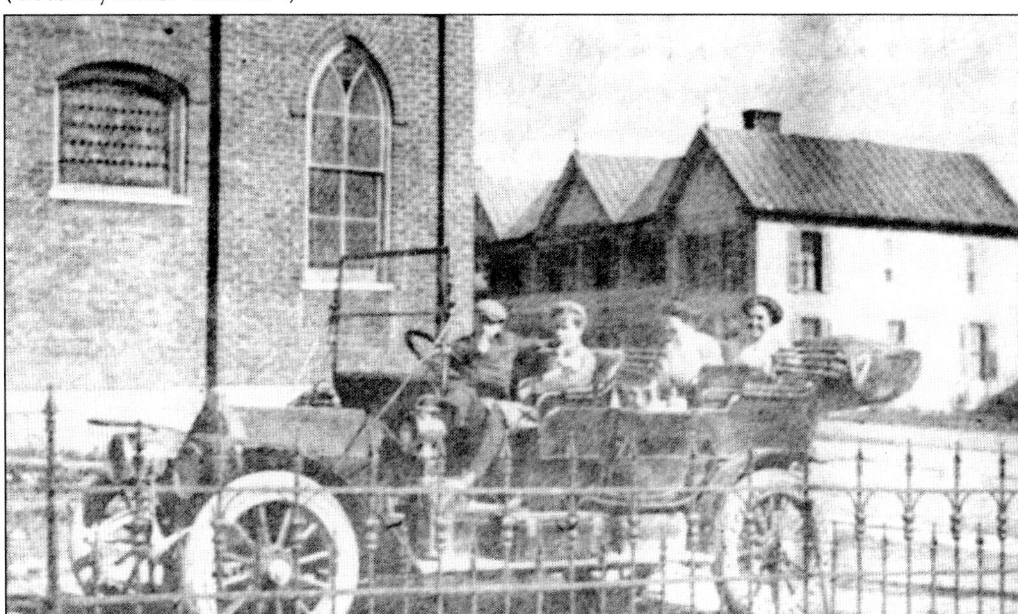

HOTEL HOLSTON. The Hotel Holston, which is the frame structure to the right, was torn down in 1923. Salvaged lumber was used to build the Mount Pleasant African Methodist Episcopal Church parsonage. The Municipal Building was built here in 1934. This photograph was taken from the yard of the J. C. Campbell residence. The corner of the Royal Oak Presbyterian Church can be seen. (Courtesy Mack Sturgill Collection.)

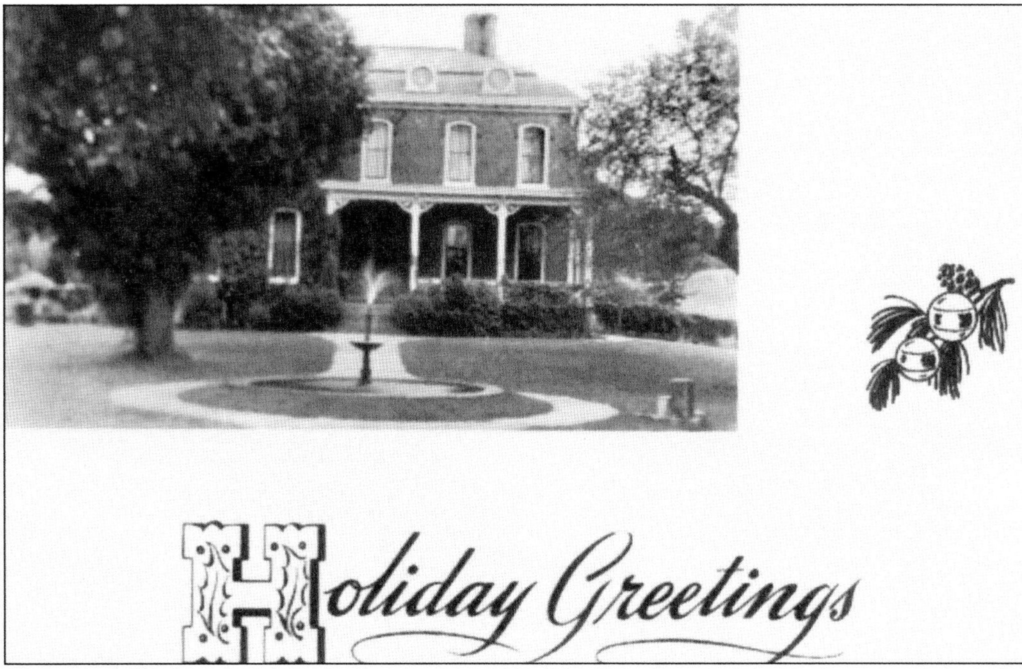

D. D. HULL HOME. In 1870, Capt. D. D. Hull purchased property from Judge George W. Jones to build this elegant brick home at the corner of Hulldale and Main Streets. This Christmas card may have been sent to friends and family by the Hull family or later owners such as W. M. Sclater, Florence Richardson, or Janie Boyd. The house was torn down in 1965. The lot eventually became the home of the Dewberry and Davis architectural firm. (Courtesy Frank Detweiler.)

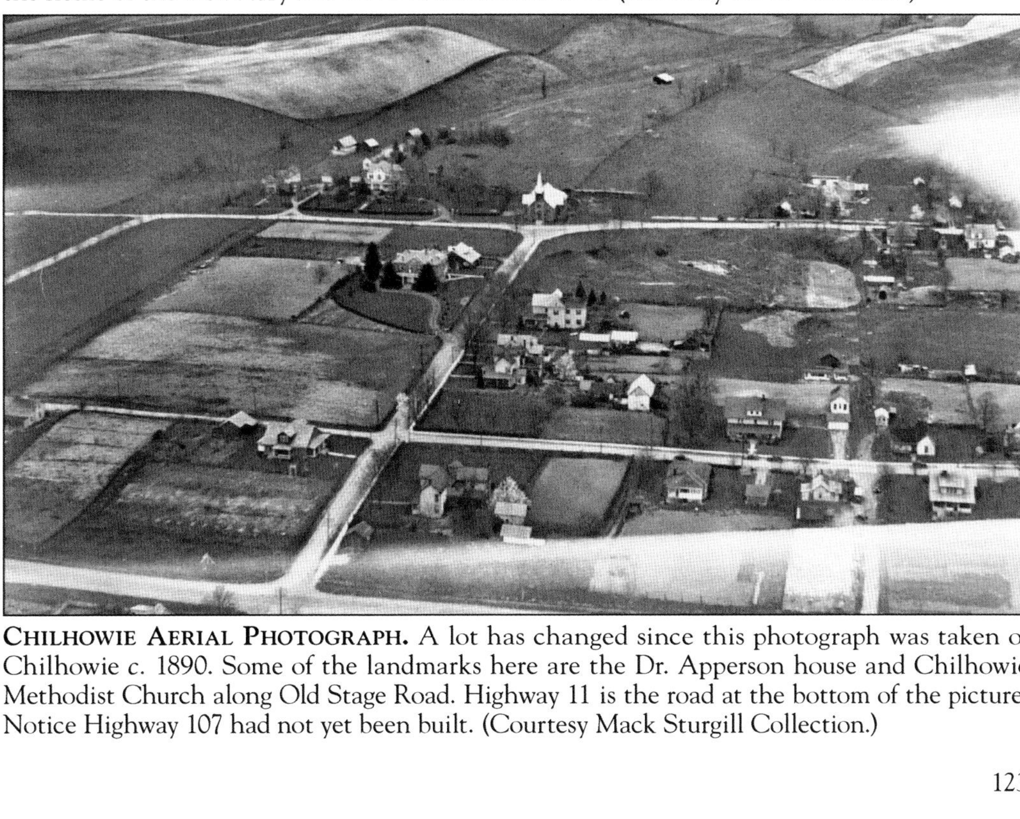

CHILHOWIE AERIAL PHOTOGRAPH. A lot has changed since this photograph was taken of Chilhowie *c.* 1890. Some of the landmarks here are the Dr. Apperson house and Chilhowie Methodist Church along Old Stage Road. Highway 11 is the road at the bottom of the picture. Notice Highway 107 had not yet been built. (Courtesy Mack Sturgill Collection.)

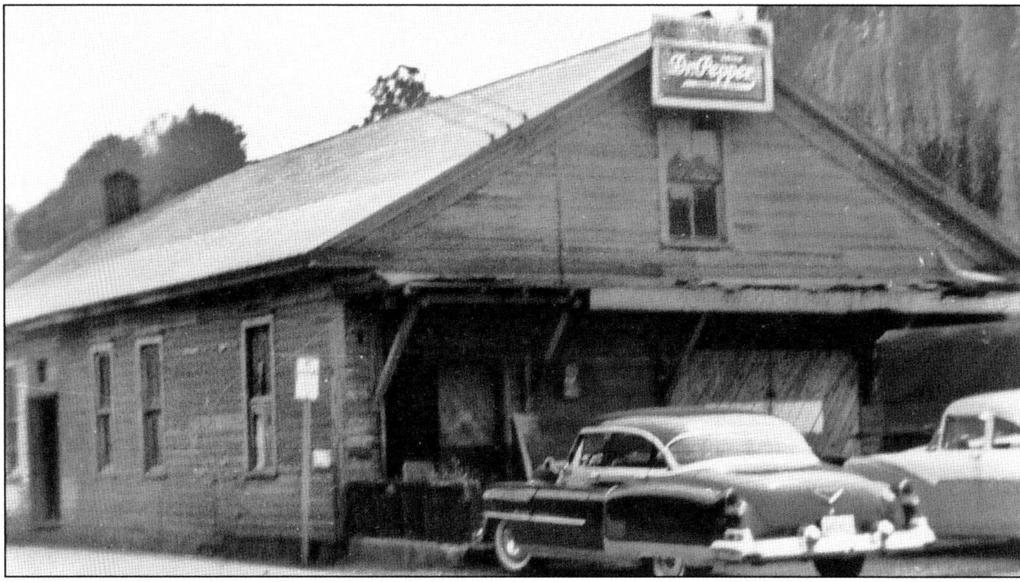

MARION AND RYE VALLEY RAILROAD DEPOT. This wooden structure was once located on the corner of Commerce and Cherry Streets and served as the depot for the Marion and Rye Valley Railroad. This rail system ran from Marion to Sugar Grove, where it intersected with Virginia Southern Railroad to form a 27-mile line. This railroad, which carried products as well as passengers, disbanded in 1931. (Courtesy Kenny Sturgill.)

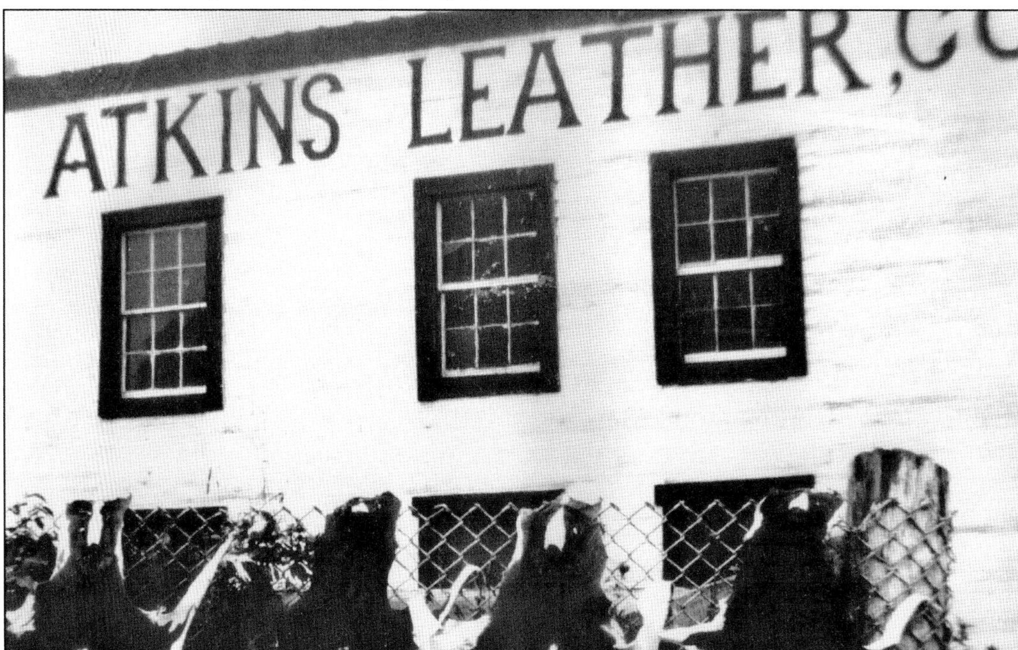

ATKINS LEATHER COMPANY. Located along Highway 11 in the Atkins area, this company was operated by A. G. Riddle and George Musser from 1922 to 1952. They bought hides (mostly of cow, goat, and sheep), cured them, and used them to make leather. This was a time-consuming process. The hides shown here are being dried. Large factories produce much of the leather used today. (Courtesy Mack Sturgill Collection.)

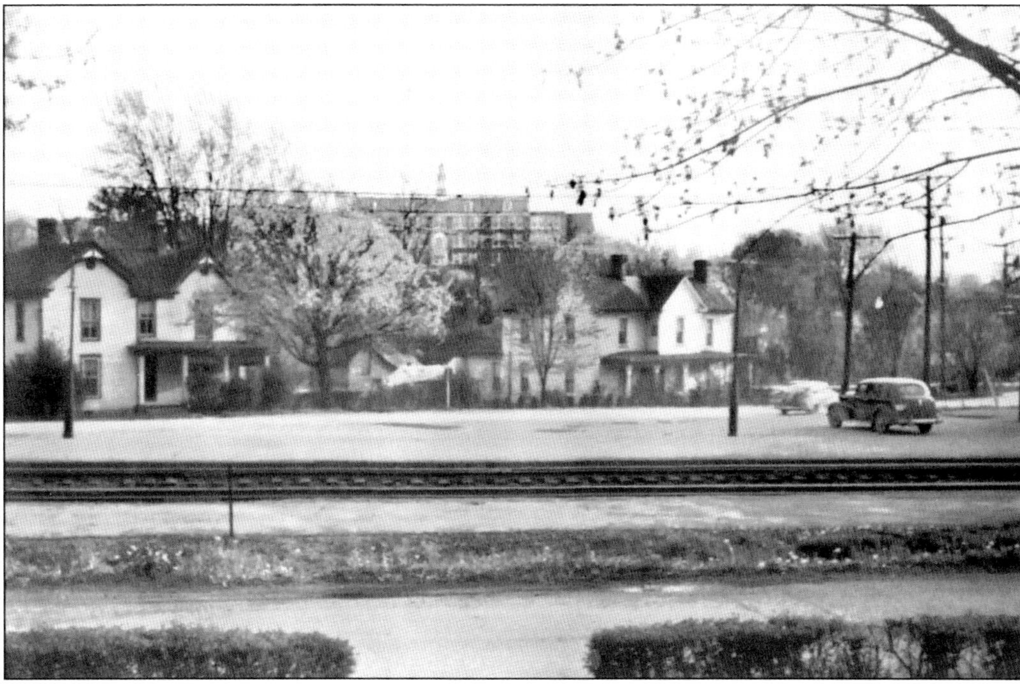

MAKING WAY FOR PROGRESS. These two large wood frame houses were once located across from the Marion Train Depot. The one on the left was built *c.* 1892 by J. R. Venable. Daisy Atkins Higginbotham built the house to the right *c.* 1898 on land given to her by her parents, Mr. and Mrs. A. T. Atkins. Both of these homes were later torn down. (Courtesy Charles W. Seaver.)

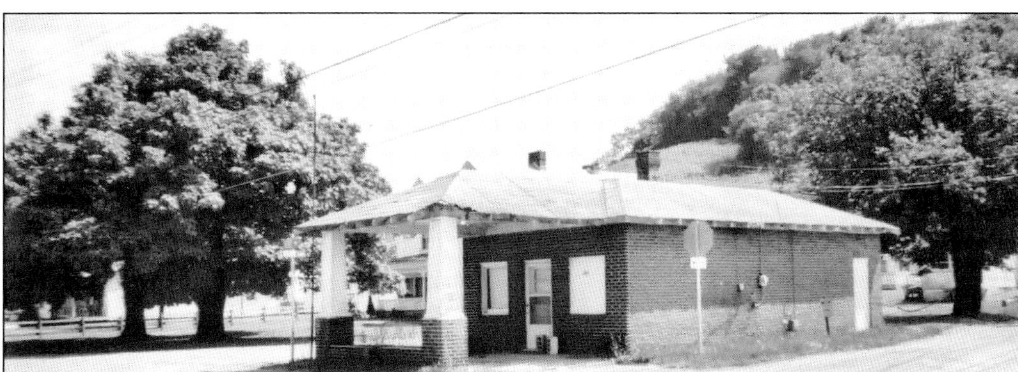

FORMER ATKINS POST OFFICE. This small, brick structure located along Highway 11 in Atkins was once Snider's Service Station and at one time served as a dwelling. Later this became the Atkins Post Office where Hugh Copenhaver served as postmaster. This building was abandoned in the early 1990s when the new, much larger post office was erected. (Courtesy Debra Williams.)

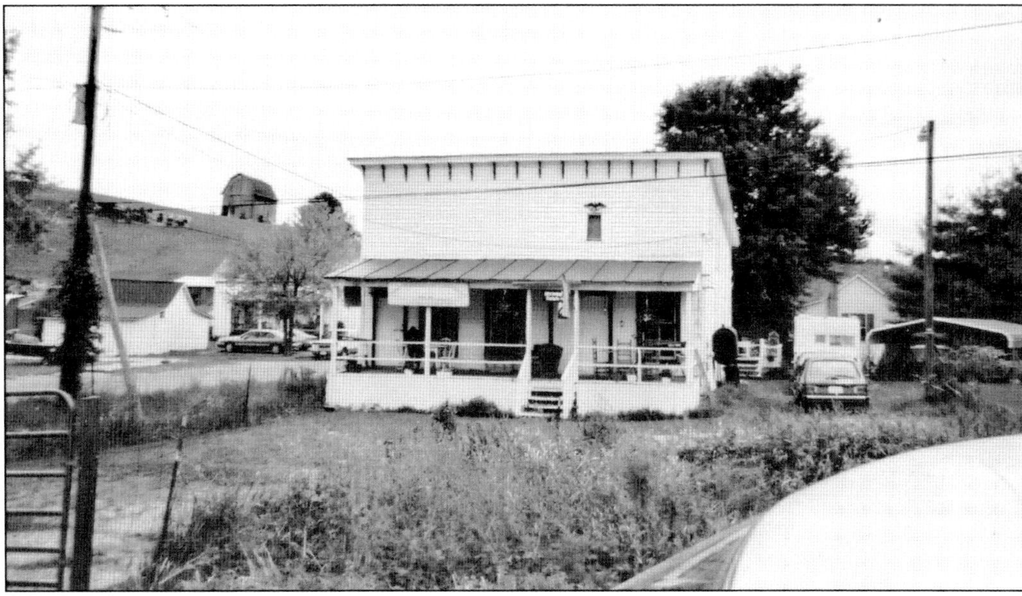

YONTS GENERAL STORE. This traditional country store was located in the Groseclose community and run by Grady Yonts. At one time, the post office was housed here. Farm supplies, seed, grain, paint, tobacco products, shoes, fabrics, as well as a long list of grocery items, candies, and sodas could all be found here. Patrons gathered around to hear the latest news by word of mouth. (Courtesy Debra Williams.)

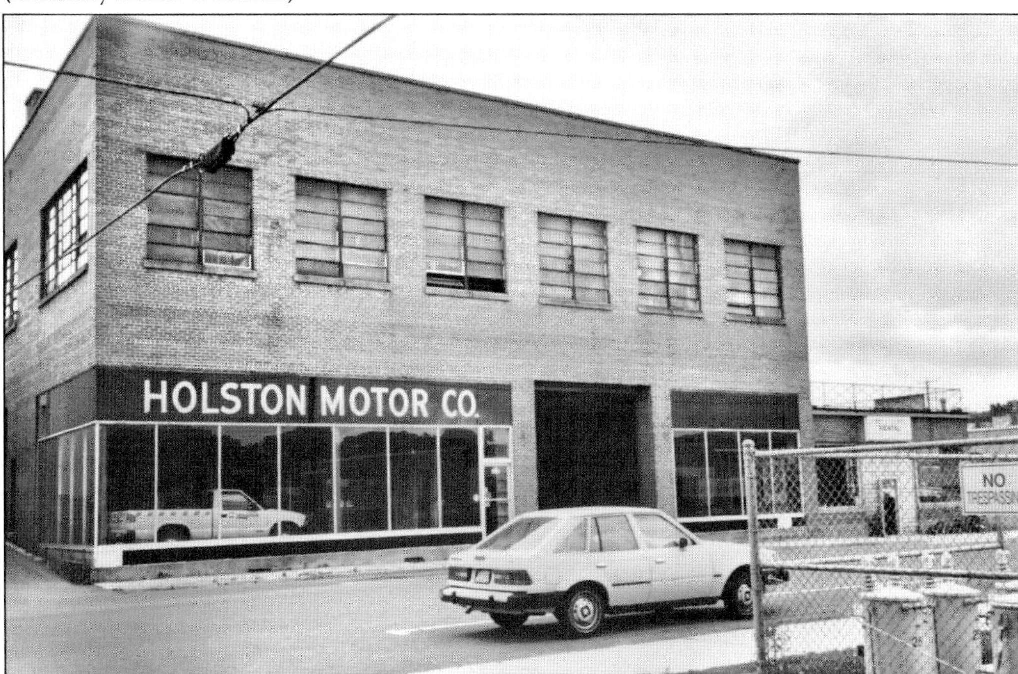

THE HOLSTON MOTOR COMPANY. Fred Killinger established this auto sales company around 1950 on Broad Street in Marion. He sold Chrysler, Dodge, and Plymouth automobiles. The company went out of business in the 1980s. T and S Auto Service and SmythNet Computer Services later located here. (Courtesy Gary and Bonnita Frazier.)

BIBLIOGRAPHY

Armstrong, Joan Tracy. *History of Smyth County, Virginia: Ante-bellum Years Through The Civil War.* Bristol, VA: McFarlane Graphics, 1986.

Byrd, Kimberly Barr, and Deborah J. Williams. *Smyth County.* Charleston, SC: Arcadia Publishing, 2005.

Harrington, R. E. *Marion Landmarks: Past and Present.* Marion, VA: Tucker Printing, 2004.

Hull, Wythe M. *The History of Marion Bottling Company, Inc.* Radford, VA: Commonwealth Press, 1985.

Kent, William B. *A History of Saltville.* Radford, VA: Commonwealth Press, 1955.

Mauck, J. Leonard. *History of Education in Smyth County.* Alexandria, VA: National Printing, 1978.

Presgraves, Jim. *Smyth County Families And History.* Pulaski, VA: B. D. Smith Printing, 1974.

Price, Charles E. *The Mystery of Ghostly Vera and other Haunting Tales of Southwest Virginia.* Johnson City, TN: Overmountain Press, 1993.

Sayers, Elizabeth Lemmon. *Smyth County, Virginia: Pathfinders and Patriots.* Marceline, MO: Walsworth, 1983.

Smyth County News. Marion, Virginia: 1970–2004.

Sturgill, Mack H. *Abijah Thomas and His Octagonal House.* Marion, VA: Tucker Printing, 1990.

———. *Hungry Mother: History and Legends.* 2nd ed. Marion, VA: Tucker Printing, 2001.

The Smyth County Heritage Book Committee and Don Mills, Inc. *Heritage of Smyth County, Virginia 1832–1997.* Marceline, MO: Walsworth, 1997.

Warmuth, Donna Akers. *Legends, Stories, and Ghostly Tales of Abingdon and Washington County, Virginia.* Boone, NC: Laurel Printing, 2005.

Wilson, Goodridge. *Smyth County History and Traditions.* Radford, VA: Commonwealth Press, 1932.